VOGUE

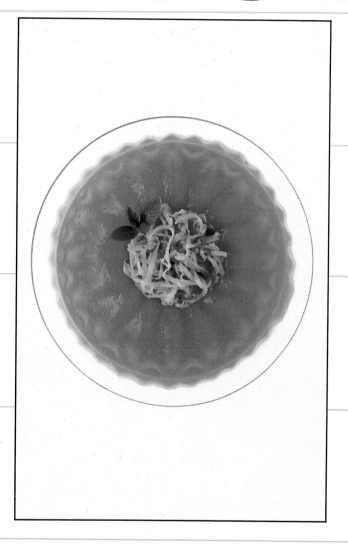

DIET
PROGRAMME

VOGUE

DIET PROGRAMME

General Editor
Deborah Hutton

Octopus Books

The contributors

DEBORAH HUTTON devised the concept for the book, wrote and edited it. She has an honours degree in English from York University and gained a job on *Vogue* after entering their annual talent competition in 1979. She has been writing health features for the magazine for 5 years and is the author of *Vogue Complete Beauty* (Octopus).

JENNY SALMON devised the 24-week programme and compiled many of the recipes. She has a bachelors degree in Home Economics, a masters degree in Nutrition and a diploma in Dietetics from Queen Elizabeth College, London, and has worked as a dietician at Whipps Cross Hospital and St. Bartholomew's Hospital in London. For the last eight years, her particular interest has been in making the complex subject of nutrition understandable to those interested in following a healthy diet but confused by conflicting views and advice. In 1983, she helped set up the KMS Partnership, a company offering a range of marketing services connected with nutrition and diet in which she is responsible for home economics projects and research and nutritional programmes. She has also written for a number of magazines, including *Vogue*, was a contributor to the highly-successful *F-Plan Diet* (Penguin) and has produced a number of books on healthy eating.

This book first published 1984 by
Octopus Books Limited
59 Grosvenor Street
London W1

ISBN 0 7064 2076 4

Printed by Gráficas Estella SA, Diputación 39,
Barcelona 15, Spain

DR BARBARA JACQUELYN SAHAKIAN contributed to the self-assessment chapter and to the general notes running throughout the book and has also acted in a consultative capacity. She has a degree in psychology from Mount Holyoke College, Massachusetts, and wrote a thesis for her doctorate at the University of Cambridge on the treatment of hyperactivity in children. Her other research interests include the treatment of memory disorders in the elderly and – particularly – the causes and treatment of eating disorders, including compulsive eating, leading to obesity, anorexia and bulimia nervosa. She has been involved in directing clinics for the treatment of eating disorders, both here and in the USA, and is currently setting up a research project at Bedford General Hospital on physiological and psychological factors in the control of appetite. She is Co-Editor of *Psychopathology Today* (Peacock Publishing) and has published over forty articles and chapters in scientific journals and books, and several features for popular magazines including an article on bulimia nervosa for *Vogue* in October 1982.

DR SHEILA BINGHAM devised the special diets and some of the recipes. She has a Bachelor of Science degree in Nutrition from Queen Elizabeth College and later gained a doctorate, also from London University, for her thesis 'The Biological Methods of Assessing Nutrition Intake'. She practised as a therapeutic dietician at University College Hospital and St. Philips Hospital, both in London, prescribing diets for general patients and those with kidney disorders. She is presently engaged in nutritional research with the Medical Research Council in Cambridge, and is particularly interested in the physiological effects of dietary fibre and the mechanisms through which it may protect against disease – such as cancer of the colon. Her thirty papers and publications include a dictionary of nutrition for the consumer, *Nutrition: Better through Eating* (Corgi, 1978).

ARABELLA BOXER devised the dinner party menus and juice diet recipes for the Special Diet section. Having had no formal training, her interest in cookery and nutrition dates from holidays spent in Southern Ireland after leaving school where she and her mother taught themselves to cook. She wrote her first recipe book, *First Slice Your Cookbook* (Penguin) in 1956 and has since written 8 others, including *Arabella Boxer's Garden Cookbook* (Weidenfeld & Nicolson), *Mediterranean Cookbook* (Dent), *Vogue Summer and Winter Cookbook* (Mitchell Beazley), and *The Sunday Times Complete Cookbook* (Weidenfeld & Nicolson). She has been *Vogue* Food Editor since 1974, and contributed the recipe section to *Vogue Complete Beauty* (Octopus) in 1982. She works regularly for the Sunday Times Magazine and has twice won the Glenfiddich Award for Food Writer of the Year.

We are grateful to Beatrix Miller, *Vogue* Editor-in-Chief, and Alex Kroll, *Vogue* Books Editor, for their help and support: Marie-Louise Avery and Penny Summers of Octopus Books for all their hard work on the manuscript and its presentation; Charlie Stebbings for his care with the photography, Dr Pat Judd for checking calorie counts, and Colin Tudge and Dr Michael O'Donnell for their permission to adapt material (pages 64 and 68 respectively) which originally appeared in *Vogue*; Caroline Ellwood for providing some additional recipes and Joanna Gibbon, *Vogue* Editorial Assistant, for her consistent help both in preparing the manuscript and checking the proofs.

CONTENTS

Introduction

Diets have fallen into disfavour. They are now said to be dangerous, self-defeating, to damage your health and to make you fat[1]; they are described as 'low grade popular infections'[2] which cause widespread misery by perpetuating an ideal of slimness that can often only be achieved at tremendous personal cost. As diets have come to be associated with fads that don't work, so the meaning of the word itself has changed. Diet as good nutrition, as a healthy and enjoyable way of eating, has come to seem like a contradiction in terms . . .

And it's not just the value of dieting, but the ideal of slimness itself that has been called into question. Feminist writers see it as part of the cultural/sexist conspiracy, 'a much larger coercion against the full and natural development of women'[3], in which to diet is to collude and to grow fat is to rebel ('Fat offends Western ideals of female beauty and, as such, every 'overweight' woman creates a crack in the popular culture's ability to make us mere products'[4]). And an increasing number of people, men as well as women, are challenging the concept that being slim is any more desirable, or indeed any better for you, than being fat.

In place of the diet books of recent years, with their unappetizingly monotonous regimens of cottage cheese and yogurt, and promises of ever more rapid weight loss, we now have a string of anti-diet books advising us to drop the subject altogether, to eat whatever we like, to make friends with food, to take up vigorous exercise, to be happy with the way we are.

But the way we are, when left to the all-too-common excesses of rich, over-refined food and an inactive sedentary lifestyle, is often rather larger than we would like. Thinness may no longer be fashionable but fitness most certainly is. Being in shape is more important than ever. The 80s message is an encouraging one – first that *anyone* can get into shape, can become fit, firm, lithe, well-muscled and effective and second that this personal best is to be achieved not through months of deprivation and undernutrition but through an active lifestyle and a healthy diet.

But how many of us are in shape? How many of us do have an active lifestyle and a healthy diet? As a nation, we are fatter and unfitter than ever before. The average weight of every man, woman and child in the West has risen alarmingly over the last 20 years, *and* we are putting the weight on at an increasingly early age. In a recent study[5] conducted in the United Kingdom, half of all 20-year-olds were found to be already too heavy, so much so that one in four was 'incurring a health risk'. The figure rises to one in two by the mid-50s.

The anti-dieting league recognizes the problem but tells us to

'The 80's message is an encouraging one – first that anyone can get into shape, can become fit, firm, lithe, well-muscled and effective and second that this personal best is to be achieved not through months of deprivation and under-nutrition but through an active lifestyle and a healthy diet'..

stop counting the calories, to start eating nutritiously, and to take to the running track – where fat and flab will magically metamorphose into muscle. But is such transformation possible without restricting the amount you eat? The top nutritionists say no. Exercise alone is not enough just as diet alone is not enough. Exercise will help transform shape more effectively than many diets but it will not help shift those extra pounds nearly as swiftly. A combined approach is needed; exercise with diet and diet with exercise and both with an increased awareness of what they can do for you. You need to be attuned to what your body needs before you can hope to give it what it wants . . .

Because the way we eat and the way we move are so fundamental to our wellbeing, the aim of this programme is as much to promote positive health as to change shape or improve fitness. The 24-week programme, for example, is not just about losing weight but about gaining new insights, about discovering how much better you feel for eating in a healthy way. Food can make you fat, full, indigested, sick, headachey, bloated and guilty, but it can also make you feel fit, inspired, vital, full of life and energy. . . The way we feel depends, to a much greater degree than most of us realize, on the way we eat.

But what type of diet will produce long-term changes in shape and wellbeing? The choice is bewildering, the claims conflicting. Ironically, much can be learned from the books telling us not to diet at all, because these books justly expose the pointlessness as well as the dangers of life spent on or between diets – the misery of not being able to trust your appetite because it seems to 'make you gain weight' as soon as you start eating in anything approaching a normal way, the futility of trying to reach and maintain an impossible goal, the self-defeating process whereby diets deplete 'energy-expensive' lean tissue, sapping vitality and lowering metabolic rate, making weight regain not just likely but inevitable. . .

The news is that there is no easy, quick and effective way of losing weight permanently, no short cuts to real changes in shape and size. *Short-term losses always lead to long-term gains.* There are no wonder foods and formulae, no miraculous combinations that by some wondrous quirk of biochemistry will balance each other out so enabling you 'to eat all you like and still lose weight'. There is nothing magical about grapefruit and eggs or bananas and milk or bunches of grapes for every meal. If you were expecting to find them here, you will be disappointed.

The only way to lose weight is to lose weight slowly AND in conjunction with an exercise programme. The new-generation diets, compiled in the light of all available evidence, place as much emphasis on what you eat as how much, on how you feel as on what you weigh. In place of limited foods to be eaten at specific times and in specific quantities, these diets encourage you to widen the variety of foods you eat, to listen to your body and to trust your own instincts, hunger and appetite included. This twenty-four week programme has been produced for people who are fatter and unfitter than they would like to be, who suspect that they could be enjoying a much enhanced level of health and vitality but understand that high-level health demands high-level motivation; who would like to gain weight and lose weight relatively swiftly but realize that there are penalties to be paid for doing it too fast. It takes time to change the habits of a lifetime.

A long-term diet, designed to promote gradual weight loss helps avoid frustrating problems with plunging metabolic rates, keeps energy high and helps instil new awareness of all the positive things that food can do for you. All you need to do right now is to start. . .

1. Claims contained in 'Dieting Makes You Fat' by Geoffrey Cannon and Hetty Einzig (Century, London, 1983)
2. 'Breaking the Diet Habit' by C. Peter Herman and Janet Polivy (Basic Books, New York, 1983)
3. 'Womansize' by Kim Chernin (The Women's Press, London 1981)
4. 'Fat is a Feminist Issue' by Susie Orbach (Hamlyn, London, 1978)
5. 'Obesity,' a Report by the Royal College of Physicians (London, 1983)

Self assessment

How can you get into shape for good? Dieting starts with a question, because if putting on weight is easy and taking it off is harder, keeping it off is harder still. Any diet can work in the short term, but only you can make those results last permanently. Use the questionnaires and charts on the following pages to enhance awareness and gain insight. Self-knowledge is the key to success.

It is no secret that few diets work. The usual pattern is to lose weight for a while, and then to regain it...often with interest. Most of us lose and gain hundreds of pounds in this way (well over our own body weight) over the course of our dieting lives.

In one New York survey, 100 people advised by their doctors to take off weight were monitored for 2 years. Only 12 lost a significant amount of weight after a year and just 2 managed to sustain it by the end of the next. This depressing result is probably rather better than average because research shows that diets are generally *more* successful when accompanied by advice and encouragement from an authoritarian figure.

Faced with these figures, the obvious conclusion is that most diets are self-defeating and over 80 per cent of people following them are wasting their time – especially if they carry exactly the same expectations and eating habits into the new diet as the one before (and the one before that... and the one before that...)

A new approach is clearly needed. It may mean settling for a goal weight a few pounds above the 'ideal' or trying a different style of dieting or radically reassessing your present eating patterns – very possibly all three.

We believe that if you want to lose weight permanently, *and are realistic in the goal you set yourself*, you can lose weight permanently. But first you must question your attitudes and examine your eating patterns. Use this chapter to help determine the right approach. Make losing weight as easy as possible by picking a diet that suits you, and avoid regaining the weight you lose by making some lasting changes to your diet and by being sensitive to those factors which have led to overeating in the past.

Ensure your future success by analysing past failures. Was the diet at fault or were you? Recognize that diets do not only fail through weakness and lack of willpower, but through their own shortcomings. Diets that severely restrict the types of food allowed, for example, can rarely be followed for more than a few days simply because the nutrients necessary for good health can only be found in a wide range of foods. So respect the instinct that rebels and bear in mind that the diets that are hardest to follow are generally the most unsound. Reproach yourself for embarking on such diets by all means, but refuse to take the blame when you break them.

Even balanced diets can have their pitfalls if unsuited to your tastes and lifestyle. Despite the promises that are often made, no diet works for everyone. Some people require absolute rigidity with foods measured out to the ounce, while others need more flexibility; some do better on short sharp blitzes but most benefit from a longer-term eating programme; some like certain foods while others detest them. We are all different.

What is necessary, then, is to have the insight to pick a diet that works for you – and a diet that works for you is one that makes you feel good for being on it. Awareness of how you feel and enjoyment of what you eat is where the new nutritional emphasis lies. A diet that enhances wellbeing while promoting weight loss is much more likely to be successful in the long-term than one which asks you to rely on feelings of virtuous deprivation to carry you through. If you feel better on the diet than you did off it, sticking to it will not be a problem – and neither will carrying its healthy principles over to your everyday way of eating once you have reached your goal.

Real awareness of how you feel on what you eat may nevertheless be rather subtler than you realize. If your reaction to reading this is to say, 'Aha, but I enjoy cream cakes and gooey chocolates', ask yourself whether that's really true. Even if you enjoy eating them at the time, how do you feel for having eaten them? Light, refreshed and full of energy or stodgy, indigested and guilty? Explore your responses to food, and become more attuned to the crucial connection between what you eat and the way you feel, by filling out the diary pages at the end of this section.

Now read on...

HOW MUCH SHOULD YOU WEIGH?

Desirable weight ranges are determined by insurance companies for the soundest business reason – they need to know how long their clients are likely to live. Their records show that, while normal-weight people have a normal life expectancy (all other things being equal), overweight people die young.

A survey compiled by the US Metropolitan Life Insurance Company over a period of 25 years has shown that people who are 10 per cent or more above the upper limit of 'acceptable' have a 50 per cent higher mortality. That means they are half as likely again to die before their time. In addition to falling prey to the killer diseases such as coronary heart disease and cancer, overweight people are more susceptible to disabling ones, such as diabetes.

But it is important to keep a sense of perspective. For, although no-one would contest that being very fat is very bad for you, being a little larger than you might like does not constitute a health hazard. In fact, being a few pounds overweight may actually be *better* for you than being a few pounds under. The 'fat equals unhealthy therefore thin equals healthy' equation flies in the face of available evidence. One major survey, carried out on the population of the town of Framingham in Massachusetts, USA, found no evidence to suggest that people who are *mildly* overweight are prejudicing their health. In fact, this group had the *best* survival record of the population – much better than the thinnest group, who were found to be more seriously at risk than the fattest . . .

Guidelines for women

Height without shoes (m)	Women Weight without clothes (kg)			
	Acceptable average	Acceptable weight range	Obese	
1.45	46.0	42–53	64	
1.48	46.5	42–54	65	
1.50	47.0	43–55	66	
1.52	48.5	44–57	68	
1.54	49.5	44–58	70	
1.56	50.4	45–58	70	
1.58	51.3	46–59	71	
1.60	52.6	48–61	73	
1.62	54.0	49–62	74	
1.64	55.4	50–64	77	
1.66	56.8	51–65	78	
1.68	58.1	52–66	79	
1.70	60.0	53–67	80	
1.72	61.3	55–69	83	
1.74	62.6	56–70	84	
1.76	64.0	58–72	86	
1.78	65.3	59–74	89	

Height without shoes (ft,in)	Women Weight without clothes (lb)			
	Acceptable average	Acceptable weight range	Obese	
4 10	102	92–119	143	
4 11	104	94–122	146	
5 0	107	96–125	150	
5 1	110	99–128	154	
5 2	113	102–131	152	
5 3	116	105–134	161	
5 4	120	108–138	166	
5 5	123	111–142	170	
5 6	128	114–146	175	
5 7	132	118–150	180	
5 8	136	122–154	185	
5 9	140	126–158	190	
5 10	144	130–163	196	
5 11	148	134–168	202	
6 0	152	138–173	208	

Bray, 1979; based on Metropolitan Life Insurance tables

ARE YOU TOO FAT?

Weight tables have been criticized for several reasons. One is that they make no assessment of fat. People come in all shapes and sizes as well as heights. You can be fit, firm and not a fraction too fat, yet be considerably heavier than someone of similar height but slighter build. It's proportion that counts.

Unfortunately, there is no easy, accurate and objective way of assessing proportion. Precise measurements of body fat require calipers and expertise. The pinch test, however, gives a rough guide. Reduce error by taking two 'pinches', one from the underside of your upper arm and the other from your hip. Add them together and divide by two to get an average and check it against the graph*, below.

Fat situated directly beneath the skin constitutes about 50 per cent of the total, so you can estimate how 'fat' you are by pinching your flesh. But make sure it is fat you are grasping, not muscle, which feels much firmer. Measure the distance between inner edges of thumb and forefinger.

WHAT IS YOUR 'BODY MASS INDEX'?

A third indication of excess weight is known as the Body Mass Index. This allows for increasing weight with increasing height and, very roughly, for differences in frame. It is expressed as follows:

$$\text{Body Mass Index} = \frac{\text{weight in kilogrammes}}{\text{height in metres}^2}$$

Check the tables, overleaf, to find the correct index for your weight and height. If the figure is under 19, you are definitely underweight and if the figure is over 24.4 you are definitely overweight – regardless of what build you are. If the figure comes within these two extreme ends of the range, however, things become more complicated because you may still be under- or overweight, depending on your build. To date, there is no completely reliable way of determining build (frame size) or its appropriate range, but the approximate ranges, given below, provide a rough guide. Assess frame size by taking two measurements – one from the tip of one shoulder to the tip of the other shoulder and the other from the tip of one shoulder to the tip (bony point) of the elbow. If these are roughly the same, assume frame size to be medium; if width is greater than length, assume frame size to be between medium and large; if the length is greater than the width, assume frame size to be between medium and small. If all this is too confusing, simply use your personal judgement and, if in doubt, choose medium.

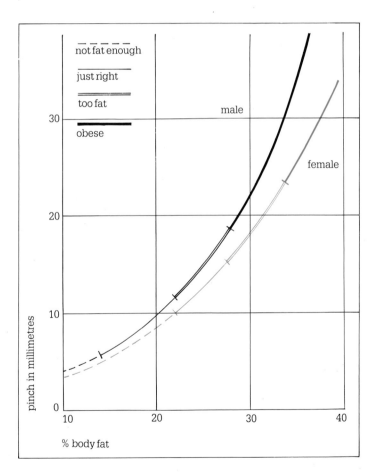

*devised from figures produced by J.V.G.A. Durnin and J. Wormersley in 'Body fat assessed from total body density and its estimation from skinfold thickness: measurements in 481 men and women aged 16 to 72 years' in the 'British Journal of Nutrition', 1974, 32, pp 77–99.

Weight ranges for adult women*

Frame	Desirable	Borderline	Overweight	Obese
Large	21.4–24	24.5–25.7	25.8–29	more than 29
Medium	20.1–22.3	22.4–23.7	23.8–26.7	more than 26.7
Small	19–20.5	20.6–22.5	22.6–24.4	more than 24.4

*approximate ranges estimated using 'Slimdicator' designed by T.J. Cole and W.P.T. James.

A GUIDE TO BODY MASS INDEX

Height in metres

Weight in kilogrammes

	1·46	1·48	1·50	1·52	1·54	1·56	1·58	1·60	1·62	1·64	1·66	1·68	1·70	1·72	1·74	1·76	1·78	1·80
45	21·1	20·5	20	19·5	19	18·5	18	17·6	17	16·7	16·3	15·9	15·6	15·2	14·9	14·5	14·2	13·9
46	21·6	21	20·4	19·9	19·4	18·9	18·4	18	17·5	17	16·7	16·3	15·9	15·5	15·2	14·8	14·5	14·2
47	22	21·5	20·9	20·3	19·8	19·3	18·8	18·4	17·9	17·5	17·1	16·6	16·3	15·9	15·5	15·2	14·8	14·5
48	22·5	22	21·3	20·8	20·2	19·7	19·2	18·7	18·3	17·8	17·4	17	16·6	16·2	15·8	15·5	15·1	14·8
49	23	22·4	21·8	21·2	20·1	20·2	19·6	19·1	18·7	18·2	17·8	17·4	17	16·6	16·2	15·8	15·5	15·1
50	23·5	22·8	22·2	21·6	21·1	20·5	20	19·5	19·1	18·6	18·1	17·7	17·3	16·9	16·5	16·1	15·8	15·4
51	23·9	23·3	22·7	22·1	21·5	21	20·4	19·9	19·4	19	18·5	18·1	17·6	17·2	16·8	16·5	16·1	15·7
52	24·4	23·7	23·1	22·5	21·9	21·4	20·8	20·3	19·8	19·3	18·8	18·4	18	17·6	17·2	16·8	16·4	16
53	24·9	24·2	23·6	22·9	22·3	21·8	21·2	20·7	20·2	19·7	19·2	18·8	18·3	17·9	17·5	17·1	16·7	16·4
54	25·3	24·7	24	23·4	22·8	22·2	21·6	21·1	20·6	20·1	19·6	19·1	18·7	18·3	17·8	17·4	17	16·7
55	25·8	25·1	24·4	23·8	23·2	22·6	22	21·5	21	20·4	20	19·5	19	18·6	18·2	17·8	17·4	17
56	26·3	25·6	24·9	24·2	23·6	23	22·4	21·9	21·3	20·8	20·3	19·8	19·4	18·9	18·5	18·1	17·7	17·3
57	26·7	26	25·3	24·7	24	23·4	22·8	22·3	21·7	21·2	20·7	20·2	19·7	19·3	18·8	18·4	18	17·6
58	27·2	26·5	25·8	25·1	24·5	23·8	23·2	22·7	22·1	21·6	21	20·5	20·1	19·6	19·2	18·7	18·3	17·9
59	27·7	26·9	26·2	25·5	24·9	24·2	23·6	23	22·5	21·9	21·4	20·9	20·4	19·9	19·5	19	18·6	18·2
60	28·1	27·4	26·7	26	25·3	24·7	24	23·4	22·9	22·3	21·8	21·3	20·8	20·3	19·8	19·4	18·9	18·5
61	28·7	27·8	27·1	26·4	25·7	25·1	24·4	23·8	23·2	22·7	22·1	21·6	21·1	20·6	20·1	19·7	19·3	18·8
62	29	28·3	27·6	26·8	26·1	25·5	24·8	24·2	23·6	23·1	22·5	22	21·5	21	20·5	20	19·6	19·1
63	29·6	28·7	28	27·3	26·6	25·9	25·2	24·6	24	23·4	22·9	22·3	21·8	21·3	20·8	20·3	19·9	19·4
64	30	29·2	28·4	27·7	27	26·3	25·6	25	24·4	23·8	23·2	22·7	22·1	21·6	21·1	20·7	20·2	19·8
65	30·5	29·7	28·9	28·1	27·4	26·7	26	25·4	24·8	24·2	23·6	23	22·5	22	21·5	21	20·5	20·1
66	31	30·1	29·3	28·6	27·8	27·1	26·4	25·8	25·1	24·5	24	23·4	22·8	22·3	21·8	21·3	20·8	20·4
67	31·4	30·6	29·8	29	28·3	27·5	26·8	26·2	25·5	24·9	24·3	23·7	23·2	22·6	22·1	21·6	21·1	20·7
68	31·9	31	30·2	29·4	28·7	27·9	27·2	26·6	25·9	25·3	24·7	24·1	23·5	22·9	22·5	22	21·5	21
69	32·4	31·5	30·7	29·9	29·1	28·4	27·6	26·9	26·3	25·7	25	24·4	23·8	23·3	22·8	22·3	21·8	21·2
70	32·8	31·9	31·1	30·3	29·5	28·8	28·1	27·3	26·7	26·1	25·4	24·8	24·2	23·7	23·1	22·6	22·1	21·6
71	33·3	32·4	31·5	30·7	29·9	29·2	28·5	27·7	27	26·4	25·8	25·1	24·5	24	23·5	22·9	22·4	21·9
72	33·8	32·8	32	31·1	30·3	29·6	28·9	28·1	27·4	26·8	26·1	25·5	24·9	24·4	23·8	23·3	22·7	22·2
73	34·2	33·3	32·4	31·6	30·8	30	29·3	28·5	27·8	27·2	26·5	25·8	25·2	24·7	24·1	23·6	23·1	22·5
74	34·7	33·7	32·8	32	31·2	30·4	29·7	28·9	28·2	27·6	26·9	26·2	25·6	25	24·5	23·9	23·4	22·8
75	35·2	34·2	33·3	32·4	31·6	30·8	30·1	29·2	28·6	27·9	27·2	26·5	25·9	25·4	24·8	24·2	23·7	23·1
76	35·6	34·7	33·7	32·9	32	31·2	30·5	29·6	29	28·3	27·6	26·9	26·2	25·7	25·1	24·5	24	23·4
77	36·1	35·1	34·2	33·3	32·4	31·6	30·9	30	29·3	28·7	28	27·3	26·6	26·1	25·4	24·9	24·3	23·7
78	36·6	35·6	34·6	33·7	32·9	32	31·3	30·4	29·7	29·1	28·3	27·6	26·9	26·4	25·8	25·2	24·6	24
79	37	36	35·1	34·1	33·3	32·5	31·7	30·8	30·1	29·4	28·7	28	27·3	26·7	26·1	25·5	25	24·3
80	37·5	36·5	35·5	34·6	33·7	32·9	32·1	31·2	30·5	29·8	29	28·3	27·6	27·1	26·4	25·8	25·3	24·6
81	38	36·9	36	35	34·1	33·3	32·5	31·6	30·9	30·2	29·4	28·7	28	27·4	26·8	26·2	25·6	25
82	38·4	37·4	36·4	35·4	34·5	33·7	32·9	32	31·2	30·5	29·8	29	28·3	27·7	27·1	26·5	25·9	25·3
83	38·9	37·8	36·8	35·9	35	34·1	33·3	32·4	31·6	30·9	30·1	29·4	28·7	28·1	27·4	26·8	26·2	25·6
84	39·4	38·3	37·3	36·3	35·4	34·5	33·7	32·8	32	31·3	30·5	29·7	29	28·4	27·8	27·1	26·5	25·9
85	39·9	38·8	37·7	36·7	35·8	34·9	34·1	33·2	32·4	31·7	30·9	30·1	29·4	28·8	28·1	27·5	26·8	26·2
86	40·3	39·2	38·2	37·2	36·2	35·3	34·5	33·5	32·8	32	31·2	30·4	29·7	29·1	28·4	27·8	27·2	26·5
87	40·8	39·7	38·6	37·6	36·7	35·8	34·9	33·9	33·2	32·4	31·6	30·8	30·1	29·4	28·8	28·1	27·5	26·8
88	41·3	40·1	39·1	38	37·1	36·2	35·3	34·3	33·5	32·8	32	31·2	30·4	29·8	29·1	28·4	27·8	27·1
89	41·7	40·6	39·5	38·5	37·5	36·6	35·7	34·7	33·9	33·2	32·3	31·5	30·7	30·1	29·4	28·8	28·1	27·4
90	42·2	41	40	38·9	37·9	37	36·1	35·1	34·3	33·5	32·7	31·9	31·1	30·5	29·8	29·1	28·4	27·8

THE SET RANGE THEORY AND WHY IT MATTERS

Statistics are great levellers. They allow only for differences in height and frame, and give 'acceptable' ranges which are often broad to a fault – over 12.5 kg (28 lb) in some cases. You may come well within them but still feel dissatisfied with your shape and no closer to knowing what your optimal weight should be.

There may be a second problem if what you feel to be your optimal weight does not coincide with the weight you naturally incline towards when eating well, but not excessively, and exercising regularly. When the weight at which you feel physiologically happiest, your 'natural' weight, is at odds with the weight at which you feel psychologically happiest, your 'ideal' weight, the seeds of an intractable weight problem are sown and a miserable life-long struggle can ensue, because every diet you pick simply pits you against yourself.

Scientists call the weight at which you feel physiologically happiest the 'set point' – a misleading term because it is more likely to be a range than any one particular weight. Whether your set range is small (as little as 1 kilo/2 pounds) or large (6 kilos/13 pounds or more) mostly depends on the genes you inherit and to a lesser, but nevertheless still appreciable, extent on your previous dieting history.

Just as some set ranges are broader than others, so some are lower or higher. This distinguishes people who put weight on very easily from those who don't. Two people of similar height can have very dissimilar set ranges – the lowest point of each representing that point beyond which they will each find it very difficult to lose weight. But even here there are differences. While some set ranges are controlled very tightly, making it difficult to dip even a kilo or so below them, others are more loosely defended. Defence takes two forms: *physiological/metabolic*, by using up energy-expensive lean tissue, reducing metabolic rate and slowing you down (see page 34) and *psychological/behavioural* by making you irritable, depressed, discontented and increasing your appetite and interest in food, especially deliciously fattening foods...

Set ranges may not be as 'set' as all that. Repeated dieting, and large weight fluctuations especially, appear to reset them upwards, possibly to create a 'safety margin' that will help protect against similar rash drops in weight in the future. So people who complain that they never had a weight problem until they started dieting may actually have a point! More positively, there are indications that regular vigorous exercise has a *lowering* effect on the set range.

Is your ideal weight within your set range or should you modify your goals?
1 *What do you weigh?* _____
2 *What would/do you weigh without restriction or excessive binges?* _____
3 *What would you like to weigh?* _____
4 *Have you ever managed to get down to this weight?...*
　more than once/once only/never
5 *...and to stay there comfortably for at least 3 months?* *yes/no*

Fortunate individuals giving the same answer to the first 3 questions have no need for this book or, indeed, for any diet book, but anyone giving very different answers to these questions, and particularly to 2 and 3, should carefully examine their reasons for wanting to be the weight they gave and should, perhaps, modify their goals.

If your answer to question 2 was very much higher than your answer to question 3, your ideal weight is likely to be some way outside your set range.

Answers to questions 4 and 5 will indicate by how much. If you have never managed to get down to this ideal weight or only with extreme difficulty, and found staying there virtually impossible, you should set yourself a more realistic goal. Use the charts given earlier and the guidelines that follow to determine this.

If your answers to 2 and 3 are some way apart, but your answer to question 4 is 'more than once' and you managed to stay there comfortably, your ideal weight is probably within your set range – just – even if your present weight is some way above it and has been for a time. Follow the long-term eating plan, losing weight steadily at a rate of no more than 1 kg (2 lb) a week, to reattain it.

ASSESS YOUR SET RANGE

Think back over past diets. How did you feel at the weights you were?

Above set range	*able to eat quite substantially without gaining very much more weight.*
Within set range	*able to maintain weight fairly easily without great deprivation; able to diet down to the lowest point of the range quite easily but further weight loss significantly harder once past it.*
Below set range	*great effort, vigilance and deprivation required to keep weight stable; growing sense of frustration; obsessive preoccupation with food even to the point of dreaming about it; high susceptibility to hunger in general and high-calorie foods in particular.*

If the above is not guide enough, there are other ways of telling whether your weight lies inside or outside your set range – and these all refer to the way you *feel*.

Life below the set range, and the sort of dieting designed to get you there, is highly stressful. The conflict between you, trying to get your weight down, and your body, trying to push your weight up, produces measurable biochemical changes, such as raised levels of stress hormones (catecholamines) in the blood. These changes are accompanied by changes in mood. As weight drops, concentration falters, sense of humour diminishes, emotions become much more highly charged and irritability and agitation increase.

Keep stress down by keeping food intake at a reasonable level and expectations realistic. If your present weight is within your set range and you are still dissatisfied with your general shape, combine diet aimed for the lower point of the range (the point at which it *begins* to become hard to lose weight and to keep it off) with a structured exercise programme to firm specific problem areas. You will be amazed by the transformation.

WHAT KIND OF EATER ARE YOU?

(To convert pounds to kilogrammes, multiply by 0.45)

1. How often do you diet? (Circle one)

Never	Rarely	Sometimes	Usually	Always

2. What is the maximum amount of weight (in pounds) you have ever lost within one month?

0–4	5–9	10–14	15–19	20+

3. What is your maximum weight gain within a week?

0–1	1.1–2	2.1–3	3.1–5	5.1+

4. In a typical week, how much does your weight fluctuate?

0–1	1.1–2	2.1–3	3.1–5	5.1+

5. Would a weight fluctuation of 5lb affect the way you live your life?

Not at all	Slightly	Moderately	Very much

6. Do you eat sensibly in front of others and binge alone?

Never	Rarely	Often	Always

7. Do you give too much time and thought to food?

Never	Rarely	Often	Always

8. Do you have feelings of guilt after overeating?

Never	Rarely	Often	Always

9. How conscious are you of what you are eating?

Not at all	Slightly	Moderately	Extremely

10. How many pounds over your desired weight were you at your maximum weight?

0–1	1–5	6–10	11–20	21

1 *Never = 0, Rarely = 1, Sometimes = 2, Usually = 3, Always = 4*

2 *0–4 = 0, 5–9 = 1, 10–14 = 2, 15–19 = 3, 20+ = 4*

3 *0–1 = 0, 1.2–2 = 1, 2.1–3 = 2, 3.1–5 = 3, 5.1+ = 4*

4 *0–1 = 0, 1.1–2 = 1, 2.1–3 = 2, 3.1–5 = 3, 5.1+ = 4*

5 *Not at all = 0, Slightly = 1, Moderately = 2, Very much = 3*

6 *Never = 0, Rarely = 1, Often = 2, Always = 3*

7 *Never = 0, Rarely = 1, Often = 2, Always = 3*

8 *Never = 0, Rarely = 1, Often = 2, Always = 3*

9 *Not at all = 0, Slightly = 1, Moderately = 2, Extremely = 3*

10 *0–1 = 0, 1–5 = 1, 6–10 = 2, 11–20 = 3, 21 = 4*

Add up total score to find your index of restraint. Now refer to the analysis.

Questionnaire adapted from 'Internal and External Components of Emotionality in Restrained and Unrestrained Eaters' devised by J. Polivy, C.P. Herman and S. Walsh in the Journal of Abnormal Psychology, 1978, 87, page 497.

What the scores mean

High scorers on this scale *(mid-20s and above)* are chronic dieters – people who find it easier to count the days off diets rather than the days on them. They are extremely weight conscious and very preoccupied with what they eat. They are 'restrained'. Anorexics and bulimics, victims of the binge/vomit disease, are very restrained indeed. In fact, some bulimics have got the highest possible restraint score of 35.

A high score also indicates an 'ideal' weight some way below the set range and an increased susceptibility to stress-induced eating (maybe as a direct result of the stress of having to keep one's weight so low). Use the blank diary pages, further on, to help determine whether this is the case.

Moderate scorers *(low 20s and high teens)* may be conscious of what they eat as much for health as for weight reasons and may rarely diet or weigh themselves.

Low scorers *(15 and below)* are people who tend to eat what they like, regardless of how nutritious or fattening it is. They are not particularly concerned with what they weigh and rarely perceive it as a 'problem'. They are 'unrestrained'. Many score as low as 5; none is likely to be reading this book.

Which diet for which score?

(High scorers *(mid 20s and above)* are advised to follow the 24-week programme from week 1, even if weight initially increases slightly as food intake returns to more normal levels. Although quantities of food included in the earlier weeks of the diet may seem large, it will help weight to stabilize and will instil more appropriate eating patterns. Keep to the diet until you reach your goal – it may only take a few weeks – and then repeat Week 1, gradually increasing food intake until you establish an appropriate maintenance level.

Lower scorers *(early 20s and below)* should use the diet plan to lose as much weight as they need, starting at week 12 or even 20. The Blitz or 14-day Special diets might appeal as a quick means to moderate weight loss if objectives are more limited or weight needs to be lost quite quickly for a special occasion.

PAST IMPERFECT, FUTURE BETTER...

Diets, like history, have a habit of repeating themselves. Writing down why your diets usually fail in the space provided below may help make this one the exception. Your first safeguard is awareness; your second, the insight to pick an appropriate diet. See suggestions, *opposite*.

WHY DO DIETS FAIL (AND HOW CAN YOU SUCCEED)?

Reason	Suggested strategy	Diet
Boredom at prospect of so much further to go	Set limited objectives, shorter deadlines: e.g. a non-edible reward for every 1.8 kg/4 lb lost or a week off a month.	Start programme at week 20; earlier if you need to lose more weight, but take a week off every 4 weeks, or even every 3 (including 2 juice diet days), then continue with the diet.
Boredom with repetitive, unappetizing food	Choose an interesting diet with unusual food combinations fresh herbs and spices, exotic fruit, seafood and good cuts of meat. Spending more on less will make what you do eat seem special. Discover the wide choice of herb teas and tisanes available. Enjoy an occasional glass of champagne.	24-week programme, starting week 1, 12 or 20, depending on goal; the Vegetarian diet for a complete change.
Lack of will power	Write failure into the diet by allowing yourself to break it. (See notes on Indulgences page 54).	24-week programme.
Lack (or loss) of incentive	Go to health spa for a few days to get started or reinspired; make a contract with a friend; join a weightwatching group or exercise class.	Start with or switch to the Blitz diet for an encouraging initial loss, then return to the longer-term programme.
Loss of confidence in ability to lose weight at all	Pick your moment, such as when returning from holiday or any time when you have extra energy and a positive attitude.	Any, as long as it is a) balanced and b) different in every respect from the ones that have preceded it, i.e. the long-term programme if you usually crash diet or the High-Fibre/Low-Fat diet if you normally pick a low-carbohydrate one.
Weight sticking	Do you really *need* to continue with the diet? Re-read notes on 'set point' on the previous page. If you decide you do, continue with the diet and take more exercise. Vow not to look at the scales for a fortnight: use a tape measure instead.	
Erratic lifestyle	Choice of diet is crucial: it MUST be flexible and easy to follow.	24-week programme. Blitz or one of the 14-day special diets. Be well prepared by buying as much as possible beforehand.
Busy professional/social life	Most diets adapt easily to restaurant menus and most restaurants will adapt easily to your wishes, providing lemon juice in place of vinaigrette, unbuttered vegetables, etc. So ask . . .	Avoid diets that dictate exactly what you must and must not eat. Follow long-term programme, using dinner party menus for entertaining.
Snacking	Be prepared. Cut fine strips of carrot, celery, apple, cauliflower, etc, each morning and keep in refrigerator. Eat lunch and breakfast in stages.	One that subdivides easily: the 3 meals in the long-term programme can break down to 6 mini ones or even more . . .
Keeping the family company	Convert them to your healthier way of eating or make sure that you provide for yourself while they eat, so you do not have to sit, watch and be tempted . . .	24-week programme (starting week 1, 12 or 20). Most meals can be made more substantial and/or appealing to children by clever additions.
Surrounded by food	Out of sight is out of mind. Remove temptation where possible and where not possible pack in opaque containers. Buy as much as you need – no more. If necessary, shop more often.	
Arguments/emotional upheavals	Awareness is your best defence. Fill in the diary section over the page to see if there is a link between your mood and the amount or *type* of food you eat. Sometimes, a particular food becomes linked subconsciously with a particular state of mind, so that we not only reward or console ourselves by eating, which is itself inappropriate, but by eating the same sort of food – invariably the stodgy, unhealthy, highly-processed and fattening kind. Help yourself to break the pattern by being more aware of it and by resolving to eat only healthy foods.	A moderate diet, such as part or all of the 24-week programme, will actually help you to break the mood/food pattern by introducing healthier foods and making you more aware of how and when you choose to indulge (see page 54).

THE DIET DIARY

We all eat for all sorts of reasons other than the need for food. Use this diary to help you determine what they are. If not actual sensations of hunger, such as stomach rumbles, what prompts you to have a meal? Convention (1 pm = 'lunchtime'), coercion, emotional stress, or have you never even thought about it?

It is important to continue with your diary for the full five days in order to get a reliable pattern. Individual days can be misleading. Remember that you are looking for factors that *consistently* determine the way you eat (or overeat) and the diary should highlight what these are. Once it does, the way forward will be clear. Combine diet with careful restructuring of lifestyle. Re-

lease nervous energy, comply with convention or mitigate boredom in more appropriate ways.

Write down everything you eat and drink in the columns provided on these pages. Don't worry if the lists seem very long. It is quite normal to be surprised, even alarmed, by the quantities you eat when everything is listed individually.

When you have completed your diary, look through it to see how well balanced and nutritious your diet is. As junk food can actually be a *cause* of overeating (see page 50), adjustments of quality as well as quantity may be in order. Bear in mind too that food, like drugs, can alter neurotransmitters in the brain and may affect mood and behaviour. Use the final column on your blank page to identify what these foods might be, noting in particular coffee, tea, alcohol and sugar-laden foods.

Day of the week: _____   Date: _____
Time: _____   Amount: _____   Food & drink: _____   Situation and mood before eating

_____   _____   _____   _____
_____   _____   _____   _____
_____   _____   _____   _____
_____   _____   _____   _____
_____   _____   _____   _____
_____   _____   _____   _____
_____   _____   _____   _____
_____   _____   _____   _____
_____   _____   _____   _____
_____   _____   _____   _____
_____   _____   _____   _____
_____   _____   _____   _____

Day of the week: _____   Date: _____
Time: _____   Amount: _____   Food & drink: _____   Situation and mood before eating

_____   _____   _____   _____
_____   _____   _____   _____
_____   _____   _____   _____
_____   _____   _____   _____
_____   _____   _____   _____
_____   _____   _____   _____
_____   _____   _____   _____
_____   _____   _____   _____
_____   _____   _____   _____
_____   _____   _____   _____
_____   _____   _____   _____

Day of the week: _____ Date: _____ Food & drink: _____ Situation and mood before eating
Time: _____ Amount: _____

_____ _____ _____ _____
_____ _____ _____ _____
_____ _____ _____ _____
_____ _____ _____ _____
_____ _____ _____ _____
_____ _____ _____ _____
_____ _____ _____ _____
_____ _____ _____ _____
_____ _____ _____ _____
_____ _____ _____ _____
_____ _____ _____ _____
_____ _____ _____ _____
_____ _____ _____ _____
_____ _____ _____ _____

Day of the week: _____ Date: _____ Food & drink: _____ Situation and mood before eating
Time: _____ Amount: _____

_____ _____ _____ _____
_____ _____ _____ _____
_____ _____ _____ _____
_____ _____ _____ _____
_____ _____ _____ _____
_____ _____ _____ _____
_____ _____ _____ _____
_____ _____ _____ _____
_____ _____ _____ _____
_____ _____ _____ _____
_____ _____ _____ _____
_____ _____ _____ _____
_____ _____ _____ _____
_____ _____ _____ _____

Day of the week: _____ Date: _____ Food & drink: _____ Situation and mood before eating
Time: _____ Amount: _____

_____ _____ _____ _____
_____ _____ _____ _____
_____ _____ _____ _____
_____ _____ _____ _____
_____ _____ _____ _____
_____ _____ _____ _____
_____ _____ _____ _____
_____ _____ _____ _____
_____ _____ _____ _____
_____ _____ _____ _____
_____ _____ _____ _____
_____ _____ _____ _____
_____ _____ _____ _____

The 24-week diet programme

HOW TO USE THE PROGRAMME

This eating programme is graduated downwards, getting stricter as it continues... 1500 calories a day for the first eight weeks, 1200 calories for the next eleven weeks and 1000 calories, as low as nutritionists recommend for extended periods, for the last five. This will help keep weight loss steady, energy and spirits up, frustration down. Plateau phases are avoided by reducing food intake as the diet progresses. Where you start depends on how much you have to lose...

Start right at the beginning, week one, if you have more than 12.5 kg (28 lb) to lose; week eight if you have between 9 and 12.5 kg (20-28 lb); week 12 if you have between 6.5 and 9 kg (14-20 lb); week 16 if you have between 3.5 and 6.5 kg (8-14 lb) and week 20 if you have 3.5 kg (8 lb) or less. Starting earlier rather than later will make for more lasting differences in weight, shape, eating habits. So allow plenty of time. If you reach your goal before the end of the programme, gradually increase intake to keep weight stable by repeating two of the early (1500-calorie) weeks before stopping the diet altogether.

Resolve now to follow the diet as closely as you can. Buy fruit, vegetables, fish and meat as fresh as possible, find shops that sell wholewheat bread and wholewheat pasta (not difficult – most supermarkets now stock them as well as health food stores) and take the trouble to follow the recipes where given.

The programme has been devised in line with the most recent research findings and recommendations. It is healthy as well as slimming – rich in complex (starchy) carbohydrates, low in refined carbohydrates and fat, moderate in protein and high in fresh fruit and vegetables, often raw for maximum nutritional value. Sugar is kept to a minimum. Salt should be kept down, too (see page 46).

Once familiar with the diet, you will find it very flexible. Breakfasts and light meals are coded according to calorific value and listed on the following pages, so as to give as wide a choice as possible. Main meals are given each day and are specially planned, week by week, to include at least one vegetarian, one fish and one iron-rich meal, some poultry and red meat. Red meat, although rich in minerals such as zinc, is limited to just once or twice a week because the latest studies advise moderation of all animal fats. Dishes in dark type have recipes which can be found in the Recipe index at the back (pages 94-123).

Lists of vegetables are given beneath each of the main meals. Where the meal contains rice, pastry, pulses, potato or pasta (as in lasagne), or where these are listed separately (as in vegetable curry and rice), choose just one; otherwise, choose three (preferably one of them potato if listed). Green and mixed salads should be very lightly dressed with a dessertspoon of Lemon and Mustard, Lemon and Tarragon, Cucumber and Yoghurt or Cottage Cheese and Chive dressings (find recipes for these in the Recipe index).

If you do not like the main meal, replace that entire day for another within the appropriate section (i.e. weeks 1-8; 9-19; 20-24), but try to keep the balance right by exchanging like for like (fish for fish, for example), and remember to switch light meals too so that the total calorific value for the day remains the same.

Each week allows a certain number of 'indulgences'. These are coded 🧁🧁🧁, listed at the top of each week and reduced as the diet progresses. The Indulgences not only make the diet more enjoyable, but also help prevent strong cravings taking a hold and sabotaging all the good work done so far. Consult the lists on page 54.

While it is important to follow the diet closely, you may have to allow yourself some latitude if you have a busy social life. Concentrate on keeping intake moderate. Choose, or ask for, simply prepared meat and fish (no rich sauces), unbuttered vegetables, salads with a little dressing, fresh fruit instead of heavy desserts. Alcohol, which counts as an indulgence, can be drunk in moderation.

Drink at least six glasses of water a day (bottled or tap) and any amount of herb teas, tisanes and tea (with lemon). Try decaffeinated coffee, or coffee with chicory, for a change and discover the huge range of herbal teas and tisanes available. They not only keep you calmer, but taste delicious too...

Cut time and trouble by making more than you need and freezing it. A number in brackets – eg lasagne (×4) – indicates that you should make 4 times the recipe quantity, and freeze 3 portions for use in future weeks.

BREAKFASTS

Different lists are given for different stages of the diet. Choose any menu and eat it at any time of day – not necessarily first thing or all at once. Try varying your breakfasts to see how well you feel and how much energy you have. From a metabolic point of view, protein is digested more efficiently in the early part of the day – so eggs, fish, even cheese and lean meat, European style, make an excellent breakfast.

WEEKS 1-12/300 CALORIES

MENU I

1 small peach/2 small fresh figs/
2 clementines/1 medium slice honeydew melon/125g (4 oz) raspberries/1 whole grapefruit
AND
1 bowl of muesli: 15g (½ oz) oatflakes, 15g (½ oz) chopped hazelnuts, 25g (1 oz) sultanas [golden raisins] and 15g (½ oz) wheatgerm, with 150 ml (¼ pint) (⅔ cup) skimmed milk

or

1 large scrambled egg with skimmed milk, 1 grilled rasher bacon [1 broiled bacon slice], 1 x 25g (1 oz) slice wholewheat toast and scraping of butter

or

125g (4 oz) smoked salmon with 2 x 25g (1 oz) slices wholwheat bread with scraping of butter, lemon juice and pepper

or

75g (3 oz) grilled [broiled] kipper fillet with 1 tomato and 1 slice wholewheat toast with scraping of butter

or

25g (1 oz) bran flakes/cornflakes/ grapenuts/raisin bran/wheatgerm with 1 tbsp plain yogurt and 150 ml (¼ pint) (⅔ cup) skimmed milk; 1 x 25g (1 oz) slice wholewheat toast with scraping of butter and 1 tsp honey, jam or marmalade

or

1 medium brown roll with 1 tsp butter and 2 tsp honey, jam or marmalade

or

1 small croissant with 1 tsp honey or jam
AND
cup of coffee (preferably decaffeinated), tea or herb tea – black with lemon or small dash of skimmed milk

MENU II

25g (1 oz) bran flakes/cornflakes/ grapenuts/raisin bran/1 Shredded Wheat/ 2 Weetabix/40g (1½ oz) bran cereal with 150 ml (¼ pint) (⅔ cup) skimmed milk

or

1 small carton plain yogurt with 2 tsp honey, 15g (½ oz) chopped hazelnuts and a sprinkling of wheatgerm

or

1 large mango

or

½ cantaloupe melon filled with 175g (6 oz) strawberries and 125g (4 oz) raspberries

or

1 large poached or coddled egg with 25g (1 oz) thinly sliced Parma ham/smoked ham
AND
2 x 25g (1 oz) wholewheat toast/1 bran muffin/3 pieces rye crispbread with 1 tsp butter, 1 tsp honey, jam or marmalade

or

1 x 25g (1 oz) slice light rye bread with ½ sliced hard-boiled egg layered with 15g (½ oz) thinly sliced Esrom, Gouda, Edam or Havarti cheese and some slices of tomato
AND
cup of coffee (preferably decaffeinated), tea or herb tea – black, with lemon or small dash of skimmed milk

MENU III

200 ml (⅓ pint) (⅞ cup) freshly squeezed orange or grapefruit juice

or

150 ml (¼ pint) (⅔ cup) apple or pineapple juice

or

2 medium oranges/2 small pears/175g (6 oz) cherries/2 small apples/1 medium banana/1 medium nectarine
AND
125g (4 oz) hot poached smoked haddock mixed with ½ chopped hard-boiled egg, chopped parsley on 1 x 25g (1 oz) slice wholewheat toast with scraping of butter

or

1 large scrambled egg made with skimmed milk, with 125g (4 oz) poached mushrooms and chopped parsley with 1 rye crispbread

or

2 grilled rashers streaky bacon [2 broiled bacon slices] with 1 grilled [broiled] tomato and 1 x 25g (1 oz) slice wholewheat toast and scraping of butter

or

1 x 25g (1 oz) slice light rye bread with 40g (1½ oz) very thinly sliced Esrom, Danbo, Jarlsberg, Edam or Gouda cheese with thin slice of orange

or

25g (1 oz) peanut butter on 1 rye crispbread
AND
cup of coffee (preferably decaffeinated), tea or herb tea – black, with lemon or small dash of skimmed milk

MENU I

150 ml (¼ pint) (⅔ cup) freshly squeezed orange or grapefruit juice/1 orange/1 pear/125g (4 oz) fresh pineapple/125g (4 oz) fresh guava/5 fresh apricots or plums/175g (6 oz) strawberries/½ fresh mango

or

1 satsuma, 125g (4 oz) raspberries or 2 fresh apricots with 2 tbsp plain yogurt
AND
1 x 40g (1½ oz) slice wholewheat toast with scraping of butter and honey, jam or marmalade

or

25g (1 oz) bran flakes/cornflakes/grapenuts/raisin bran/2 Weetabix/1 large Shredded Wheat with 150 ml (¼ pint) (⅔ cup) skimmed milk and no sugar

or

1 medium poached, boiled or coddled egg with 2 rye crispbreads and scraping of butter

or

75g (3 oz) smoked salmon with squeeze of lemon juice and black pepper/50g (2 oz) smoked ham, both with 1 rye crispbread and scraping of butter

or

2 grilled rashers streaky bacon [2 broiled bacon slices] with 1 tomato
AND
cup of coffee (preferably decaffeinated), tea or herb tea – black, with lemon or small dash of skimmed milk

MENU II

25g (1 oz) bran flakes/cornflakes/grapenuts/raisin bran/2 Weetabix/1 large Shredded Wheat with 150 ml (¼ pint) (⅔ cup) skimmed milk, no sugar

or

75g (3 oz) dried and soaked prunes with 2 tbsp plain yogurt

or

1 medium banana/125g (4 oz) paw-paw with 150g (5 oz) carton plain yogurt

or

2 fresh nectarines

or

2 grilled rashers streaky bacon [2 broiled bacon slices], 1 tomato and 125g (4 oz) poached mushrooms
AND
1 rye crispbread with scraping of butter and jam, honey or marmalade
AND
cup of coffee (preferably decaffeinated), tea or herb tea – black, with lemon or small dash of skimmed milk

MENU III

½ medium grapefruit/½ medium ogen melon/1 medium satsuma
AND
2 x 25g (1 oz) slices wholewheat toast, scraping of butter and jam, honey or marmalade

or

2 grilled rashers streaky bacon [2 broiled bacon slices], 1 tomato and 125g (4 oz) poached mushrooms

or

1 x 25g (1 oz) slice light rye bread/2 slices rye crispbread with 25g (1 oz) thinly sliced Esrom, Danbo, Jarlsberg, Edam or Gouda cheese

or

1 large boiled, poached or coddled egg with 1 x 25g (1 oz) slice wholewheat toast and scraping of butter
AND
cup of coffee (preferably decaffeinated), tea or herb tea – black, with lemon or small dash of skimmed milk

There is no good evidence to decree that you must start the day with something to eat, though most people feel better for doing so – but exactly what and how much they feel better for eating varies considerably. In one British study, a group of volunteers were all asked to change their breakfast habits for a few weeks – the large breakfast eaters having very little or nothing at all and the small breakfast eaters having a full meal. The result? Everyone felt *worse* for the change. Mental alertness, and concentration were particularly affected. It seems we naturally incline to what suits us best.

LIGHT MEALS

A 650 CALORIES

■ Watercress soup/Carrot soup/Celery soup/Potato, carrot and onion soup WITH 2 slices wholewheat bread and butter, 50g (2 oz) any cheese AND green salad with **French dressing**

■ Gazpacho/Cucumber and mint soup/Orange and tomato soup/Consommé WITH 125g (4 oz) French bread and 25g (1 oz) butter

■ **Three bean salad** with **French** or **Blue cheese dressing** WITH 150g (5 oz) grapes/small carton plain yogurt and 2 tsp honey

■ Salad Niçoise: 75g (3 oz) tuna (drained), 125g (4 oz) cold cooked new potato, 125g (4 oz) green beans, 1 tomato, 10 olives, 1 sliced hard-boiled egg, watercress, chopped lettuce, **French dressing** WITH 2 slices wholewheat/rye bread/wholewheat roll and butter

■ Special salad: 1 sliced hard-boiled egg, 25g (1 oz) browned pine nuts, 1 slice bread made into croûtons, tomatoes, chicory [endive], lettuce, radicchio, watercress, 40g (1½ oz) any hard cheese (grated), **Thousand Island** or **Lemon and tarragon dressing**

■ Club sandwich: 2 slices wholewheat toast, 50g (2 oz) any cheese, 2 grilled rashers streaky bacon [broiled bacon slice], 1 hard-boiled egg, 1 tsp mayonnaise salad/garnish WITH apple or banana

■ Toasted cheese: 2 slices wholewheat bread toasted on one side, spread with 1 tsp mustard (optional) and 50g (2 oz) any hard cheese grilled [broiled] WITH large mixed salad with 1 tbsp **French dressing** AND 1 banana/small carton natural yogurt and 1 tsp honey

■ Sandwiches: 3 slices wholewheat bread (fresh or toasted) WITH: 50g (2 oz) any cheese/150g (5 oz) chicken with 1 tsp mayonnaise/125g (4 oz) sardines with 1 tsp mayonnaise/100g (3½ oz) cooked ham/ 75g (3 oz) smoked salmon and little cream cheese/1 hard-boiled egg with 50g (2 oz) tuna and a little mayonnaise AND small carton plain yogurt and 2 tsp honey/150g (5 oz) grapes/apple and orange

■ 2 large eggs scrambled with skimmed milk, 2 grilled rashers streaky bacon [broiled bacon slices], 1 tomato, 2 slices wholewheat toast and butter AND 1 apple/75g (3 oz) grapes/1 orange

■ Soufflé cheese omelette/Spinach soufflé WITH wholewheat roll and butter, green salad with **French** or **Egg and caper dressing** AND 1 apple/75g (3 oz) grapes/1 orange

■ Quick pizza WITH mixed salad with **French** or **Blue cheese dressing** AND banana/small carton plain yogurt with 1 tsp honey

■ 2 poached eggs WITH 50g (2 oz) any hard cheese (grated) and 2 slices wholewheat toast and butter AND 1 orange/1 pear/1 apple/2 peaches

■ Wholewheat fettuccine/macaroni/rigatoni/shells/spaghetti with **Cheese and ham** or **Tomato and basil sauce** WITH green salad and 50g (2 oz) any chopped browned nuts and **French dressing**

■ 175g (6 oz) jacket potato WITH: 40g (1½ oz) sour cream, 75g (3 oz) smoked salmon, mixed salad and **Lemon and mustard** or **Herb dressing**/3 grilled [broiled] rashers streaky bacon, 40g (1½ oz) any hard cheese grated WITH large mixed salad with above dressings

■ 1 sliced avocado pear WITH 1 pink grapefruit and a little **French dressing** AND 1 slice wholewheat bread with scraping of butter

■ 150g (5 oz) grilled [broiled] beefburger with 25g (1 oz) any cheese, melted, WITH 1 wholewheat roll, lettuce, cucumber and tomato

■ 1 medium smoked trout, 2 slices wholewheat bread and butter WITH green salad and **Herb dressing** AND 1 orange/2 tangerines/4 plums

■ 150g (5 oz) smoked mackerel WITH green salad and **French Lemon and tarragon dressing** AND apple and orange/large banana

B 550 CALORIES

■ French onion soup WITH large mixed salad and 25g (1 oz) any chopped nuts with 1 tbsp **French** or **Blue cheese dressing**

■ Gazpacho/Cucumber and mint soup/Orange and tomato soup/Consommé WITH 75g (3 oz) French bread and butter

■ Minestrone/Corn and fish chowder/Cream of onion soup WITH 2 slices wholewheat bread and butter, 25g (1 oz) any cheese AND apple and orange/1 banana and a few nuts/150g (5 oz) grapes/small carton plain yogurt and 1 tsp honey

■ Melon, pear and cucumber salad/Mediterranean seafood salad/Curried mushroom salad/Fennel and orange salad/ Chinese cabbage and chicken salad WITH 75g (3 oz) French bread and butter/wholewheat roll and butter AND apple and orange/150g (5 oz) grapes/small carton plain yogurt and 2 tsp honey

■ **Three bean salad** WITH 1 tbsp **French, Blue cheese** or **Lemon and tarragon dressing** AND 1 slice wholewheat toast and butter

■ Salad Niçoise: as A but with 50g (2 oz) tuna

■ Avocado salad: ½ avocado pear, 25g (1 oz) Mozzarella cheese, 1 grilled rasher streaky bacon [broiled bacon slice], tomato, lettuce, cucumber, watercress, endive [chicory], 1 tbsp **French** or **Egg and caper dressing**

■ Club sandwich: as A but without fruit

■ Toasted cheese sandwich: as A but without fruit/yogurt

■ Toasted peanut butter sandwich: 2 slices wholewheat toast and 50g (2 oz) peanut butter and small carton plain yogurt with 1 tsp honey

■ Sandwiches: as A but without fruit or yogurt

■ 2 large scrambled eggs WITH 2 grilled rashers streaky bacon [broiled bacon slices], 1 slice wholewheat toast and butter AND 1 apple/ 1 orange and a few grapes/6 plums/75g (3 oz) grapes

■ Quick pizza WITH mixed salad and 1 tbsp **French** or **Egg and caper dressing**

■ Smoked salmon quiche/Tomato and courgette [zucchini] pie WITH mixed salad and 1 tbsp **French** or **Blue cheese dressing** AND 1 banana/1 apple and a few grapes/small carton plain yogurt with 1 tsp honey and sprinkling of wheatgerm

■ Wholewheat pasta as A but WITH 15g (½ oz) chopped nuts

■ **Lasagne** WITH green salad and **French dressing** AND 1 orange/ 2 tangerines/4 plums

■ **Jacket potatoes** with fillings 2 or 4 (page 107) WITH mixed salad, a sprinkling of nuts and 1 tbsp **Lemon and mustard** or **Herb dressing**

■ Corn on the cob WITH 25g (1 oz) butter and 2 slices wholewheat bread or toast

■ 1 large globe artichoke/150g (5 oz) asparagus WITH 40g (1½ oz) melted butter/3 tbsp **French dressing** AND 2 slices wholewheat/rye bread, 40g (1½ oz) any cheese/75g (3 oz) smoked salmon

■ ½ avocado pear sliced WITH ½ pink grapefruit, sprinkled with parsley and a little **French dressing** AND 1 wholewheat roll and butter AND 40g (1½ oz) any cheese

■ 1 large slice cantaloupe melon or 4 fresh figs WITH 75g (3 oz) Parma ham AND 2 slices wholewheat bread with butter, 25g (1 oz) any cheese

■ 100g (4 oz) grilled [broiled] beefburger WITH 1 wholewheat roll/175g (6 oz) cottage cheese AND mixed salad with **French** or **Blue cheese dressing**

Light meals are coded A, B, C or D according to calorific value and listed below. Each list gives a wide variety of ideas and includes food which can either be prepared simply at home or well in advance and taken to the office with you...

 400 CALORIES

 300 CALORIES

- French onion soup WITH 1 slice wholewheat bread and butter
- Watercress soup/Carrot soup/Celery soup/Potato, carrot and onion soup WITH 1 slice wholewheat/rye bread and butter, 25g (1 oz) any cheese
- Gazpacho/Cucumber and mint soup/Orange and tomato soup/Consommé WITH 1 slice wholewheat/rye bread and butter AND mixed salad with sprinkling chopped nuts and Lemon and tarragon or Egg dressing
- As first five salads from B WITH 1 slice wholewheat/rye bread and butter AND fruit/yogurt as listed
- Small serving Three bean salad without dressing
- Salad Niçoise: 50g (2 oz) tuna (drained), 125g (4 oz) green beans, 1 sliced hard-boiled egg, 1 tomato, lettuce, watercress, 10 olives, French dressing WITH 1 crispbread and scraping of butter
- Sandwiches: 2 slices wholewheat bread (fresh or toasted) with scraping of butter WITH: 50g (2 oz) any hard cheese/75g (3 oz) lean ham/40g (1½ oz) peanut butter/125g (4 oz) prosciutto/50g (2 oz) chicken liver, duck or game pâté/65g (2½ oz) tuna (drained)/3 grilled rashers streaky bacon [broiled bacon slices]/1 hard-boiled egg with 25g (1 oz) tuna and a little mayonnaise/100g (4 oz) smoked salmon/75g (3 oz) prawns [shrimps] with 1 tsp mayonnaise/75g (3 oz) sardines (drained) AND lettuce, tomato, cucumber, watercress garnish
- 65g (2½ oz) taramasalata with 1 piece warmed or toasted pitta bread
- 2 scrambled eggs WITH 25g (1 oz) smoked salmon and 1 slice wholewheat toast and butter
- Soufflé cheese omelette/Spinach soufflé WITH mixed salad and sprinkling chopped browned nuts and 1 tbsp French or Thousand Island dressing
- French vegetable quiche WITH large mixed salad and a little French or Herb dressing
- 2 poached eggs WITH 2 slices wholewheat toast and butter
- Leek and thyme quiche WITH mixed salad and French, Egg and caper or Thousand Island dressing
- Wholewheat pasta, as B but with no dressing on salad
- 175g (6 oz) jacket potato WITH 50g (2 oz) sour cream and 75g (3 oz) smoked salmon/2 rashers grilled streaky bacon [broiled bacon slices] and 20g (¾ oz) any hard cheese (grated), mixed salad and Herb dressing/Fillings 1 or 3 (page 107) WITH small green salad 15g (½ oz) chopped nuts and Lemon and tarragon dressing/ Fillings 2 or 4 WITH green or mixed salad and Blue cheese or French dressing
- ½ mango/½ cantaloupe melon/5 figs/large pear WITH 50g (2 oz) prosciutto or Parma ham AND 1 slice dark rye bread/2 crispbreads with scraping of butter
- ½ large avocado pear WITH ½ pink grapefruit sprinkled with chopped parsley and 1 tbsp French dressing AND 1 piece rye crispbread
- 150g (5 oz) artichoke hearts WITH 1 hard-boiled egg with lettuce, endive [chicory], cucumber sprinkled with chopped browned nuts and French or Egg and caper dressing
- 1 medium grilled [broiled] kipper WITH 1 piece wholewheat toast and butter
- 120g (4 oz) grilled [broiled] beefburger WITH 1 slice wholewheat bread/120g (4 oz) cottage cheese/mixed salad with Cucumber and yogurt or Herb dressing
  1 small smoked trout WITH mixed salad and French dressing AND 1 slice wholewheat bread and butter

- French onion soup WITH 1 crispbread
- Watercress soup/Carrot soup/Celery soup/Potato, carrot and onion soup WITH 1 slice wholewheat rye bread and butter
- Gazpacho/Cucumber and mint soup/Orange and tomato soup/Consommé WITH 1 slice wholewheat/rye bread and butter and 50g (2 oz) any cheese
- Minestrone/Corn and fish chowder/Cream of onion soup WITH 1 slice wholewheat or rye bread
- Lentil soup WITH 2 slices wholewheat bread and scraping of butter. As first five salads from B WITH 1 slice wholewheat/rye bread and scraping of butter
- Crunchy salad
- Brown rice and nut salad AND 1 apple/1 orange/75g (3 oz) grapes/ small carton plain yogurt
- Sandwiches: 2 slices wholewheat bread (fresh or toasted) with a scraping of butter WITH: 25g (1 oz) hard cheese/40g (1½ oz) cooked ham/50g (2 oz) chicken/50g (2 oz) corned beef/1 hard-boiled egg/ 50g (2 oz) prawns [shrimps]/1½ grilled rashers streaky bacon [broiled bacon slices] AND lettuce, tomato, cucumber, watercress garnish
- Toasted bacon sandwich: 2 slices wholewheat toast with 2 grilled rashers streaky bacon [broiled bacon slices] and tomato (optional) AND 1 apple/orange/75g (3 oz) grapes
- Open sandwich: 1 slice pumpernickel and scraping of butter WITH 50g (2 oz) smoked cheese/50g (2 oz) prawns [shrimps] with lettuce and cucumber and 1 tbsp mayonnaise/50g (2 oz) chicken with ¼ avocado, watercress and tomato
- 2 scrambled eggs WITH 1 slice wholewheat toast/50g (2 oz) smoked salmon
- Soufflé cheese omelette/Spinach soufflé WITH lettuce, watercress and tomato salad
- 2 egg omelette WITH 75g (3 oz) poached mushrooms
- Leek and thyme quiche
- Spinach and cottage cheese quiche WITH mixed salad and 1 tbsp French dressing
- Smoked salmon quiche/Tomato and courgette [zucchini] pie WITH green salad and 1 tbsp Lemon and tarragon or Herb dressing
- Piperade WITH green salad and 1 tbsp French dressing
- 1 Baked egg WITH 2 slices wholewheat toast (no butter)
- 40g (1½ oz) wholewheat pasta WITH Americana sauce/7g (¼ oz) butter with garlic, parsley or basil/2 tsp pesto sauce AND mixed salad and 1 tbsp French or Lemon and tarragon dressing
- 175g (6 oz) jacket potato WITH: Filling 1 (page 107) Fillings 2 or 3 WITH small carton plain yogurt and 1 apple/Filling 4 WITH mixed salad (no dressing)
- ½ avocado pear with 1 tbsp French dressing
- ½ mango/½ cantaloupe melon/5 figs/large pear WITH 75g (3 oz) prosciutto ham AND 1 rye crispbread
- 75g (3 oz) smoked salmon with lemon juice and black pepper WITH 2 slices wholewheat bread and scraping of butter
- 1 small smoked trout WITH mixed salad and 1 tbsp French or Lemon and tarragon dressing
- 1 large globe artichoke/150g (5 oz) asparagus WITH 40g (1½ oz) melted butter/3 tbsp French dressing

MONDAY

A

Lamb noisette with garlic and rosemary
Vegetables: jacket baked potato, swede (rutabaga), Brussels sprouts, mangetout, green beans or cauliflower

150 g/5 oz carton plain yogurt with tsp honey

NB Soak fruit for tomorrow

TUESDAY

B

Courgette (zucchini) and tomato pie (×2)
Vegetables: spinach, boiled parsnip, green beans, broccoli or green salad

Winter fruit compote

WEDNESDAY

A

Mediterranean seafood sauce (×5)
75 g/3 oz boiled tagliatelle (25 g/1 oz/½ cup raw weight)
Vegetables: green or mixed salad, courgettes (zucchini) or green beans

Strawberry sorbet (×5)

THURSDAY

A

Liver provençal
75 g/3 oz boiled brown rice (25 g/1 oz/2 tbsp raw weight)
Vegetables: spinach, green beans or carrots

Banana, honey and nut fool (×6)

NB Soak prunes for tomorrow

FRIDAY

B

Pork fillet (tenderloin) with prunes
Vegetables: mashed potato (with skimmed milk), **red cabbage with apple**, green beans, braised celery, cauliflower or marrow (squash)

150 g/5 oz carton natural yogurt with 2 tsp honey and 25 g/1 oz wheatgerm

SATURDAY

B

1 cup consommé

Poached salmon steak
Vegetables: boiled new potato, courgettes (zucchini), peas, mangetout or green salad

100 g/4 oz grapes

SUNDAY

A

75 g/3 oz roast chicken (about 3 slices) with **Parsley and thyme stuffing** and 2 tbsp **Low fat gravy**
Vegetables: boiled potato, broccoli, carrots, cabbage, mangetout or 2 baked tomatoes

25 g/1 oz Camembert, Brie or smoked cheese with 1 rye crispbread

Fill in your weight, below. Charts are given every two weeks but you can make a weekly note, too, if you like... No more often than that though, because weight is not lost at a constant rate and daily fluctuations may reflect random variations rather than real changes.

In women, these random variations are largely caused by temporary shifts in body water that take place throughout the menstrual cycle as hormone levels rise and fall. A rise in oestrogen and progesterone just before menstruation, for example, causes the body to retain more water and become heavier. So be aware of this and know that a small gain in weight at this time reflects a gain in water, not fat.

Always use the same scales and weigh yourself on the same day each week, or fortnight, and at the same time. Keep scales on a solid flat surface, not carpet, and move them as little as possible. If you are serious about monitoring your weight, invest in proper quality scales. Although larger and heavier than the commercial type, they will fit in the corner of a bathroom or walk-in cupboard and have the advantage of a locking mechanism to keep everything stable while being moved.

Check scales for accuracy if they have been moved about or stored away: place a fixed known weight on the centre and take your reading directly in line with the indicator. If the reading is not exactly that of the fixed weight, your scales need adjusting. You may be able to do this yourself, but if the scales have been damaged, dropped or allowed to rust badly, they may need servicing or even replacing.

NB Weighing yourself has its limitations. Scales do not show whether you are losing lean or fat or just plain water and that's important, because it is what you lose that determines your shape at the end of the diet. So keep a subjective eye on your shape. Combine exercise with diet to firm up problem areas and use a measuring tape as an additional guide to progress.

Early weight losses on crash diets may be dramatic but they are deceptive, being losses not of fat but of glycogen, a granular carbohydrate stored in the liver and muscles, which binds with three times its weight in water.

Three pounds of water lost for every pound of glycogen! No wonder crash dieters feel their diet is working. But what they do not appreciate is that glycogen is always replaced, water retained again, and weight regained on a return to more normal eating.

There is, anyway, a limit to how much glycogen you can lose. Non-dieters probably have 2.7-3.6 kg (6-8 lb) of glycogen in their bodies, of which they might lose half. Habitual dieters have rather less because their systems have not had the chance to replenish themselves. Once glycogen stores are depleted, weight loss slows down and may even stop. The honeymoon period of rapid weight loss can never last indefinitely, even if you jump from one diet to another. Very restricted diets rarely require you to follow them for more than a fortnight because once the glycogen stores have been stripped they will appear to have stopped 'working'. Follow them for that amount of time and you will lose lots of weight but you will also regain it almost immediately.

The way to lasting weight loss is to keep glycogen levels stable and that means keeping intake moderate and the proportion of starchy carbohydrates reasonably high. This is why this diet starts off so gently and places such emphasis on wholemeal foods such as wholewheat bread and pasta. Although the amount of weight lost in the early stages may be disappointing in comparison with previous diets, at least you can be confident that every pound lost is a true pound lost and not just a fleeting phenomenon. You will appreciate the difference when the diet is over and you manage to keep off the weight you have lost.

*keeping glycogen levels up will also make you feel better, more energetic, see page 63.

some arithmetic . . .

1 kg (2.2 lb) of glycogen	= 4000 Calories
1 kg (2.2 lb) of water	= zero Calories
1 kg (2.2 lb) of fat	= 7000 Calories

If you lose 1 kg (2.2 lb) of glycogen, you will lose 4 kg (9 lb) overall because you will also lose 3 kg (6.6 lb) of water. This loss represents just 4000 calories. It can be regained in the space of one weekend.

If you lose 4 kg (9 lb) of fat, the loss will register identically on the scales, but this time represents 28,000 calories. This could only be regained after several *weeks* of overeating . . .

As the upper limit to the rate at which you can mobilize fat out of the fat cells, into the bloodstream and out of the body is about 1000 calories a day (that means burning 1000 calories more than you eat), and as it takes a deficit of 7000 calories to shift a kilogram of fat, the most you should aim to lose in a week is one kilogram (2.2lb). Any more will be glycogen/water or lean tissue . . . Neither is advisable.

	Weight	Bust	Waist	Hips	Thighs
Start					
Week 2					

A — MONDAY

175 g/6 oz fillet (tenderloin) or rump steak grilled (broiled) with herbs, all fat removed
Vegetables: poached mushrooms, cabbage with caraway seeds, or green beans

½ medium ogen melon filled with 175 g/6 oz fresh strawberries or segments of 1 large orange

A — TUESDAY

Fish pie (×3)
Vegetables: green beans, 2 grilled (broiled) tomatoes, spinach, carrots or green salad

150 g/5 oz carton any fruit yogurt

B — WEDNESDAY

Braised kidneys (×3)
75 g/3 oz boiled brown rice (25 g/1 oz/2 tbsp raw weight)
Vegetables: carrots, cauliflower, marrow (squash), peas or mixed salad

1 mashed banana sprinkled with 25 g/1 oz hazelnuts

A — THURSDAY

Wholewheat pan pizza (×3)
Vegetables: green or mixed salad, braised fennel or spinach

1 stewed cooking apple, sweetened to taste, with 25 g/1 oz chopped dates and 150 g/5 oz carton natural yogurt

C — FRIDAY

Trout with almonds
Vegetables: boiled new potato, broccoli, mangetout, green beans or mixed salad

25 g/1 oz any hard cheese with 2 water biscuits

A — SATURDAY

Wholewheat macaroni with cheese and ham
Vegetables: 2 grilled (broiled) tomatoes, peas, broccoli, green or mixed salad

Fruit salad: 100 g/4 oz fresh pineapple, 100 g/4 oz grapes and 1 sliced banana

NB Soak fruit for tomorrow

B — SUNDAY

Chicken florentine
Vegetables: boiled new potato, swede (rutabaga), leeks, carrots, Brussels sprouts or poached mushrooms

150 g/5 oz any dried fruit (figs, apricots, prunes)

MONDAY

A

Middle Eastern rice
Vegetables: green or mixed salad

150 g/5 oz carton plain yogurt with tsp honey

TUESDAY

C

Liver with orange (×2)
75 g/3 oz boiled brown rice (25 g/1 oz/2 tbsp raw weight)
Vegetables: broccoli, courgettes (zucchini), spinach or green salad

25 g/1 oz any hard cheese and 1 apple or pear

WEDNESDAY

B

Leek and thyme quiche
Vegetables: green beans, broccoli, green or mixed salad

Orange and pear fruit salad

THURSDAY

A

Sole with lemon and prawns (shrimp)
Vegetables: boiled new potato, 2 baked tomatoes, broccoli, leeks or green salad

100 g/4 oz stewed plums, sweetened to taste, with 150 g/5 oz carton plain yogurt

NB Marinate chicken for tomorrow

FRIDAY

B

Skewered chicken
Vegetables: jacket baked potato, carrots, broccoli, mangetout, 2 grilled (broiled) tomatoes, cauliflower or leeks

Peach and orange sorbet (×6)

SATURDAY

A

Spinach soufflé
Vegetables: boiled new potato, green or mixed salad, green beans, courgettes (zucchini) or poached mushrooms

1 nectarine or 100 g/4 oz grapes

SUNDAY

C

Lamb with apricot stuffing
Vegetables: green beans, cabbage, marrow (squash), cauliflower or carrots

Banana, honey and nut fool (×5)

 **WEEK 4**

The metabolic flame burns energy in the form of accumulated sugar and fat reserves, and it burns brightest when you move fastest, eat most. When you diet, your metabolic rate drops sharply – by 6 per cent by the end of the first week and by 15-20 per cent at the end of the third. Raise it by keeping active...

 A

Sole florentine
Vegetables: boiled new potato, braised celery, peas, carrots, broccoli or mixed salad

1 stewed cooking apple, sweetened to taste, with 150 g/5 oz carton plain yogurt

MONDAY

B

Wholewheat spaghetti with chicken livers
Vegetables: green or mixed salad, peas, green beans or tomatoes

25 g/1 oz any blue cheese and 1 pear

TUESDAY

A

Veal escalope with tomatoes
Vegetables: boiled new potato, spinach, cauliflower, cabbage, courgettes (zucchini) or green beans

150 g/5 oz carton plain yogurt with 2 tsp honey and 25 g/1 oz wheatgerm

WEDNESDAY

 C

Lasagne (×4)
Vegetables: green or mixed salad, spinach or poached mushrooms

25 g/1 oz dates, 25 g/1 oz walnuts and large apple

NB Soak fruit for tomorrow

THURSDAY

 A

Vegetable curry (×4)
65 g/3 oz boiled brown rice (25 g/1 oz/2 tbsp raw weight)
Vegetables: green or mixed salad

Winter fruit compote

FRIDAY

 B

Ham with cider sauce
Vegetables: jacket baked potato, broad (fava) beans, carrots, green beans or mangetout

Autumn baked apple

SATURDAY

 A

1 cup consommé
Herb chicken
Vegetables: boiled potato, broccoli, cauliflower, peas, courgettes (zucchini) or spinach

100 g/4 oz fresh pineapple or 1 large orange

SUNDAY

33

WEEK 5

MONDAY
C

Pork curry (×2)
75 g/3 oz boiled brown rice (25 g/1 oz/2 tbsp raw weight)
Vegetables: sliced cucumber with 3 tbsp plain yogurt, green or mixed salad

1 banana and 25 g/1 oz raisins or 15 g/½ oz walnuts and 150 g/5 oz carton plain yogurt

TUESDAY
A

Liver provençal
75 g/3 oz boiled brown rice (25 g/1 oz/2 tbsp raw weight)
Vegetables: green or mixed salads, green beans

1 apple or large orange or pear

WEDNESDAY

A

Spinach roulade
Vegetables: poached mushrooms, green beans, 2 baked tomatoes, sweetcorn (kernel corn) or mixed salad

½ grapefruit with crunchy topping (25 g/1 oz wheatgerm, 1 tsp honey with cinnamon and spices to taste) placed under hot grill

THURSDAY

B

Bitkis (×4)
Vegetables: green beans, carrots, cauliflower, green or red cabbage, green or mixed salad

50 g/2 oz hard cheese with celery or cucumber

NB Soak fruit for tomorrow

FRIDAY

B

Baked fish with ginger
Vegetables: mashed potato, **red cabbage with apple**, carrots, leeks, broccoli, braised celery or mangetout

150 g/5 oz dried fruit (apricots, figs, prunes, etc)

SATURDAY

B

Fillet steak (tenderloin) with green peppercorns and herbs
Vegetables: jacket baked potato, green beans, cauliflower, carrots, green or mixed salad

Fruit salad: 100 g/4 oz fresh chopped pineapple, 50 g/2 oz grapes and ½ banana

SUNDAY

C

2 lamb cutlets, grilled (broiled), with 2 tsp redcurrant jelly, all fat removed
Vegetables: baked jacket potato, swede (rutabaga), sweetcorn (kernel corn), cauliflower, carrots or peas

25 g/1 oz any hard cheese with a water biscuit

	Weight	Bust	Waist	Hips	Thighs
Week 4					
Week 6					

Dieting slows down the metabolic rate and the more drastic the diet, the greater the slowdown. Anyone who has watched the scales sticking after just a few days' dieting will know this; and will know also that the only way to persuade the scales on down again is by scaling the diet down too. To lose more you have to eat less...and less...and less...until you end up subsisting on virtually nothing.

The dilemma is common, the reasons more complex, but the truth is that any diet that takes you, *or threatens to take you,* below your natural comfortable weight will become progressively harder as your body becomes more and more determined to defend its rightful healthy weight – that which psychologists call the 'set point'. Crash diets, which shock your body into the most spirited defence, are the least effective of all. Keep metabolism on an even keel by following a diet that reduces the quantities of food so gently that your body has a chance to adapt naturally to the new level without over-reacting.

'Metabolic rate' refers to the basal, or resting, rate. This is taken when the body is still. It is a measure of internal activity – the amount of energy used simply to keep the body going, to maintain essential biochemical processes such as oxygen exchange, protein synthesis and tissue repair.

The basal rate is the figure on which all other energy calculations depend, such as how much an hour's jogging or yoga is worth. Because basal rates can vary considerably from person to person, so can the amount of energy used by various activities. Charts stating that an hour's jogging uses so many calories, and an hour's running so many more, fail to take this into account. An hour's activity will never be worth exactly the same for everyone in terms of calories used or weight lost.

WHAT INFLUENCES YOUR METABOLIC RATE? As a rule, the larger and heavier you are and the more lean tissue you have, the higher your metabolic rate. Lean tissue (organs and muscle) is a key factor because there is much more going on there than in fat, which is relatively inert. Women, who have a higher ratio of fat to muscle than men and tend to be smaller and lighter, generally have lower metabolic rates.

IS THE SURVIVAL OF THE FITTEST ALSO THE SURVIVAL OF THE FATTEST? If those with the most adaptable metabolisms were best able to survive drought and famine and so to pass on their genes, as Darwin suggested, then yesterday's natural survivors are the overweight population of today...

Three things cause metabolism to drop when dieting:

1. You are getting lighter.

2. The body cannot distinguish between fashion and famine and reacts as though dieting were the latter, conserving its energy by functioning in a lower metabolic gear. This happens very quickly, probably after just four days.

3. As part of the emergency alert, metabolically-expensive lean tissue is jettisoned and inactive fat conserved, so lowering metabolic rate still further.

Metabolic rate not only drops when you diet, but also rises when you *overeat*. This was first noted in 1902 by a psychologist called Neumann who carried out an experiment on himself, eating about 2000 calories more than usual every day for several months. He found that although he put on weight to begin with, his weight soon stabilized at its new, higher level and ceased to rise thereafter.

Recent research suggests that the mechanism which allowed him to do this derives from a tissue known as brown fat, which has the function of burning off extra calories as heat rather than storing them as fat.

Brown fat may be a critical factor in determining who stays slim and who gets fat. People who tend to put on weight easily seem to have less brown fat, or less *active* brown fat, than people who eat all they like and still remain lean. In one experiment, where fat and lean people were exposed to cold, the lean group was found to be able to maintain their body temperature through the *internal* generation of heat, while that of the fat group dropped.

 MONDAY

Mediterranean seafood sauce (×4)
75 g/3 oz boiled brown rice (25 g/1 oz/2 tbsp raw weight)
Vegetables: peas, spinach or green salad

150 g/5 oz carton plain yogurt with 25 g/1 oz chopped dates and 25 g/1 oz raisins

 TUESDAY

Pork casserole
Vegetables: jacket baked potato, peas, **red cabbage with apple**, green beans, green or mixed salad

Apple or pear with 75 g/3 oz grapes

 WEDNESDAY

Smoked salmon quiche (×2)
Vegetables: green or mixed salad, green beans, courgettes (zucchini) or cucumber salad

1 fresh mango or 2 large oranges

 THURSDAY

Indian chicken
Vegetables: boiled new potato, braised fennel, green beans, marrow (squash), green or mixed salad

25 g/1 oz Stilton or 40 g/1½ oz Danish Blue and 1 apple or pear

 FRIDAY

Steak and kidney casserole (×3)
75 g/3 oz boiled tagliatelle (25 g/1 oz/½ cup raw weight)
Vegetables: green beans, braised fennel, spring greens, carrots or broccoli

Peach and orange sorbet (×5)

 SATURDAY

Lasagne (×3)
Vegetables: green or mixed salad

Fruit salad: 100 g/4 oz fresh pineapple, 100 g/4 oz grapes and 1 banana

NB Soak fruit for tomorrow

 SUNDAY

Chinese stuffed pepper (×2)
Vegetables: leeks, cauliflower, poached mushrooms, courgettes (zucchini), salsify or mixed salad

Winter fruit compote

WEEK 7

MONDAY

 B

Lamb kebab
75 g/3 oz boiled brown rice (25 g/1 oz/2 tbsp raw weight)
Vegetables: poached mushrooms, green or mixed salad

25 g/1 oz Gouda or Edam and 2 water biscuits

TUESDAY

 B

Liver stroganoff (×2)
75 g/3 oz boiled tagliatelle (25 g/1 oz/½ cup raw weight)
Vegetables: cauliflower, mangetout, Brussels sprouts, swede (rutabaga), green or mixed salad

Orange and pear fruit salad

WEDNESDAY

 C

French vegetable quiche (×2)
Vegetables: green or mixed salad, spinach, green beans or celeriac

150 g/5 oz carton plain yogurt with 25 g/1 oz chopped dates, 25 g/1 oz hazelnuts and few raisins

THURSDAY

 A

Skewered chicken
Vegetables: boiled new potato, sweetcorn (kernel corn), broccoli, green or mixed salad or poached mushrooms

1 apple, large orange or pear

FRIDAY

 A

Poached salmon steak
Vegetables: boiled new potato, mangetout, cauliflower, green beans or green salad

Baked apple with blackcurrant sauce

SATURDAY

 B

Chilli con carne (×2)
Vegetables: boiled new potato, carrots, cabbage, braised celery, green or mixed salad

Banana, honey and nut fool (×4)

SUNDAY

C

Barbecue lamb (×2)
Vegetables: jacket baked potato, courgettes (zucchini), cauliflower, spring greens, leeks or broccoli

25 g/1 oz Camembert, Brie or smoked cheese and 1 apple or pear

Activity is the key. Lose weight through a combination of diet and exercise and your shape will change dramatically...

A — MONDAY

Wholewheat pan pizza (×2)
Vegetables: green or mixed salad, spinach, mangetout or green beans

Fresh fruit salad: apple, orange, ½ medium ogen melon and 100 g/4 oz grapes

A — TUESDAY

Baked fish with ginger
Vegetables: boiled new potato, poached mushrooms, celeriac, cauliflower, mangetout, green or mixed salad

Peach and orange sorbet (×4)

B — WEDNESDAY

Cannelloni
Vegetables: **Pepperoni, ratatouille**, green or mixed salad

50 g/2 oz any hard cheese with 1 water biscuit

NB Soak prunes for tomorrow

B — THURSDAY

1 cup consommé
Pork fillet (tenderloin) with prunes
Vegetables: Brussels sprouts, **red cabbage with apple**, boiled parsnip, green beans, broccoli or cauliflower

1 banana

C — FRIDAY

Chicken florentine
Vegetables: boiled new potato, broad (fava) beans, spinach, cauliflower or broccoli

150 g/5 oz carton plain yogurt with 1 chopped apple and 25 g/1 oz chopped dates

A — SATURDAY

Steak au poivre: 175 g/6 oz fillet (tenderloin) or rump steak, grilled (broiled) with 12 black peppercorns pressed onto meat, fat removed
Vegetables: jacket baked potato, puréed swede (rutabaga), spinach, green or mixed salad

150 g/5 oz stewed rhubarb, sweetened to taste, and 150 g/5 oz carton plain yogurt

B — SUNDAY

Chicken véronique
Vegetables: boiled new potato, carrots, spring greens, courgettes (zucchini) or mangetout

50 g/2 oz any hard cheese and cucumber or celery

MONDAY

Skate with capers: 175 g/6 oz wing of skate, grilled (broiled) and served with 6 capers heated with 7 g/¼ oz butter
Vegetables: boiled new potato, green beans, poached mushrooms, salsify or braised celery

100 g/4 oz grapes or 1 banana

TUESDAY

Beef goulash (×4)
75 g/3 oz boiled tagliatelle (25 g/1 oz/½ cup raw weight)
Vegetables: 2 baked tomatoes, mangetout, spring greens, green or mixed salad

Baked apple with blackcurrant sauce

WEDNESDAY

Spinach soufflé
Vegetables: courgettes (zucchini), leeks, 2 baked tomatoes, green or mixed salad

Green fruit salad

THURSDAY

Pork curry
75 g/3 oz boiled brown rice (25 g/1 oz/2 tbsp raw weight)
Vegetables: green beans, green or mixed salad

25 g/1 oz Camembert with 2 rye crispbreads

FRIDAY

Stuffed aubergine (eggplant)
Vegetables: jacket baked potato, peas, carrots, mangetout, celeriac or green salad

1 peach, 1 small orange or 50 g/2 oz grapes

SATURDAY

Lasagne (×2)
Vegetables: spinach, green or mixed salad

½ grapefruit with crunchy topping (see Week 5 Day 3)

SUNDAY

Chicken with almonds
Vegetables: mashed potato, braised celery, spinach, peas, broccoli or green beans

1 large slice cantaloupe melon

Most diets concentrate on how much weight you can expect to lose in a given period and do not bother too much about where that weight is coming from, but new research is showing that the *type* of weight you lose is as important, from the point of view of your final shape, as the *amount*.

Studies at the University of Glasgow have shown that if you lose weight by dieting alone and take no exercise, up to one-third of the weight lost will be lean tissue (mainly muscle) not fat. This proportion rises with the severity of the diet. On an extended fast about half the weight lost is lean.

As muscle keeps you firm and fat makes you flabby, the most effective strategy is one which enables you to lose nearly 100 per cent fat while keeping, or even gaining, muscle. Do this by following a moderately restricted, nutritious eating plan and by keeping active both while losing weight and afterwards. Switching surplus fat for stronger muscles will result in a leaner, better-looking body and your metabolic rate will not drop as low . . .

	Weight	Bust	Waist	Hips	Thighs
Week 8					
Week 10					

Fat is not just bulkier than muscle, but lighter too. If you habitually crash diet, you may gradually alter the composition of your body, upping the ratio of fat to lean, so although you may not weigh any more you will look different. Slimness is not just a matter of what the scales indicate, but of the shape you are in. You can be lean, or fat, but the more you crash diet, the more your chances of switching from the first to the second increase...

Q. Which exercise is the best to take up?

A. Any regular, fairly vigorous exercise, such as swimming, cycling, running or aerobic dancing, will help shed fat and conserve muscle. Choose an activity that you enjoy and which fits in with your way of life. Build up the time spent exercising and the level of intensity as you get fitter. This may also have a second, weight reducing effect by keeping your metabolic rate raised for some hours after the exercise has finished...

NB *'Passive exercise' is no substitute for active, on-your-feet exercising; nor is massage. Machines claiming to act by electrical stimulation of the muscle will not produce a visible slimming effect. 'The amount of energy dissipated by the muscle contractions is minimal,' states the Royal College of Physicians' 1983 report 'Obesity', 'and it is clear that the public should be advised against the use of these devices, which are often expensive as well as being ineffective techniques for slimming...'*

MONDAY

Liver with orange
Vegetables: boiled new potato, green beans, carrots, peas or green salad

25 g/1 oz grapes

TUESDAY

175 g/6 oz fillet (tenderloin) or rump steak, grilled (broiled) with herbs, all fat removed
Vegetables: watercress salad, green beans, swede (rutabaga), salsify, asparagus, 2 baked tomatoes or cauliflower

50 g/2 oz fresh pineapple

WEDNESDAY

100 g/4 oz **stuffed roast shoulder of lamb** (about 3 thin slices), all fat removed, with 2 tbsp **low fat gravy**
Vegetables: braised celery, **red cabbage with apple**, Brussels sprouts, carrots, broccoli, or boiled parsnip

1 apple, large orange or pear

THURSDAY

Wholewheat spaghetti with tomato and basil
Vegetables: peas, courgettes (zucchini), celeriac, green or mixed salad

1 banana

FRIDAY

Cottage pie (×2)
Vegetables: carrots, cabbage, leeks, marrow (squash), swede (rutabaga) or green beans

1 peach, 3 plums or 50 g/2 oz grapes

SATURDAY

Sole with herbs and wine
Vegetables: boiled new potato, mangetout, salsify, green beans, broccoli or green salad

25 g/1 oz smoked cheese and 1 water biscuit

SUNDAY

Pork chop with cider
Vegetables: boiled parsnip mashed with pepper and 1 tsp butter, **red cabbage with apple**, carrots, green beans, leeks or peas

Red fruit salad

WEEK 11

MONDAY

Bitkis (×3)
Vegetables: green salad, poached mushrooms, courgettes (zucchini), green beans or butter beans

Green fruit salad

TUESDAY

2 lamb cutlets, grilled (broiled), with 2 tsp redcurrant jelly, all fat removed
Vegetables: jacket baked potato, ratatouille, spinach, courgettes (zucchini), 2 grilled (broiled) tomatoes, broccoli or cauliflower

WEDNESDAY

Aubergine (eggplant) pie
Vegetables: green beans, poached mushrooms, sweetcorn (kernel corn) or green salad

½ grapefruit

THURSDAY

Herring with mustard sauce
Vegetables: boiled new potato, mangetout, salsify, broad (fava) beans, green beans or green salad

1 apple, large orange or pear

FRIDAY

Chilli con carne
Vegetables: boiled new potato, carrots, green beans, green or mixed salad

25 g/1 oz any hard cheese with celery

SATURDAY

Sole with lemon and prawns (shrimp)
Vegetables: boiled new potato, mangetout, broccoli, watercress, peas or mixed salad

1 fresh mango or 2 oranges

SUNDAY

Chicken florentine
Vegetables: green beans, broccoli, baked onion, cauliflower, 2 baked tomatoes or braised fennel

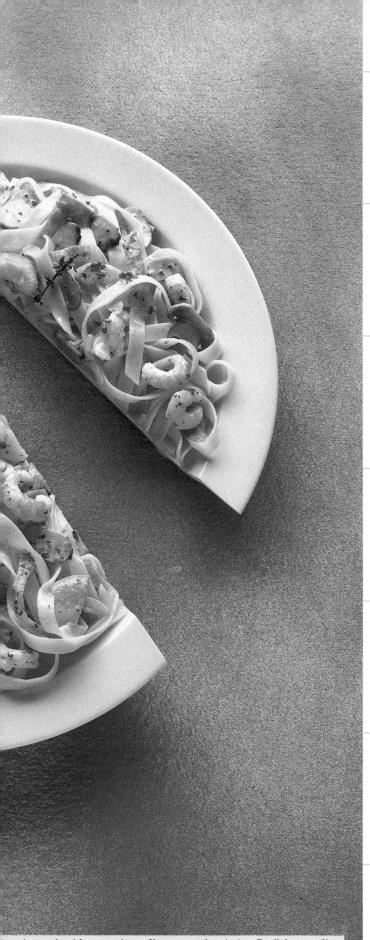

Liver provençal

75 g/3 oz boiled tagliatelle (25 g/1 oz/½ cup raw weight)
Vegetable: green or mixed salad or spinach

150 g/5 oz carton plain yogurt with 2 tsp honey and sprinkling of wheatgerm

MONDAY

Smoked haddock roulade (×2)

Vegetables: courgettes (zucchini), mangetout, broccoli, green or mixed salad

100 g/4 oz passion fruit, 175 g/6 oz fresh strawberries or 50 g/2 oz grapes

TUESDAY

French vegetable quiche

Vegetables: spinach, green beans, sweetcorn (kernel corn), green or mixed salad

½ grapefruit or 1 clementine

WEDNESDAY

Chicken véronique

Vegetables: boiled new potato, green salad, broccoli, spring greens, cauliflower or green beans

25 g/1 oz Camembert or Brie and 1 rye crispbread

THURSDAY

Cannelloni

Vegetables: 2 grilled (broiled) tomatoes, **ratatouille**, green or mixed salad

50 g/2 oz fresh pineapple or 50 g/2 oz grapes

FRIDAY

Trout with almonds

Vegetables: boiled new potato, green beans, salsify, peas, broccoli, asparagus or green salad

150 g/5 oz carton plain yogurt with 2 tsp honey

SATURDAY

Beef goulash (×3)

75 g/3 oz boiled brown rice (25 g/1 oz/2 tbsp raw weight)
Vegetables: 2 baked tomatoes, carrots, Brussels sprouts, spring greens or marrow (squash)

1 peach or medium slice honeydew melon

SUNDAY

...eep in touch with sensations of hunger and satiation. Don"t let any diet ...ictate meal times or sizes. Eat when hungry and, once hunger is ...atisfied, STOP.

	Weight	Bust	Waist	Hips	Thighs
Week 12					
Week 14					

MONDAY

 C

Wholewheat macaroni with cheese and ham
Vegetables: spinach, mangetout, peas, poached mushrooms or green salad

Strawberry sorbet (×4)

TUESDAY

 A

Vegetable curry (×2)
75 g/3 oz boiled brown rice (25 g/1 oz/2 tbsp raw weight)

1 tangerine/satsuma or peach

WEDNESDAY

 B

Bitkis (×3)
Vegetables: carrots, green beans, braised fennel, green or mixed salad

100 g/4 oz grapes

THURSDAY

 B

Fish pie (×2)
Vegetables: broccoli, mangetout, carrots, green or mixed salad

½ grapefruit

FRIDAY

 D

Beef carbonnade
Vegetables: jacket baked potato, **red cabbage with apple**, broccoli, peas or spring greens

150 g/5 oz carton plain yogurt with 1 peach, 100 g/4 oz raspberries or 50 g/2 oz grapes

NB Marinate the chicken for tomorrow

SATURDAY

 C

Skewered chicken
Vegetables: jacket baked potato, 2 grilled (broiled) tomatoes, courgettes (zucchini), green or mixed salad

25 g/1 oz any hard cheese with celery or cucumber

SUNDAY

  D

2 lamb cutlets, grilled (broiled), with 2 tsp redcurrant jelly, all fat removed
Vegetables: new potato, baked onion, peas, sweetcorn (kernel corn), cauliflower, carrots or mixed salad

½ ogen melon

Although 'hunger' and 'appetite' are often used interchangeably, there are some important distinctions. While hunger is a physiological sensation, caused by lack of food and allied to specific processes such as stomach contractions, appetite is less well defined and appears to be governed as much by external cues as internal ones.

For example: the food itself – how appealing it looks, how good it smells and how much you like it; your mood (how excited/tense/depressed/distracted/bored you are); a multitude of other external factors, largely influenced by conditioning, such as 'If it's 1 pm, it must be lunchtime...'

There is now good evidence that people who are overweight tend to be more susceptible to these factors. Hunger seems to be less important in determining the way they eat, appetite more.

> **EXPERIMENT** with hunger when you eat... stopping every so often, waiting a few moments, then sitting back and asking, 'Am I still hungry?' Is the hunger still there or has it gone? Look for an absence of the sensation, not a feeling of fullness or physical discomfort. If you are still hungry, eat a little more; then repeat the test.

A third of the adult British population attempts to slim each year and spends over £200 *million* on slimming products designed to help them do so – more often to the profit of the manufacturers than to themselves.

Most slimming products aim to suppress appetite. Few work in the long term. They can be divided, as follows, into three groups:

1. FIBRE-BASED BULKING AGENTS containing bran, guar gum or methyl cellulose, which swell in the stomach when swallowed with water, supposedly producing a sensation of fullness. In practice, a substantial amount of fibre would have to be taken in this way – much more than the maximum doses in these products – and the stomach soon adapts to the sensation of distension anyway.

2. SWEETS designed to raise blood/sugar levels so rapidly and substantially that they will signal to the brain that hunger is satisfied. In reality, the body reacts quickly to

return these levels to normal by secreting insulin which facilitates the removal of glucose from the blood into the cells, so any effect on appetite is very brief.

3. ANAESTHETIC CHEWING GUM which numbs the mouth so that pleasure derived from food, such as taste and texture, is minimized and the food, theoretically, loses its appeal. The sheer number of different factors influencing the appetite are stacked against this one too, as is the fact that the anaesthetic effect wears off quite quickly.

The most rigid diets are often the most appealing because their iron rules provide the discipline that dieters usually lack, but they do have their dangers. One of the less obvious is that they alienate you from feelings of hunger and satiation by stipulating exactly when and what and how much you must eat. You cannot afford to acknowledge hunger if hungry most of the time...

Years spent crash dieting may cause you to abandon hunger as a cue for eating and to depend upon less reliable cues, such as availability, mood or time of day. This may not be apparent while the current diet is going well and weight is being lost, but once you have finished the diet or your willpower falters, disordered eating habits can wreak havoc. The compulsive eating trap is a common one. One-third of all patients attending US obesity clinics describe episodes of binge eating after crash dieting and the true proportion is probably a lot higher than that.

AVOID regular use of laxatives. They won't speed weight loss, can become addictive and may be dangerous as they deplete the body of essential minerals, particularly potassium. Loss of potassium is especially hazardous because it can affect the heart by inducing spontaneous contraction of the cardiac muscle. Other side-effects include dehydration, impaired kidney function, epilepsy and even death.

MONDAY

Steak and kidney casserole (×2)
75 g/3 oz boiled brown rice (25 g/1 oz/2 tbsp raw weight)
Vegetables: green beans, braised celery or peas

100 g/4 oz passion fruit, 175 g/6 oz fresh strawberries or 50 g/2 oz grapes

TUESDAY

Mediterranean seafood sauce (×3)
75 g/3 oz boiled tagliatelle (25 g/1 oz/½ cup raw weight)
1 vegetable: green or mixed salad

Green fruit salad

WEDNESDAY

Piperade
Vegetables: jacket baked potato, spinach, broccoli, green beans, green or mixed salad

Autumn baked apple

THURSDAY

Sole florentine
Vegetables: boiled new potato, 2 grilled (broiled) tomatoes, poached mushrooms or green salad

Banana, honey and nut fool (×3)

FRIDAY

Stuffed pepper with tomato sauce (×2)
75 g/3 oz boiled pasta shells (25 g/1 oz/½ cup raw weight)
Vegetable: green salad

25 g/1 oz Stilton or 40 g/1½ oz Danish Blue and 1 apple or pear

SATURDAY

Chicken with peach and ginger
Vegetables: boiled new potato, spinach, mangetout, broccoli, cauliflower or green salad

150 g/5 oz carton plain yogurt with 2 tsp honey and sprinkling wheatgerm

SUNDAY

175 g/6 oz fillet (tenderloin) or rump steak, grilled (broiled) with herbs, all fat removed
Vegetables: 2 grilled (broiled) tomatoes, cauliflower, green beans, red cabbage with apple, green or mixed salad

½ ogen melon or 1 tangerine/satsuma

WEEK 15

MONDAY

B

Lamb kebab
75 g/3 oz boiled brown rice (25 g/1 oz/2 tbsp raw weight)
Vegetables: peas, poached mushrooms, spinach or green salad

Red fruit salad

TUESDAY

C

Liver stroganoff
75 g/3 oz boiled tagliatelle (25 g/1 oz/½ cup raw weight)
Vegetables: broccoli, green beans, leeks or green salad

Strawberry sorbet (×3)

WEDNESDAY

C

Spinach roulade
Vegetables: poached mushrooms, 2 grilled (broiled) tomatoes, sweetcorn (kernel corn), green beans, broccoli or salsify

150 g/5 oz carton any fruit yogurt

THURSDAY

B

Sole with lemon and prawns (shrimp)
Vegetables: boiled new potato, green beans, mangetout, peas, cauliflower or green salad

1 apple, large orange or pear

NB Soak fruit for tomorrow

FRIDAY

C

Sweet and sour chicken
Vegetables: beansprouts, poached mushrooms, mangetout, green beans, cauliflower or peas

Winter fruit compote

SATURDAY

A

Chinese stuffed pepper
Vegetables: green or mixed salad

Green fruit salad

SUNDAY

D

100 g/4 oz **stuffed roast shoulder of lamb** (about 3 slices) with 2 tbsp **low fat gravy**
Vegetables: jacket baked potato, baked onion, green beans, cauliflower or **red cabbage with apple**

25 g/1 oz Camembert, Brie or smoked cheese with celery or a few grapes

 A MONDAY

Wholewheat pan pizza
Vegetables: green or mixed salad

150 g/5 oz stewed rhubarb or 100 g/4 oz stewed plums, sweetened to taste, with 150 g/5 oz carton plain yogurt

 B TUESDAY

Baked fish with ginger
Vegetables: boiled new potato, mangetout, poached mushrooms, green beans or green salad

100 g/4 oz grapes or 1 banana

 C WEDNESDAY

Cannelloni
Vegetables: **pepperoni**, spinach, green or mixed salad

1 apple, large orange or pear

 B THURSDAY

Herb chicken
Vegetables: boiled new potato, mangetout, spring greens, peas, broccoli or carrots

1 peach, 100 g/4 oz raspberries, 3 plums or 50 g/2 oz grapes

 D FRIDAY

Herring with mustard sauce
Vegetables: boiled new potato, mangetout, sweetcorn (kernel corn), green or mixed salad

Banana, honey and nut fool (×2)

 D SATURDAY

Braised kidneys (×2)
75 g/3 oz boiled brown rice (25 g/1 oz/2 tbsp raw weight)
Vegetables: carrots, mangetout or green salad

25 g/1 oz Camembert, Brie or smoked cheese and 1 rye crispbread

 C SUNDAY

175 g/6 oz fillet (tenderloin or rump steak), grilled (broiled) with 6 crushed black peppercorns pressed onto both sides, all fat removed
Vegetables: spinach, green beans, broccoli, marrow (squash), 2 baked tomatoes or green salad

1 apple or pear with 75 g/3 oz grapes

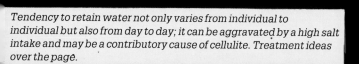

Tendency to retain water not only varies from individual to individual but also from day to day; it can be aggravated by a high salt intake and may be a contributory cause of cellulite. Treatment ideas over the page.

45

WEEK 17

MONDAY

2 lamb cutlets, grilled (broiled), all fat removed
Vegetables: 2 grilled (broiled) tomatoes, green beans, courgettes (zucchini), spinach or poached mushrooms

Green fruit salad

TUESDAY

Oriental red mullet
Vegetables: boiled new potato, broad (fava) beans, braised celery, **ratatouille** or mixed salad

Strawberry sorbet (×2)

WEDNESDAY

Chicken with peach and ginger
Vegetables: mashed potato, mangetout, courgettes (zucchini), braised fennel, peas or green salad

½ grapefruit

THURSDAY

Vegetable lasagne
Vegetables: spinach, green beans, peas or green salad

½ ogen melon or 1 tangerine/satsuma

FRIDAY

Liver provençal
Vegetables: baked jacket potato, cauliflower, peas, braised celery, swede (rutabaga) or carrots

150 g/5 oz carton plain yogurt

SATURDAY

Fish pie
Vegetables: spinach, mangetout, green beans, carrots or green salad

Autumn baked apple

SUNDAY

175 g/6 oz fillet (tenderloin) or rump steak, grilled (broiled) with herbs, all fat removed
Vegetables: mashed potato, broccoli, **ratatouille, red cabbage with apple** or green salad

Peach and orange sorbet (×3)

CUTTING DOWN YOUR SALT INTAKE

	Eat freely
Meat	beef, rump and sirloin steak, lamb, pork, veal, chicken duck, grouse, partridge, pheasant, turkey, venison
Fish	cod (raw or grilled), halibut, eel, trout, herring roe
Dairy foods	unsalted butter, cod liver oil, vegetable oils
Cereals	barley, flour, rice, rye, soya flour, spaghetti, puffed or shredded wheat
Fruit	all fruit except those listed, *right*
Vegetables	artichokes, asparagus, aubergines (eggplant), French (green) and runner (string) beans, Brussels sprouts, cauliflower, chicory, endive, leeks, lettuce, marrow (squash), onions, parsnips, peas, green peppers, potatoes, salsify, spring greens, tomatoes
Nuts	almonds, Brazil nuts, hazelnuts, peanuts, walnuts
Drinks	herbal teas, fruit juices, lager, cider, red wine, rosé wine sparkling wine
Seasonings	mustard, pepper

Cellulite may be a cosmetic problem, and not a medical one, but it is a problem all the same – especially to the women who have it.

A lamentable lack of scientific research has led beauticians to concentrate more on cures than on causes for these infuriatingly intractable pockets of fat, though whether there is a proven cure is doubtful. In fact, there is no good evidence that *any* of the remedies on offer at exclusive salons have a significant effect. Self-help, however, might, *see opposite*.

Cellulite is sometimes described as 'fat gone wrong' because, unlike ordinary fat which disappears with dieting, cellulite tends to become *more* marked and visible as weight is lost. If this is your problem now, a combination approach – directed at reducing excess water, restoring circulation, purifying the system and firming contours – is in order. But don't expect to see results for at least 3 months: it is a long, slow process.
1. **EXERCISE** can help by firming muscles, boosting circulation. Particularly recommended: running, skipping, cycling (indoor cycles especially), jumping and trampolining.
2. **DIET** can have very positive effects. Cut right down on salt (see listings *above*), using a seasoning substitute to make food palatable. Eat plenty of raw vegetables, fresh fruits and (particularly) foods high in vitamin B6 (known to be helpful for counteracting puffiness and bloating): lamb's

moderation	Avoid
, pigeon, offal (ox, lamb, pig or calf sweetbreads	canned meat, kidney, chicken liver, pork pie, bacon, ham, salami, sausages
ɔck, lemon sole, plaice, whiting, ɡ, mackerel, salmon, whitebait, els	kipper, canned salmon, sardines, crab and tuna, lobster, scampi, oysters, scallops, smoked fish, prawns (shrimps)
egg yolk, yogurt, cheese	salted butter, dried milk and margarine
macaroni, oatmeal, muesli, rye reads, bread	most brand cereals, oatcakes, biscuits (crackers) and pastry
currants, melons, passion fruit, apricots and figs, raisins and as (golden raisins)	olives in brine
beans, kidney beans, broccoli, age, cucumber, lentils, mushrooms, potatoes, canned tomatoes, sprouts, beetroot (beet), carrots, ɣ, radishes, watercress, spinach	canned carrots, peas, potatoes, sweetcorn (kernel corn); 'instant' potato
nuts, desiccated coconut	salted peanuts
ght beers, white wine, sherry, outh	brand hot chocolate and milk-based drinks
ɪr, vinegar, chutneys	baking powder, yeast and beef extract, bottled sauces, tomato purée, salt

liver, mackerel, nuts, wholegrains and wheatgerm.

3. MASSAGE helps stimulate the tissues directly under the skin, so *possibly* freeing trapped waste deposits and eliminating pockets of water, but you do not need the expensive variety from beauty salons. Rub the area briskly with a rough flannel or, European-style, with a natural-fibre brush, in long, firm strokes towards the heart for 5 minutes every day; then wash or shower.

NB Reducing salt intake will have health benefits, too. A high intake may lead to high blood pressure, a major contributory factor to coronary heart disease. As much as 30 per cent of the population may be at risk.

Professor Arnold Bender of the University of London's Queen Elizabeth College, and a leading authority on salt in the diet, says that we all get more than enough salt in our diet because about one-third of the salt we consume is *already* present in the food we eat and that is enough to satisfy our physiological needs. Another third is added during cooking to make food more palatable, the final third to 'season' it once on the plate...

	Weight	Bust	Waist	Hips	Thighs
Week 16					
Week 18					

MONDAY

Bitkis
75 g/3 oz boiled brown rice (25 g/1 oz/2 tbsp raw weight)
Vegetables: green or mixed salad, green beans or courgettes (zucchini)

100 g/4 oz grapes

TUESDAY

Lamb with garlic and rosemary
Vegetables: boiled new potato, courgettes (zucchini), 2 baked tomatoes, green beans, **red cabbage with apple** or asparagus

½ grapefruit with crunchy topping (see Week 5 Day 3)

WEDNESDAY

Mediterranean seafood sauce (×2)
75 g/3 oz boiled tagliatelle (25 g/1 oz/½ cup raw weight)
Vegetables: spinach, peas, mangetout, mixed or green salad

Banana, honey and nut fool

THURSDAY

175 g/6 oz fillet (tenderloin) or rump steak, grilled (broiled) with herbs, all fat removed
Vegetables: jacket baked potato, **ratatouille**, green beans, cauliflower or green salad

25 g/1 oz Camembert, Brie and 1 rye crispbread

FRIDAY

Aubergine (eggplant) pie
75 g/3 oz pasta shells (25 g/1 oz/½ cup raw weight)
Vegetables: green or mixed salad

150 g/5 oz carton plain yogurt with 1 tsp honey

SATURDAY

Lasagne
Vegetables: spinach, green or mixed salad

Peach and orange sorbet (×2)

SUNDAY

Barbecue lamb
Vegetables: poached mushrooms, **red cabbage with apple**, broccoli, cauliflower, sweetcorn (kernel corn), spinach or green salad

Autumn baked apple

MONDAY

Skate with capers: 150 g/5 oz wing of skate, grilled (broiled) and served with 6 capers heated with 7 g/¼ oz butter
Vegetables: boiled new potato, broccoli, salsify, mangetout, or green salad

½ ogen melon filled with 100 g/4 oz fresh chopped pineapple or segments of large orange

TUESDAY

Beef goulash (×2)
Vegetables: jacket baked potato, 2 baked tomatoes, carrots, peas, green beans, marrow (squash) or cabbage

150 g/5 oz carton plain yogurt with 2 tsp honey and sprinkling wheatgerm

WEDNESDAY

Courgette (zucchini) and tomato pie
Vegetables: broccoli, carrots, spinach, spring greens, mangetout or green salad

1 apple, large orange or pear

THURSDAY

Kidneys in red wine
75 g/3 oz boiled brown rice (25 g/1 oz/2 tbsp raw weight)
Vegetables: cauliflower, swede (rutabaga), spring greens, leeks, peas or green salad

1 banana

FRIDAY

Stuffed pepper with tomato sauce
Vegetables: poached mushrooms, carrots, green or mixed salad

1 peach, 100 g/4 oz fresh raspberries or 2 tangerines/satsumas

SATURDAY

Smoked salmon quiche
Vegetables: mangetout, green beans, green or mixed salad

Peach and orange sorbet

SUNDAY

Chicken with almonds
Vegetables: braised celery, courgettes (zucchini), mangetout, broccoli or green beans

25 g/1 oz Danish Blue or Roquefort and 1 water biscuit

A

Vegetable curry (×2)
75 g/3 oz boiled brown rice (25 g/1 oz/2 tbsp raw weight)
Vegetables: green or mixed salad or sweetcorn (kernel corn)

100 g/4 oz fresh pineapple

D

175 g/6 oz fillet (tenderloin) or rump steak, grilled (broiled) with herbs, all fat removed
Vegetables: jacket baked potato, 2 grilled (broiled) tomatoes, watercress, braised fennel, swede (rutabaga), salsify or mixed salad

1 apple, large orange or pear

D

Lamb with garlic and rosemary
Vegetables: jacket baked potato, Brussels sprouts, cauliflower, broccoli, baked onion or braised celery

½ ogen melon or 1 tangerine/satsuma

D

Smoked haddock roulade
Vegetables: courgettes (zucchini), spinach, 2 grilled (broiled) tomatoes, poached mushrooms or cauliflower

Green fruit salad

D

Cottage pie
Vegetables: cabbage, carrots, swede (rutabaga), mangetout, leeks or green salad

1 small banana

D

Wholewheat macaroni with cheese and ham
Vegetables: peas, broccoli, 2 grilled (broiled) tomatoes, green or mixed salad

1 peach, 3 plums or 50 g/2 oz grapes

D

Chicken florentine
Vegetables: mashed potato, broad (fava) beans, braised leeks, braised fennel, **red cabbage with apple**, green beans or green salad

100 g/4 oz grapes

One of the most enduring dietary myths… eating half a grapefruit before a meal helps burn off fat. More myths over the page…

MONDAY

Liver provençal
75 g/3 oz boiled tagliatelle (25 g/1 oz/½ cup raw weight)
Vegetables: spinach, carrots, peas, marrow (squash), spring greens or mangetout

½ grapefruit

TUESDAY

Skewered chicken
Vegetables: 2 grilled (broiled) tomatoes, mangetout, poached mushrooms, green or mixed salad

50 g/2 oz fresh pineapple

WEDNESDAY

Baked fish with ginger
Vegetables: boiled new potato, broccoli, braised fennel, leeks or green beans

1 banana

THURSDAY

Piperade
Vegetables: braised celery, fennel, cauliflower, green beans, green or mixed salad

50 g/2 oz grapes

FRIDAY

Lamb kebab
Vegetables: jacket baked potato, braised celery, courgettes (zucchini), poached mushrooms or green salad

150 g/5 oz carton natural yogurt with 2 tsp honey and sprinkling wheatgerm

SATURDAY

Sole florentine
Vegetables: boiled new potato, carrots, cauliflower, 2 grilled (broiled) tomatoes or mangetout

1 apple, large orange or pear

SUNDAY

Beef goulash
75 g/3 oz boiled tagliatelle (25 g/1 oz/½ cup raw weight)
Vegetables: green beans, carrots, marrow (squash), baked onion, peas or green salad

½ ogen melon or 1 tangerine/satsuma

---

8 more myths...

A calorie is a calorie is a calorie. All calories may be equally fattening but they are not equally nourishing, see opposite.

Margarine is less fattening than butter. Both contain exactly the same number of calories (80 per 10 g).

Yogurt is not fattening. Natural fat-free or low-fat yogurts are relatively low in calories (about 70 in a small carton) but whole milk or fruit-flavoured yogurts are almost twice that. Despite their health-giving image, fruit yogurts are also extremely high in sugar (about 17 per cent).

Fruit is not fattening. Bananas have twice the calories of apples and cherries and 4 times the calories of grapefruit. Although most fruits have little or no fat, avocados contain large amounts.

Slimming breads are less fattening than other breads. Unless the information on the wrapper states how low the bread is in calories (and it's lower per slice than the average), it may not be any less fattening. Some granary breads are less fattening than 'slimming' breads and much better for you.

There's no difference between honey and sugar. Both are fattening, but honey contains fructose, which is sweeter than sugar (sucrose), so you use less of it, and water, which makes it lower in calories anyway.

Eating foods in certain combinations activates enzymes which prevents them being absorbed by the gut... (Judy Mazel, 'Beverly Hills Diet', 1981). 'Blatantly wrong-headed and potentially dangerous' ('British Journal of Hospital Medicine', February, 1982).

Eating carrots is the healthiest way to keep slim. Eating excessive quantities of carrots can be bad for you. Complications include amenorrhoea (absent or irregular periods), temporary infertility and discoloration of the skin, which actually turns orange.

The US Department of Agriculture has cautioned that it is difficult to get all the nutrients we need on less than 1600 calories a day. This means that slimmers, whose diets are always some way below this, must make extra sure that what they eat is nutritious and well-balanced.

Even people subsisting on diets containing much more than 1600 calories may not be getting all the nutrients necessary to good health – the correct balance of amino acids in protein, for example, or the right fatty acids or enough of the fibre, vitamins, minerals and trace elements that their bodies require to function at their best. Today's typical highly-refined diet overfeeds and undernourishes, putting on weight while taking away vitality and wellbeing. In addition to providing next-to-nothing nutritionally, it also draws heavily upon valuable stores of certain key nutrients – most notably magnesium and the B vitamins, especially B1 (thiamin). In one Japanese study, early signs of the thiamin-deficiency disease, beriberi, were found among affluent and apparently 'well-fed' teenagers living on junk food diets.

NB Under-nutrition can lead to overeating. If your diet is composed largely of refined foods and 'empty' calories, such as those contained in sugar and alcohol, you may have to eat 1000 calories or more *over* the basic 1600 or so that you need just to get the vital nutrients that your body requires. It is much more difficult to become slim and to remain slim on an unbalanced diet because hunger is influenced by quality of food as well as quantity. If the quality of what you eat is inadequate, messages of hunger will continue to be sent until the shortfall is made up.

IMPORTANT. Now that you are on the last phase of the diet, with calories cut to just 1000, each calorie must count for as much as possible. There is no room in your diet for junk foods of limited nutritional value. Increase nutrient density by taking a daily multivitamin and mineral tablet, eating organically grown fruit and vegetables raw or very briefly cooked and buying all foods as fresh as possible.

	Weight	Bust	Waist	Hips	Thighs
Week 20					
Week 22					
Week 24					

MONDAY

Soufflé cheese omelette
Vegetables: **ratatouille**, broccoli, poached mushrooms, green or mixed salad

25 g/1 oz grapes

TUESDAY

Trout with almonds
Vegetables: boiled new potato, braised fennel, mangetout, green beans, green or mixed salad

100 g/4 oz fresh pineapple

WEDNESDAY

100 g/4 oz fillet (tenderloin) or rump steak, grilled (broiled) with herbs, all fat removed
Vegetables: boiled new potato, **ratatouille**, spring greens, green or mixed salad

½ grapefruit with crunchy topping (See Week 5 Day 3)

THURSDAY

Cannelloni
Vegetables: 2 grilled (broiled) tomatoes, **pepperoni**, green or mixed salad

1 tangerine/satsuma or 1 oz fresh pineapple

FRIDAY

Braised kidneys
75 g/3 oz boiled brown rice (25 g/1 oz/2 tbsp raw weight)
Vegetables: carrots, broccoli, marrow (squash), peas or mixed salad

1 small peach or 25 g/1 oz grapes

SATURDAY

Chicken with peach and ginger
Vegetables: green salad, mangetout, green beans, salsify, peas or courgettes (zucchini)

Green fruit salad

SUNDAY

Lamb with garlic and rosemary
Vegetables: jacket baked potato, 2 baked tomatoes, **red cabbage with apple**, cauliflower or spring greens

1 small slice melon

MONDAY

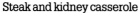

Mediterranean seafood sauce
75 g/3 oz boiled tagliatelle (25 g/1 oz/½ cup raw weight)
Vegetables: green or mixed salad, courgettes (zucchini) or green beans

75 g/3 oz fresh pineapple or 50 g/2 oz grapes

TUESDAY

Tarragon chicken: 225 g/8 oz chicken portion, cooked in foil with skin removed and a slice of onion, a sprig of fresh tarragon, seasoning and lemon juice.
Vegetables: boiled new potato, braised celery, broccoli or leeks

1 banana

WEDNESDAY

Steak and kidney casserole
Vegetables: green beans, mangetout, 2 baked tomatoes, spinach, Brussels sprouts or spring greens

Red fruit salad

THURSDAY

Vegetable curry
75 g/3 oz boiled brown rice (25 g/1 oz/2 tbsp raw weight)
Vegetables: green or mixed salad

½ grapefruit

FRIDAY

Smoked salmon roulade
Vegetables: boiled new potato, braised fennel, green beans, peas, spinach or green salad

1 apple, orange or pear

SATURDAY

Wholewheat spaghetti with chicken livers
Vegetables: peas, 2 grilled (broiled) tomatoes, spinach, green or mixed salad

1 small peach, 2 plums or 25 g/1 oz grapes

SUNDAY

Lamb kebab
Vegetables: jacket baked potato, swede (rutabaga), parsnip, **red cabbage with apple,** cauliflower, carrots or green salad

Strawberry sorbet

Knowing when to stop dieting is as important as being able to keep to your diet. The key is comfort: stop at a weight you can comfortably maintain. You will know you have gone too far if you find it a constant struggle to keep to your new weight.

 Chicken florentine
Vegetables: courgettes (zucchini), carrots, leeks, broccoli, cauliflower or beetroot (beet)

½ ogen melon or 1 tangerine/satsuma

MONDAY

 Spinach soufflé
Vegetables: green beans, 2 grilled (broiled) tomatoes, poached mushrooms, green or mixed salad

150 g/5 oz carton plain yogurt

NB Soak prunes for tomorrow

TUESDAY

 Pork fillet with prunes
Vegetables: cabbage, spinach, braised celery, marrow (squash), spring greens, baked onion or carrots

1 apple, large orange or pear

WEDNESDAY

 200 g/7 oz plaice (flounder) fillet, grilled (broiled) with herbs
Vegetables: boiled new potato, mangetout, green beans, peas, 2 grilled (broiled) tomatoes, poached mushrooms or green salad

75 g/3 oz fresh pineapple

THURSDAY

 Wholewheat spaghetti with tomato and basil
Vegetables: spinach, peas, green beans, green or mixed salad

1 peach, 3 plums, 100 g/4 oz raspberries or 50 g/2 oz grapes

FRIDAY

 Indian chicken
Vegetables: boiled new potato, courgettes (zucchini), asparagus, green or mixed salad

½ grapefruit

SATURDAY

 150 g/5 oz fillet (tenderloin) or rump steak, grilled (broiled) with herbs, all fat removed
Vegetables: **red cabbage with apple**, Brussels sprouts, green beans, green or mixed salad

1 banana or 100 g/4 oz grapes

SUNDAY

INDULGENCES

As temptation is a part of any diet, there are no forbidden fruits on this one. Some high-calorie foods are allowed every week, even in the final stages when overall calorie count is cut right down.

These Indulgences are meant to encourage a more flexible attitude to food. Being allowed to 'break' your diet from time to time and indulge in a favourite food, or drink, should help avoid the all-or-nothing starve/stuff mentality that sabotages many diets almost as soon as they have started. If all foods are allowed there can be no excuse for defaulting.

Each week of the diet gives a code of indulgences allowed. Check particular favourites against these lists and, if your heart's desire is not on them, work out exactly how much you can allow yourself within the stated limit.

100 CALORIES

50g (2 oz) dried apricots

1 mashed banana with 1 tsp sugar

50g (2 oz) chestnuts

½ medium ogen melon with 50g (2 oz) port OR 25g (1 oz) port and 75g (3 oz) strawberries OR 175g (6 oz) strawberries

1 large nectarine

125g (4 oz) fresh pineapple with 2 tsp single (light) cream

250g (8 oz) fresh cherries

1 passion fruit with 125g (4 oz) paw-paw OR 2 medium peaches

3 small dried figs

2 fresh figs with 125g (4 oz) grapes

100g (3½ oz) palm hearts with lemon juice and chopped parsley

25g (1 oz) Austrian smoked cheese with 1 rye crispbread

25g (1 oz) Lancashire/Double Gloucester/Roquefort cheese

40g (1½ oz) sausage roll (made with shortcrust pastry)

2 grilled (broiled) fish fingers

25g (1 oz) Parma ham with 1 large fresh peach

125g (4 oz) prawns (shrimps) in shells with lemon juice and 25g (1 oz) wholewheat bread

25g (1 oz) smoked cod's roe with lemon juice, on 25g (1 oz) wholewheat toast

2 tsp mayonnaise

2 Bourbon biscuits (cookies)

1 shortbread biscuit (cookie)

1 plain cup cake

1 small jam tart

50g (2 oz) chocolate ice cream

100g (3½ oz) chocolate frozen mousse

75g (3 oz) fruit yogurt

1 thin pancake (crêpe) with lemon juice and ¾ tsp sugar

75g (3 oz) egg custard

1 large meringue with 1 tbsp whipping cream

25g (1 oz) fruit pastilles

150 ml (¼ pint) (⅔ cup) grape juice

1 cup of Ovaltine: 1 tsp Ovaltine with 200 ml (⅓ pint) (⅞ cup) skimmed milk

1 cup hot chocolate: 2 tsp drinking chocolate and 200 ml (⅓ pint) (⅞ cup) skimmed milk

300 ml (½ pint) (1¼ cups) Coca Cola

4 tbsp (2 fl oz) (¼ cup) spirit (any) mixed with slimline tonic/bitter lemon/soda

300 ml (½ pint) (1¼ cups) dry or sweer cider

1 large glass of champagne

300 ml (½ pint) (1¼ cups) lager generous glass dry or medium sherry

25g (1 oz) any liqueur, except Chartreuse

Crudités: 1 tbsp garlic mayonnaise with 50g (2 oz) each pepper and carrots and 125g (4 oz) celery

½ medium avocado pear with black pepper and lemon juice

1 medium corn on the cob with 1 tsp butter

25g (1 oz) Caerphilly, Cheddar, Cheshire, Emmenthal, Camembert or cream cheese with 1 plain Digestive biscuit (Graham cracker) or water biscuit (cracker)

25g (1 oz) Stilton with 1 water biscuit (cracker)

50g (2 oz) Ricotta cheese with 1 water biscuit (cracker)

Bacon sandwich: 2 grilled rashers streaky bacon (2 broiled bacon slices), 1 sliced tomato and 1 x 25g (1 oz) slice wholewheat bread

35g (1½ oz) taramasalata with 1 x 25g (1 oz) slice wholewheat toast

12 fresh oysters, lemon juice and 1 x 25g (1 oz) slice wholewheat bread and scraping of butter

75g (3 oz) smoked salmon, lemon juice, black pepper, 1 x 25g (1 oz) slice wholewheat bread and scraping of butter

25g (1 oz) caviar/Danish lumpfish roe with 25g (1 oz) cream cheese on 1 rye crispbread

20g (¾ oz) peanut butter on ½ muffin/1 x 25g (1 oz) slice wholewheat toast/2 rye crispbreads

1 grilled (broiled) pork sausage and 1 tbsp tomato ketchup

4 snails cooked with butter, garlic and parsley

25g (1 oz) pistachio nuts

30g (1¼ oz) peanuts

75g (3 oz) potato crisps (chips)

25g (1 oz) potato rings

2 pancakes with scraping of butter and 2 tsp honey, jam or marmalade

1 crumpet with scraping of butter and 2 tsp honey, jam or marmalade

1 cheese scone

1 plain scone with scraping of butter and 2 tsp honey, jam or marmalade

1 currant scone with scraping of butter

1 iced cup cake

1 small Danish pastry

1 small éclair

½ jam doughnut or 1 ring doughnut

1 mince pie

50g (2 oz) treacle tart

1 large meringue with 2 tbsp whipping cream and 175g (6 oz) raspberries

50g (2 oz) fruit cake

125g (4 oz) plum pie

100g (3½ oz) apple strudel

60g (2¼ oz) chocolate cake

1 chocolate and 1 plain Digestive biscuit (Graham cracker)

3 plain Digestive biscuits (Graham crackers)

4 coconut biscuits (cookies)

1 x 25g (1 oz) bowl bran flakes/ cornflakes/grapenuts/ raisin bran/Shredded Wheat/any bran cereal OR 2 Weetabix with 150 ml (¼ pint) (⅔ cup) whole milk

25g (1 oz) popcorn

45g (1¾ oz) milk or plain chocolate

40g (1½ oz) chocolate-coated peppermint creams

Hot chocolate: 2 tsp drinking chocolate, 150 ml (8 fl oz) (1 cup) skimmed milk and 25g (1 oz) whipping cream

200 ml (⅓ pint) (⅞ cup) Bloody Mary

90 ml (3 fl oz) (6 tbsp) Vodka cocktail

⅓ bottle wine (red/rosé/white – dry/medium/sparkling)

Special diets

Diets are not just about eating less but about eating well. Good nutrition, always important, is especially vital when breastfeeding or pregnant or when following a restricted diet for health or ethical reasons. In this chapter you will find healthy eating plans for prospective and nursing mothers, a high-fibre, very low-fat diet (highly recommended for men) and a vegetarian diet, designed both for those already committed to this healthy way of eating and for those anxious to try something new. A healthy diet that keeps interest up, boredom down, has the best possible chance of success.

There are diets for other special circumstances too. If you want to lose a little weight quickly for a holiday or special occasion, for example, you can follow one of the short sharp Blitz diets, safe in the knowledge that you are not undernourishing yourself – though you should be aware that this is not the best way of losing weight in the long term. Re-read the introduction to find out why. The 24-hour juice fasts will refresh and revitalize, whether or not you want to lose weight, and make an excellent break from too much rich, heavy food and alcohol. Try one for a day and see how much better you feel... An analysis of essential nutrients – calories, carbohydrates, protein, fibre, relevant vitamins and minerals – is given for each diet. Figures in brackets after each nutrient indicate the recommended daily allowance (U.K. only).

JUICE DIETS

These fruit and vegetable juices will provide a refreshing rest from the excesses of rich food, unbalanced eating patterns and an unhealthy lifestyle. Set aside one day when demands are not too great. Allow yourself 3 cocktails, all the same or different, and alternate with plentiful glasses of water.

Providing it is undertaken for a period of no more than two days, fasting can be a great relief to the system – particularly if it is habitually overloaded with alcohol and rich or refined foods. In general, you can expect to feel bad on the first day, better on the second. These feelings of general malaise (headaches, irritability, weakness) are thought to be due both to lack of food and to withdrawal symptoms of foods to which one is 'allergically addicted'. These masked allergies are very difficult to track down and should only be investigated under the direction of an environmentally and nutritionally orientated doctor. Yet another possible explanation for these symptoms is that after a period without food the metabolism switches to a state called ketosis, in which it starts burning fats rather than sugars. This can release fat-soluble toxins which may have some transient bad effects as they are swept out of the system.

Prolonged fasting can have some serious side-effects: protein, mineral and vitamin deficiencies, fainting, dizziness, possible liver disorder and even death. Most doctors now consider that prolonged fasts should only be taken as a means of weight control under the strictest medical supervision.

	Vegetable I	Vegetable II	Fruit I	Fruit II
Calories	81	56	133	187
Protein	38%	29%	5%	6%
Fat	5%	7%	NONE	NONE
Carbohydrate	57%	64%	95%	94%
Fibre (g)	14.3	5.1	5.6	6.9
Vitamin C (mg)	48.3	163.6	23.8	84.3
Potassium (mg)	1443	993	463	879
Magnesium (mg)	95	47	24	35
Sodium (mg)	587	41	8	10

Fasting may help clear the mind and cleanse the system but it is not an effective long-term strategy for losing weight. When you fast, as much as 65 per cent of the weight lost is due to a breakdown of lean tissue – *not fat*. The result is a far from ideal body shape and a steep drop in metabolic rate – as much as 40 per cent on extended fasts – making some weight regain inevitable once the fast is broken.

VEGETABLE JUICES
Weigh vegetables after trimming. Wash them well, especially the ones that grow above the ground, which may have been sprayed with harmful chemicals. Shake dry.

FRUIT JUICES
Wash all fruit carefully, remembering that even if it looks clean, it has probably been sprayed with chemicals. Remove stones (pits), but leave apple cores, skin, etc.

Vegetable Juice I

Metric/Imperial	American
75 g/3 oz spinach, leaves and tender stalks only	3 oz spinach, leaves and tender stalks only
150 g/5 oz carrots	5 oz carrots
150 g/5 oz fennel	5 oz fennel
75 g/3 oz celery	3 oz celery

Put all ingredients through a juicer.

Fruit Juice I

Metric/Imperial	American
2 dessert apples (preferably Cox's or Granny Smith's)	2 Granny Smith apples
2 apricots or 2-3 plums	2 apricots or 2-3 plums
½ mango or paw-paw, or 2 passion fruit, or 1 lime	½ mango or paw-paw, or 2 passion fruit, or 1 lime

Put all ingredients through a juicer.

Vegetable Juice II

Metric/Imperial	American
175 g/6 oz tomatoes	6 oz tomatoes
125 g/4 oz cucumber	4 oz cucumber
75-125 g/3-4 oz green pepper or chicory	3-4 oz green pepper or endive
25 g/1 oz watercress or parsley	1 oz watercress or parsley

Put all ingredients through a juicer.

Fruit Juice II

Metric/Imperial	American
1 large ripe pear	1 large ripe pear
1 large orange	1 large orange
125 g/4 oz black grapes	4 oz black grapes

Put all ingredients through a juicer.

On fasts and juice diets you tend to lose a great deal of retained fluid and, with it, the important minerals potassium, magnesium and sodium. These fruit and vegetable juices have been specially formulated to compensate for this and so keep levels up...

5-DAY BLITZ

Low- or no-carbohydrate diets should be 'strongly discouraged' says the Royal College of Physicians in its 1983 report, *Obesity*, even if you only want to follow them for a short period of time. To lose weight rapidly, choose a diet high in starchy carbohydrates (wholewheat bread, wholegrain cereals and pasta, lentils and pulses) and low in fats instead, like the diets given here.

	BREAKFASTS	LIGHT MEALS	MAIN MEALS
DAY 1	None	Milk: 600 ml/1 pint (2½ cups) whole milk Fruit: 3 oranges (100 g/3½ oz each) and 2 apples (125 g/4 oz each)	None
DAY 2	BREAKFAST ALLOWANCE FROM DAY 2: 25 g/1 oz Shredded Wheat, Weetabix, Weetaflakes *or* Puffed Wheat, with 10 g/⅓ oz bran	Tomato sandwich: 100g/3½ oz tomatoes, 1 tsp low calorie mayonnaise and 50 g/2 oz wholewheat bread Fruit: 120 g/4 oz apple	Fillet steak: 125 g/4 oz fillet (tenderloin), grilled (broiled), using no oil. Season well and remove all fat. Vegetable: 100 g/3½ oz broccoli Strawberry ice: blend together 150 g/5 oz fresh or frozen strawberries, 6 tbsp water, and 10 g/⅓ oz dried skimmed milk until smooth. Freeze for about 3 to 4 hours until firm.
DAY 3	As day 2	Cheese and pepper sandwich: 50 g/2 oz chopped green pepper, 100 g/3½ oz cottage cheese and 50 g/2 oz wholewheat bread Fruit: 100 g/3½ oz orange	Fillet of plaice (flounder): 150 g/5 oz fillet, grilled (broiled) with a sprinkling of freshly chopped herbs. Serve with slices of lemon. Vegetable: 100 g/3½ oz carrots Stewed apples: 150 g/5 oz apples cooked with 15 g/½ oz raisins (no sugar)
DAY 4	As day 2	Cucumber and egg sandwich: 50 g/2 oz chopped cucumber, 50 g/2 oz hard-boiled egg, 1 tsp low calorie mayonnaise and 50 g/2 oz wholewheat bread Fruit: 150 g/5 oz pear	Paprika chicken: remove the skin from 100 g/3½ oz chicken breast and coat with French (Dijon-style) mustard and paprika to taste. Grill (broil) under a gentle heat until thoroughly cooked. Vegetable: 100 g/3½ oz cabbage Fruit: 100 g/3½ oz cherries or grapes
DAY 5	As day 2	Smoked salmon and watercress sandwich: 60 g/2½ oz smoked salmon, 50 g/2 oz chopped watercress, 1 tsp low calorie mayonnaise, lemon juice and 50 g/2 oz wholewheat bread Fruit: 125 g/4 oz apple	Eggs and spinach: 2 medium eggs poached and served with 100 g/3½ oz boiled and chopped spinach. Season well. Vegetable: 50 g/2 oz grilled (broiled) tomato Fruit: 1 banana

DAILY ALLOWANCE FROM DAY 2: 600 ml/1 pint (2½ cups) skimmed milk; unlimited water and herb teas. 1 daily multivitamin plus iron.

On short, sharp diets it is especially important to weigh all foods precisely, checking scales for accuracy against a light object of known weight before starting. If your scales are not accurate, a specialist dealer will calibrate them properly for you.

10-DAY BLITZ

Short sharp diets can be great for getting into shape for a holiday or special occasion, but they must be followed by several weeks of moderate eating if you want to keep the weight off for any length of time.

Weight that is lost very quickly tends to be regained very quickly too, partly because the loss is largely glycogen instead of fat (see page 31) and partly because of a long-term drop in basal metabolic rate.

	BREAKFASTS	LIGHT MEALS	MAIN MEALS
DAY 1	BREAKFAST ALLOWANCE: 25 g/1 oz Shredded Wheat, Weetabix, Weetaflakes *or* Puffed Wheat, with 7 g/¼ oz bran.	Cheese and caper sandwich: 50 g/2 oz cottage cheese, 15 g/½ oz capers and 50 g/2 oz wholewheat bread Fruit: 1 apple	**Pork casserole:** follow recipe on page 113 but leave out the soy sauce and sugar and add 50 g/2 oz mushrooms 5 minutes before the end of cooking. Vegetables: 100 g/3½ oz carrots Oranges and figs: simmer 50 g/2 oz dried figs in 4 tbsp orange juice for 20 minutes or until soft. Allow to cool and mix with 100 g/3½ oz fresh orange slices.
DAY 2 As day 1		Liver pâté and tomato sandwich: 50 g/2 oz **liver pâté** (see Breastfeeding Diet, page 78) and 100 g/3½ oz sliced tomatoes with 50 g/2 oz wholewheat bread Fruit: 100 g/3½ oz cherries or grapes	Baked jacket potato: 150 g/5 oz potato with 100 g/3½ oz seasoned cottage cheese. **Ratatouille** (page 114) Baked apple: 100 g/3½ oz apple filled with 15 g/½ oz raisins
DAY 3 As day 1		Baked beans on toast: 100 g/3½ oz baked beans and 50 g/2 oz tomato on 50 g/2 oz wholewheat toast Fruit: 1 pear	**Indian chicken** (page 106) Salad: 100 g/3½ oz lettuce, watercress, cucumber and green pepper Banana and prunes: 100 g/3½ oz chopped banana mixed with 50 g/2 oz stewed prunes
DAY 4 As day 1		Corn and cheese sandwich: 50 g/2 oz cottage cheese, 40 g/1½ oz sweetcorn (kernel corn) flavoured with Tabasco (hot pepper sauce) with 50 g/2 oz wholewheat bread Fruit: 1 orange	Plaice (flounder) in orange sauce: (see High fibre, Low fat Diet, Day 9, page 67) Vegetables: 100 g/3½ oz broccoli or green beans Banana and melon: 50 g/2 oz chopped banana mixed with 100 g/3½ oz chopped melon
DAY 5 As day 1		Cucumber sandwich: 50 g/2 oz sliced cucumber, 1 tsp low calorie mayonnaise with 50 g/2 oz wholewheat bread Fruit: 1 orange	**Lamb with garlic and rosemary** (page 108) Vegetable: 100 g/3½ oz shredded white cabbage cooked in just enough boiling water to cover. Serve well seasoned with freshly ground black pepper. Fruit: 1 grapefruit

DAILY ALLOWANCE: 600 ml/1 pint (2½ cups) skimmed milk; unlimited water and herb teas; 1 daily multivitamin plus iron

It is a well known and accepted fact that dieting depresses the metabolism. Not so well known or accepted is the fact that it may remain depressed once the diet is over – *even if all the weight that was lost has been regained*. If metabolic rate does not recover to 100 per cent each time, it is not surprising that it gets more and more difficult to lose weight with each successive diet.

In one Scottish experiment, set up to assess the effects of yo-yoing weight levels on metabolic rate, volunteers were over-fed one month and under-fed the next so that their weight gains and losses would reflect the typical pattern of on/off dieters. After 18 months, when the results were analysed, every one of the volunteers showed a measurable drop in metabolic rate – one by as much as 15 per cent – even though they were back at the weight at which they had started.

Diets of less than 750 calories a day are nearly always self-defeating because glycogen levels become so depleted that most of the lost weight is regained almost immediately. People who fast or go on very stringent diets may, on breaking them, step up their intake to as little as 1,000 calories and still find themselves regaining weight over the next day or days.

A rapid loss of glycogen is not a good idea. It interferes with concentration and makes you feel listless, lethargic, depressed, headachy and hungry. Keep some carbohydrate in your diet and you will feel much better.

BREAKFASTS	LIGHT MEALS	MAIN MEALS	
As day 1	Soup julienne: mix 2 tsp beef extract with 200 ml/⅓ pint (⅞ cup) boiling water. Add 25 g/1 oz diced carrot and simmer for 10 minutes. Add 25 g/1 oz sliced leek and seasoning, and continue cooking until the vegetables are just tender. 75 g/3 oz wholewheat bread with 15 g/½ oz low fat spread Fruit: 1 pear	Fillet steak: 150 g/5 oz fillet (tenderloin), grilled (broiled), using no oil. Season well and remove all fat. Vegetables: 100 g/3½ oz grilled (broiled) mushrooms, 50 g/2 oz grilled (broiled) tomatoes and 100 g/3½ oz peas. Stewed apple: 100 g/3½ oz apple stewed without sugar	DAY 6
As day 1	Tomato sandwich: 100 g/3½ oz sliced tomatoes, 1 tsp low calorie mayonnaise and 50 g/2 oz wholewheat bread Fruit: 1 peach	**Kidneys in red wine** (page 108) Brown rice: 40 g/1½ oz boiled Salad: 100 g/3½ oz lettuce, watercress, cucumber and green pepper Orange jelly: dissolve 7 g/¼ oz (1 envelope) gelatine in 7 tbsp fresh orange juice. Leave in the refrigerator for 2 hours until set.	DAY 7
As day 1	Ham sandwich: 50 g/2 oz lean ham, 50 g/2 oz shredded lettuce, 1 tsp low calorie mayonnaise and 50 g/2 oz wholewheat bread Fruit: 1 apple	Baked fish: wrap 200 g/7 oz cod steak in foil with 50 g/2 oz sweetcorn (kernel corn), 2 sliced tomatoes, a little celery salt and freshly ground black pepper. Bake in a moderately hot oven, 200°C (400°F) or Gas Mark 6, for 15 minutes. Vegetable: 100 g/3½ oz broccoli Raspberry yogurt: 100 g/5 oz plain yogurt mixed with 100 g/3½ oz fresh or frozen raspberries NB Soak apricots for tomorrow	DAY 8
As day 1	Liver pâté and tomato sandwich: 50 g/2 oz **liver pâté** (see Breastfeeding Diet, page 78), 100 g/3½ oz sliced tomatoes and 50 g/2 oz wholewheat bread Fruit: 1 apple	Poached egg and potato: 1 poached egg with 150 g/5 oz mashed potato made with skimmed milk. Coleslaw: 50 g/2 oz cabbage, 25 g/1 oz grated carrot, 15 g/½ oz grated onion and 7 g/¼ oz shredded red pepper mixed with 7 g/¼ oz sultanas (golden raisins), 2 tsp low fat dressing (page 110) and seasoning. Fruit compote: 25 g/1 oz dried apricots stewed and mixed with 50 g/2 oz chopped banana	DAY 9
As day 1	Crab and tomato sandwich: 50 g/2 oz fresh or canned crabmeat, 50 g/2 oz sliced tomatoes, 1 tsp low calorie mayonnaise and 50 g/2 oz wholewheat bread Fruit: 1 pear	Lemon chicken escalope: remove the skin from 125 g/4 oz chicken breast and beat well. Coat with 7 g/¼ oz wholemeal flour and fry for 5 minutes each side in 2 tsp oil. Remove and keep warm. Add the juice of 1 lemon and seasoning to the pan. Bring to the boil, pour over chicken. Vegetable: 100 g/3½ oz runner (string) beans Blackberry and port mousse: stew 75 g/3 oz fresh or frozen blackberries with 1 tsp sugar until tender. Blend with 1 tbsp plain yogurt, 1 tsp lemon juice and 1 tsp port. Sprinkle over 7 g/¼ oz (1 envelope) gelatine and stir until dissolved. Leave in a cool place to set.	DAY 10

Calories 1200 • Protein 27% • Fat 16% (maximum recommended intake 35%) • Carbohydrate 57% • Fibre 33 g • Vitamin A 1069 mg (RDA) • Calcium 1187 mg

HIGH FIBRE, LOW FAT

The average westerner eats some 20 g/¾oz of fibre per 2000 calories. Although this diet contains nearly half that in terms of calories, its fibre content is more than half as much again.

In this diet, half your fibre comes from cereals and wholewheat bread and half from fruit, vegetables, beans and pulses. Once you have lost weight, keep to the principles and increase the quantities for an excellent weight-maintenance eating plan.

In its report on Dietary Fibre, the Royal College of Physicians has suggested that substantial health benefits may be gained by increasing the amount of fibre which we eat, particularly in the form of cereals.

Lack of fibre in the diet has been implicated in at least 12 diseases, from cancer of the colon and diverticulitis to gallstones and varicose veins. These diseases are known as the 'diseases of civilisation' because they are much commoner in industrialized countries than in less-developed ones, such as those in rural Africa, where fibre intake is 3 or 4 times higher.

Hand in hand with lack of fibre and a highly refined diet goes a surfeit of fat. It is no coincidence that many diseases which are linked with excessive fat intake, such as coronary heart disease, have also been linked with a low fibre intake.

Fibre regulates the rate at which food is broken down, digested and released into the bloodstream, so helping to ensure a smooth running digestive system and (good news for slimmers) providing a continuous supply of energy which keeps you feeling fuller longer...

Food in its natural state is high in fibre. If you take away the fibre, you are left with the pure 'refined' sugar. This 'refined' sugar rushes into the bloodstream and loads the body with far more sugar than it is capable of dealing with at any one time because it cannot produce enough insulin to keep the blood/sugar ratio at a sensible level. If you continually do this, the cells that produce the insulin may eventually give up the struggle and the result will be maturity-onset diabetes – a disease which is more common in developed countries, such as Britain and the USA, than in less-developed countries where food is still largely eaten in its natural state.

In the past, doctors were reluctant to accept that fibre might have some subtle beneficial effects because they considered that it was merely 'roughage' – indigestible food that passed unaltered through the gut and out the other end. Its laxative effects were attributed to the fact that it increased bulk and helped push everything along.

Although there is some truth in this, we now know that fibre is much more than an inert bulking agent and that it is actually broken down and, indeed, digested in the colon. Some of the by-products of this process have a chemical effect on the muscles of the colon wall, inducing them to be more active and helping to guard against constipation.

Fibre has another vital protective function, by giving the bacteria that colonize the lower reaches of the intestine something to work on. Highly refined food, which is digested well before it reaches the colon, does not keep the bacteria fully occupied with the result that they may start to produce toxic substances and carcinogens (cancer-producing agents).

As fibre is metabolized in the colon it produces breakdown products known as volatile fatty acids (VFAs). Cows and sheep are known to be able to re-absorb them and to use them as their chief source of energy, explaining why they can subsist quite happily on vast amounts of fibre in the form of grass or even straw. There is now some evidence that human beings produce VFAs too and that people on extremely high-fibre diets may derive a proportion of their energy from fibre, just as cows do. It is intriguing to think that, with just a little change in physiology, we might have been as well able to live on grass as we do now on bread.

As Vitamin A is found mainly in fats, such as butter and fish oils, you should be aware of alternative sources when you limit your fat intake. Eat more yellow or orange fruits and vegetables (carrots, apricots, etc) and dark green vegetables, such as watercress, spring greens and spinach.

Don't just rely on bran for fibre. Oats, wheat, pulses, fruits and vegetables (jacket baked potatoes especially) are all high in fibre and are now thought preferable to bran, because bran contains phytate – a gummy substance which binds key minerals calcium, iron and zinc and prevents their absorption into the system. As little as one tablespoon of bran has been shown to reduce calcium absorption. Although wholemeal flour also contains phytate, it is inactivated by baking.

	BREAKFASTS	LIGHT MEALS	MAIN MEALS
DAY 1	BREAKFAST ALLOWANCE: 25 g/1 oz Shredded Wheat, Weetabix, Weetaflakes *or* Puffed Wheat	Tomato and peanut sandwich: 20 g/¾ oz peanut butter, 50 g/2 oz sliced tomato and 75 g/3 oz wholewheat bread Fruit: 2 pears	**Sweet and sour pork** Brown rice: 40 g/1½ oz boiled Vegetables: 100 g/3½ oz raw beansprouts Figs and oranges: soak 25 g/1 oz dried figs in 6 tbsp fresh orange juice for about 4 hours or until soft. If wished, simmer gently for 20 minutes, then cool and mix with 100 g/3½ oz fresh orange segments. NB Soak beans for tomorrow.
DAY 2	As day 1	Poached egg: 1 poached egg and 1 grilled (broiled) tomato on 75 g/3 oz wholewheat toast with 15 g/½ oz low fat spread 150 g/5 oz plain yogurt NB Soak lentils and make stock for tomorrow.	**Beef and bean casserole** Vegetable: 150 g/5 oz jacket baked potato Orange jelly: 150 ml/¼ pint (⅔ cup) fresh orange juice set with 1 tsp gelatine
DAY 3	As day 1	**Lentil soup** (page 109) 75 g/3 oz wholewheat bread Fruit: 2 pears	**Wholewheat pan pizza** (page 123) Coleslaw: 100 g/3½ oz grated white cabbage and 100 g/3½ oz grated carrot mixed with 20 g/¾ oz **low fat dressing** (page 110) and seasoning Fruit: 100 g/3½ oz grapes NB Soak prunes for tomorrow.
DAY 4	As day 1	Ham and lettuce sandwich: 50 g/2 oz cooked ham, 50 g/2 oz lettuce and 75 g/3 oz wholewheat bread with 15 g/½ oz low calorie mayonnaise Fruit: 2 apples	**Fish pie** (page 104) Use sweetcorn (kernel corn) in place of peas Vegetables: 100 g/3½ oz runner (string) beans Stewed prunes: 100 g/3½ oz prunes stewed without sugar
DAY 5	As day 1	Baked beans on toast: 200 g/7 oz baked beans and 50 g/2 oz grilled (broiled) tomato on 75 g/3 oz wholewheat toast Fruit: 1 banana	Lamb kebabs: 100 g/3½ oz cubed lean lamb, 25 g/1 oz quartered onion, 50 g/2 oz small whole tomatoes, 50 g/2 oz whole mushrooms and bay leaves, arranged alternately on a skewer, seasoned and grilled (broiled) or barbecued Brown rice: 40 g/1½ oz boiled Salad: 100 g/3½ oz watercress, 100 g/3½ oz chicory (endive) and 50 g/2 oz orange segments with 2 tsp **low fat dressing** (page 110) Raspberry yogurt: 150 g/5 oz fresh raspberries
DAY 6	As day 1	Cheese and pickle sandwich: 40 g/1½ oz Edam cheese, 2 tsp pickle and 75 g/3 oz wholewheat bread Fruit: 2 apples	**Lemon chicken escalope** (see 10-day Blitz Diet, page 63). Use 150 g/5 oz chicken. Vegetables: 100 g/3½ oz boiled potato and 100 g/3½ oz broccoli Apple compote: 150 g/5 oz apple stewed with 25 g/1 oz raisins
DAY 7	As day 1	Prawn and lettuce sandwich: 100 g/3½ oz prawns (shrimp), 50 g/2 oz lettuce and 20 g/¾ oz low calorie mayonnaise with 75 g/3 oz wholewheat bread	Roast meat: 100 g/3½ oz lean roast meat with 2 tbsp **low fat gravy** (page 110) Vegetables: 150 g/5 oz jacket baked potato, 100 g/3½ oz carrots and 100 g/3½ oz peas Peaches with plum sauce: 100 g/3½ oz stewed plums, stoned (pitted) and puréed, and served with 100 g/3½ oz poached, sliced fresh peaches NB Soak haricot beans for tomorrow.

DAILY ALLOWANCE: 600 ml/1 pint (2½ cups) skimmed milk

BREAKFASTS	LIGHT MEALS	MAIN MEALS	
WEEK 2		Bean and tuna fish salad: mix 50 g/2 oz cooked and cooled haricot beans with 50 g/2 oz drained tuna, 25 g/1 oz finely chopped onion, lemon juice, crushed garlic, freshly chopped parsley and seasoning. Vegetables: 150 g/5 oz boiled new potato and 100 g/3½ oz green pepper *Note*: to prepare the pepper, cut it in half, remove pith and seeds, and flatten. Place under a preheated grill (broiler) until the skin is blackened. Remove skin and serve at once. Banana yogurt: 150 g/5 oz plain yogurt with 100 g/3½ oz banana.	DAY 8
As day 1	Tomato sandwich: 100 g/3½ oz tomatoes, 20 g/¾ oz low calorie mayonnaise and 75 g/3 oz wholewheat bread Fruit: 2 apples		
As day 1	Lentil soup (page 109) 75 g/3 oz wholewheat bread Fruit: 1 pear	Plaice in orange sauce: poach 200 g/7 oz plaice (flounder) fillet in 120 ml/4 fl oz (½ cup) fresh orange juice. Remove fish and keep warm. Thicken sauce with 1 tsp cornflour (cornstarch) mixed with 1 tsp water and season well. Serve with orange slices. Vegetables: 150 g/5 oz boiled new potato and 100 g/3½ oz runner (string) beans Fruit: 100 g/3½ oz grapes or cherries NB Soak beans for tomorrow.	DAY 9
As day 1	Beetroot open sandwich: 75 g/3 oz curd cheese, 2 tsp horseradish sauce and 100 g/3½ oz pickled or fresh sliced beetroot (beet) on 75 g/3 oz wholewheat bread Fruit: 2 oranges	Chilli con carne (page 101) Vegetable: 150 g/5 oz jacket baked potato Baked apple: 100 g/3½ oz apple, filled with 25 g/1 oz raisins and served with 65 g/2½ oz plain yogurt NB Soak apricots for tomorrow.	DAY 10
As day 1	Crab and beansprout sandwich: 50 g/2 oz fresh or canned crabmeat, 50 g/2 oz beansprouts and 75 g/3 oz wholewheat bread with 20 g/¾ oz low calorie mayonnaise Fruit: 200 g/7 oz grapes	Poached chicken Vegetables: 100 g/3½ oz carrots and 150 g/5 oz boiled potato Stewed apricots: 50 g/2 oz dried apricots soaked overnight and stewed in a little water until soft. Serve with 15 g/½ oz chopped walnuts.	DAY 11
As day 1	Cucumber salad: slice ½ cucumber lengthways, scoop out the centre and chop. Mix with 50 g/2 oz curd cheese, 40 g/1½ oz chopped red pepper, 6 stoned (pitted) black olives and seasoning. Fill cucumber halves. 75 g/3 oz wholewheat bread Fruit: 2 pears	Beef goulash (page 98) Vegetables: 150 g/5 oz jacket baked potato and 100 g/3½ oz cauliflower Blackcurrant yogurt: 100 g/3½ oz fresh or frozen blackcurrants stewed until soft and cooled. Mix with 150 g/5 oz plain yogurt and add a little saccharine, if wished. NB Soak lentils for tomorrow.	DAY 12
As day 1	Tuna and tomato sandwich: 75 g/3 oz tuna, 100 g/3½ oz sliced tomato and 75 g/3 oz wholewheat bread Fruit: 1 banana	Vegetable curry (page 121) 40 g/1½ oz green mango chutney Brown rice: 40 g/1½ oz boiled Yogurt and cucumber: 50 g/2 oz chopped cucumber mixed with 50 g/2 oz plain yogurt. Chill before serving. Fruit: 200 g/7 oz melon	DAY 13
As day 1	Cheese and sweetcorn sandwich: 75 g/3 oz cottage cheese, 50 g/2 oz sweetcorn (kernel corn), 25 g/1 oz shredded lettuce and 75 g/3 oz wholewheat bread Fruit: 100 g/3½ oz grapes or cherries	Roast beef: 100 g/3½ oz lean roast beef served with 2 tbsp low fat gravy (page 110). Vegetables: 150 g/5 oz jacket baked potato, 150 g/5 oz peas and 100 g/3½ oz cauliflower Fruit salad: 150 g/5 oz sliced fresh peaches with 100 g/3½ oz fresh strawberries *OR* Cheese and biscuits: 25 g/1 oz Edam cheese with 1 Digestive biscuit (Graham cracker)	DAY 14

Calories 1200 • Protein 27% (minimum recommended intake 10%) • Fat 16% • Carbohydrate 57% • Fibre 31 g • Vitamin B1 (thiamin) 1.2 mg (RDA 0.9 mg). Vitamin B2 (riboflavin) 2 mg (RDA 1.3 mg) • Vitamin B12 2.8 μg (RDA 2 μg) • Iron 12 mg (RDA 12 mg)

VEGETARIAN

Variety is the keynote of the vegetarian diet. Eat from as wide a range of foods as possible – mixing fruit with vegetables, nuts, seeds, cereals, eggs and dairy products – and you will have a diet that is lower in fat, higher in fibre and as adequate in protein as any other diet. And remember, vegetarians tend not only to be healthier and longer-living, but slimmer too...

Protein, often seized upon as a major problem for vegetarians, is the one component of the diet most of us get more than enough of. In recognition of this, official bodies, such as the Food and Agriculture Organisation, are now *reducing* their recommended intake of protein.

A second misconception is that because meat contains most protein it also contains the best. Eggs, milk, fish, cheese and whole rice (in that order) *all* provide better quality protein than red meat and poultry; while vegetable sources, such as nuts, seeds, grains and pulses, also provide some.

Vegans, who do not eat dairy foods, eggs or fish, should take care to mix their plant proteins. Of the 22 amino acids in protein, there are 8 that the body cannot make and that must therefore be found in the diet. The egg is a uniquely valuable protein source because it contains all 8, and in the right concentrations, while grains and pulses contain different and complementary amino acids. Combine them, as with beans on toast or lentil curry with rice, to get the protein you need.

MAKE SURE YOU GET ENOUGH of vitamins B12, B1, B2 and D and iron... especially if you are a vegan. B12 is particularly important for people choosing to make their diet completely free of animal products (dairy foods, eggs, even honey) because these are the major nutritional sources of the vitamin. Although supplementation is usually necessary, there are recorded cases of British vegans living 14 to 17 years without any form of B12 supplement, and still maintaining apparently normal levels of the vitamin. This has led nutritionists to theorize that some people are able to manufacture and absorb B12 in their own gut. But this emphatically does not apply to everyone.

B1 (thiamin) and B2 (riboflavin) can be found in pulses, yeast, wheatgerm (an excellent source of most of the B vitamins) and cereals and should not be a problem if the diet is varied. You should also be getting sufficient vitamin D if you get enough sunshine, as the primary source of the vitamin is sunlight; secondary sources are fatty fish, margarine and fish oil. The best, easily absorbed source of iron is meat and fatty fish like sardines. Secondary sources are eggs, soya and dark green vegetables. Taking a Vitamin C-rich fruit or vegetable with your meal will help increase iron uptake from your food by as much as 4 times.

Vegetarian diets can protect against high blood pressure. One study in Israel revealed that only 2 per cent of a group of vegetarians had high blood pressure compared with 26 per cent in a meat-eating group of similar age and social circumstance. In Australia a group of men actually *lowered* their abnormal blood pressures by switching to a vegetarian diet for 6 weeks. When they returned to eating meat, their blood pressures rose to their previous levels.

It is now generally agreed that excessive meat consumption and over-indulgence in animal fats can contribute to a damaging effect on the arteries, to coronary heart disease and to a whole number of cancers, including those of the bowel, colon, ovary, breast, pancreas and prostate. Eliminating meat from the diet automatically cuts out a major source of fat. We have become accustomed to thinking of meat as protein, but in fact even lean meat, with a little visible fat removed, still contains large amounts of fat up to 60 per cent or more of the total weight once water is discounted. Even if not intending to eliminate meat from the diet entirely, we should all cut down. Once a day is more than adequate, twice excessive.

NB *VERY RESTRICTIVE VEGETARIAN DIETS, SUCH AS MACROBIOTIC DIETS, NEED CAREFUL PLANNING AND SUPPLEMENTATION. GET PROFESSIONAL NUTRITIONAL ADVICE BEFORE EMBARKING ON THEM.*

The ultimate vegetarian . . . Luckily, human herbivores don't have to rely on rabbit food to enjoy the health benefits that can be derived from a vegetarian diet, see left. Find protein in nuts, beans, pulses, wholegrains, lentils and dairy foods too.

	BREAKFASTS	LIGHT MEALS	MAIN MEALS
DAY 1	BREAKFAST ALLOWANCE: 25 g/1 oz Shredded Wheat, Weetabix, Weetaflakes *or* Puffed Wheat	Tomato sandwich: 100 g/3½ oz sliced tomatoes, 50 g/2 oz shredded lettuce, 2 tsp low calorie mayonnaise and 75 g/3 oz wholewheat bread Fruit: 2 apples	Eggs on vegetable purée Vegetable: 200 g/7 oz jacket baked potato Fruit: 1 pear Cheese: 50 g/2 oz Camembert
DAY 2	As day 1	Cottage cheese and fennel sandwich: 50 g/2 oz chopped fennel, 100 g/3½ oz cottage cheese and 75 g/3 oz wholewheat bread Fruit: 2 oranges	**Vegetable curry** (page 121) served with 40 g/1½ oz mango chutney. Brown rice: 50 g/2 oz boiled Fruit: 100 g/3½ oz fresh or frozen raspberries
DAY 3	As day 1	Beetroot open sandwich: 75 g/3 oz curd cheese mixed with 2 tsp horseradish sauce, 100 g/3½ oz sliced beetroot (beet) or tomato and 75 g/3 oz wholewheat bread Fruit: 1 apple	**Wholewheat pan pizza** (page 123) Salad: 150 g/5 oz lettuce, watercress, green pepper and cucumber Fruit: 1 pear NB Soak beans for tomorrow.
DAY 4	As day 1	Poached egg: 1 poached egg with 1 grilled (broiled) tomato on 75 g/3 oz wholewheat toast Fruit: 1 peach or pear	**Mixed bean salad** Salad: 150 g/5 oz watercress, grated carrot and chicory (endive) Ginger yogurt: 150 g/5 oz plain yogurt mixed with 50 g/2 oz chopped, crystallized stem (preserved) ginger
DAY 5	As day 1	Cheese and peanut sandwich: 15 g/½ oz sugar-free peanut butter mixed with 20 g/¾ oz curd cheese and 50 g/2 oz chopped apple with 75 g/3 oz wholewheat bread Fruit: 1 orange	Broccoli with cheese sauce: cook 150 g/5 oz broccoli tips until just tender. Prepare 150 ml/¼ pint (⅔ cup) **white sauce** (page 123) and add 50 g/2 oz grated Cheddar cheese. Pour the cheese sauce over the freshly cooked broccoli. Vegetable: 150 g/5 oz jacket baked potato Fruit: 200 g/7 oz melon
DAY 6	As day 1	Grapes and blue cheese sandwich: 25 g/1 oz seeded and halved grapes, 75 g/3 oz blue cheese, 25 g/1 oz curd cheese and 75 g/3 oz wholewheat bread Fruit: 100 g/3½ oz banana	**Gnocchi with tomato sauce** (page 105) Fruit: 1 pear
DAY 7	As day 1	100 g/3½ oz cooked, canned or fresh salsify Tomato salad: 100 g/3½ oz sliced tomatoes, freshly chopped basil, seasoning and **low fat dressing** (page 110) with 50 g/2 oz olives Fruit: 100 g/3½ oz grapes	Vegetable omelette: prepare an omelette using 2 eggs, a little skimmed milk, 2 tsp freshly chopped chives and seasoning. Cook in a non-stick frying pan (skillet) and fill with 100 g/3½ oz cooked broad (fava) beans or peas. Orange yogurt: 150 g/5 oz plain yogurt mixed with 100 g/3½ oz fresh orange segments

DAILY ALLOWANCE: 600 ml/1 pint (2½ cups) skimmed milk

BREAKFASTS	LIGHT MEALS	MAIN MEALS	
As day 1	Pickle and cheese sandwich: 50 g/2 oz Edam cheese, 25 g/1 oz sweet pickle and 75 g/3 oz wholewheat bread Fruit: 2 apples NB Soak lentils for tomorrow.	Stuffed tomatoes: slice the tops and scoop out the seeds from 2 large tomatoes. Fill with curd cheese flavoured with Tabasco (hot pepper sauce) and paprika, and sprinkle with freshly chopped herbs. Vegetable: 150 g/5 oz jacket baked potato Blackcurrant and banana dessert: stew 100 g/3½ oz fresh or frozen blackcurrants, cool, and purée in a blender. Stir in 50 g/2 oz chopped banana and serve chilled.	DAY 8
As day 1	Lentil soup (page 109) 75 g/3 oz wholewheat bread Fruit: 1 pear	Vegetable lasagne (page 121) Wholewheat pasta: 50 g/2 oz boiled Spiced grapefruit: 100 g/3½ oz fresh grapefruit, sprinkled with cinnamon and browned under a hot grill (broiler)	DAY 9
As day 1	Baked beans on toast: 150 g/5 oz baked beans and 50 g/2 oz tomato on 75 g/3 oz wholewheat toast Fruit: 1 orange	Cheese pie Red cabbage with apples (page 115) Fruit: 1 pear	DAY 10
As day 1	Avocado cheese sandwich: 40 g/1½ oz sliced avocado, 50 g/2 oz cottage cheese and 75 g/3 oz wholewheat bread Fruit: 2 apples NB Soak lentils for tomorrow.	Middle Eastern rice (page 111) Chicory and orange salad: 100 g/3½ oz chicory (endive) and 100 g/3½ oz fresh orange segments tossed in low fat dressing (page 110) Fruit: 200 g/7 oz melon	DAY 11
As day 1	Lentil soup (page 109) 75 g/3 oz wholewheat bread Fruit: 2 pears	Courgettes au gratin Hot beetroot: 100 g/3½ oz thinly sliced cooked beetroot (beet) heated through with the juice of 1 lemon or small orange Fruit and cheese: 200 g/7 oz sliced fresh plums with 50 g/2 oz curd cheese NB Soak lentils for tomorrow.	DAY 12
As day 1	Cheese and pineapple sandwich: 50 g/2 oz cottage cheese, 25 g/1 oz chopped pineapple and 75 g/3 oz wholewheat bread Fruit: 2 apples	Wholewheat spaghetti with tomato and basil sauce (page 123). Add 25 g/1 oz cooked lentils to the sauce. Oranges and figs: soak 50 g/2 oz dried figs in 6 tbsp orange juice for 4 hours or until soft. If wished, simmer gently for 20 minutes, then cool and mix with 100 g/3½ oz fresh orange slices.	DAY 13
As day 1	Cheese and tomato sandwich: 50 g/2 oz curd cheese, 50 g/2 oz finely chopped green pepper, 50 g/2 oz sliced tomato and 75 g/3 oz wholewheat bread Fruit: 100 g/3½ oz grapes	Mushroom omelette: prepare an omelette using 2 eggs and skimmed milk. Fill with 100 g/3½ oz poached mushrooms. 50 g/2 oz wholewheat bread with 15 g/½ oz low fat spread Salad: 150 g/5 oz mixed green vegetables Yogurt with raisins: 150 g/5 oz plain yogurt mixed with 15 g/½ oz raisins	DAY 14

PREGNANCY

Because eating well is essential when pregnant or breastfeeding, these diets are healthy eating programmes rather than stringent slimming regimens. They are designed to be as easy and flexible as possible. There is no need to weigh out quantities exactly; just follow the broad outlines of the diet using standard recipes where none are given and cutting down on fat and sugar where possible. If you want to use fat in your recipes and/or on bread or potatoes, substitute skimmed milk for half or even all the whole milk allowance.

There is increasing evidence that the nutritional status of *both* partners, but the woman especially, is important to the future health of the unborn child – particularly around the time of conception – when sperm and eggs are developing and cells are fusing and dividing. These processes draw on the body's *immediate* nutritional reserves, which must be adequate for the biochemical changes involved in the development of the fetus to go ahead normally.

Diet before conception as well as afterwards must therefore be a priority to give your baby the best possible start in life. Stop smoking, cut alcohol consumption right down and preferably out altogether, and revise your diet – making sure it is high in protein, iron and zinc (red meat is an outstandingly good source of all these), wholegrains and folic acid – well before stopping contraception. Folic acid, extremely important to the very early development of the fetus, can be found in most vegetables, liver, oranges, melons, avocados, nuts, broccoli and Brussels sprouts – the last two are particularly good sources. Eat them briefly cooked or raw in salads.

Feelings of nausea, with or without actual vomiting, often occur during early pregnancy. Help yourself by eating little and often. A dry biscuit (cracker) or piece of toast taken with a little tea or fruit juice can sometimes help reduce the sickness, particularly if taken on waking. As prolonged and frequent episodes of vomiting can deplete important nutrients, you should consult your doctor if vomiting persists.

As long as women are fairly active and well-fed before they conceive*, they need to eat very little more once they do become pregnant, according to on-going studies in Scotland, Holland, Thailand and the Gambia. These reveal that when women eat according to instinct, and not according to what they are told by their doctors, they raise their intake very little – by 100 calories a day or even less – with the exception of a brief period around the middle of their pregnancy when intake may rise more steeply.

These findings, which conflict very strongly with the old advice to 'eat for two', suggest that there is a biological control operating during pregnancy which conserves energy by slowing down the general level of activity, lowering metabolic rate and instituting other biochemical changes – rather in the same way that starvation/crash dieting is now understood to do (see page 34). Previous estimates of food requirements during pregnancy,

which have ignored this biological control factor, have therefore tended to be unrealistically high.

Many women date their weight problems from pregnancy and it is possible that if they feel they must eat much more than they want to when they become pregnant, they could be setting themselves up for weight problems later on. The key, it now appears, is to have the confidence to be guided by your body and listen to its needs. Your doctor will let you know if he considers you need to put on more weight at any stage. In the meantime, think more in terms of the quality of what you eat than the quantity. The diet here will give a guide.

*Women who have a very sedentary lifestyle and are already subsisting on low-calorie intakes, say around 1,600, are an exception and will need to raise intake more substantially.

Obstetricians routinely advise a weight increase of around 12.5 kg (28 lb) over a pregnancy – though even here there are wide variations in the amount of weight gained with no apparent effects on the birthweight of the baby. If overweight at the start of pregnancy, however, it is possible that your obstetrician will advise restricting weight gain to about 7 kg (15½ lb) so that your weight after delivery will actually be less than at the start of your pregnancy. Let yourself be guided by your doctor.

BREAKFAST ALLOWANCES FOR DIET OVER THE PAGE:
A
1 egg (boiled, poached or scrambled);
2 slices wholewheat toast with 15 g/½ oz low fat spread and 25 g/1 oz marmalade;
150 ml/¼ pint (⅔ cup) unsweetened orange or grapefruit juice

B
40 g/1½ oz Shredded Wheat, Weetaflakes, Allbran or Weetabix and 1 tsp sugar (if necessary);
150 ml/¼ pint (⅔ cup) unsweetened orange or grapefruit juice

Vitamin C increases the amount of iron absorbed from your food by as much as 400 per cent. As iron is crucial to the growth of the developing child, eating iron-rich foods with fresh fruit and vegetables will ensure optimal uptake...

	BREAKFASTS	LIGHT MEALS	MAIN MEALS
DAY 1		Tongue and tomato sandwich: 60 g/2½ oz tongue, 100 g/3½ oz sliced tomato and 75 g/3 oz wholewheat bread with 15 g/½ oz low fat spread Fruit: 1 orange	**Lasagne** (page 108) Salad: watercress and **low fat dressing** (page 110) Fruit: 150 g/5 oz pear Cheese: 60 g/2½ oz Camembert
DAY 2		Cheese and Indian pineapple salad: 50 g/2 oz pineapple, 60 g/2½ oz apple and 50 g/2 oz celery, diced and mixed together with 20 g/¾ oz low calorie mayonnaise, seasoning, pinch of curry powder and freshly chopped mixed herbs. Serve with 100 g/3½ oz cottage cheese, 75 g/3 oz wholewheat bread and 15 g/½ oz low fat spread.	Lamb's liver: coat 150 g/5 oz lamb's liver in seasoned flour. Soften 50 g/2 oz sliced onion in 10 g/⅓ oz oil and add the liver. Take care not to overcook. Season and serve at once. Vegetables: 150 g/5 oz boiled potato and boiled cabbage Stewed apple and custard: 150 g/5 oz stewed apple with 150 g/5 oz custard
DAY 3		Poached egg: 1 poached egg on 75 g/3 oz wholewheat toast with 15 g/½ oz low fat spread Vegetable: 1 tomato Fruit: 1 banana Tea: 60 g/2½ oz fruit cake	**Watercress soup** (page 122) **Lamb with apricot stuffing** Vegetables: 150 g/5 oz boiled potato and 100 g/3½ oz green beans **Green fruit salad** (page 106)
DAY 4		Kipper pâté: blend together 100 g/3½ oz cooked kipper fillet, 25 g/1 oz cottage cheese, crushed garlic, nutmeg, pepper and juice of ¼ lemon. Chill and serve with slices of lemon, 75 g/3 oz wholewheat bread with 20 g/¾ oz low fat spread Salad: 50 g/2 oz watercress Fruit: 100 g/3½ oz grapes or cherries Tea: 60 g/2½ oz scone with 15 g/½ oz low fat spread and 30 g/1¼ oz jam (jelly)	Beef kebab: 150 g/5 oz cubed lean beef and as many small whole tomatoes, mushrooms and onion quarters as desired. Season and grill (broil) to taste. Brown rice: 60 g/2½ oz boiled Salad: 100 g/3½ oz mixed green vegetables **Strawberry sorbet** (page 118) NB Soak apricots for tomorrow.
DAY 5		Cheese and lettuce sandwich: 60 g/2½ oz Cheddar cheese, 60 g/2½ oz shredded lettuce, 1 tbsp low calorie mayonnaise and 75 g/3 oz wholewheat bread Fruit: 2 apples	**Wholewheat spaghetti with chicken livers** (page 123) (but leave out the sherry) Apricot dessert: 150 g/5 oz stewed apricots mixed with 10 g/⅓ oz walnuts and 150 g/5 oz plain yogurt. Serve chilled.
DAY 6		Tuna and tomato sandwich: 60 g/2½ oz tuna, 100 g/3½ oz sliced tomatoes and 75 g/3 oz wholewheat bread with 15 g/½ oz low fat spread Fruit: 1 banana Tea: 2 Digestive biscuits (Graham crackers)	Beef goulash (page 98) Vegetables: 200 g/7 oz jacket baked potato and 150 g/5 oz broccoli **Winter fruit compote** (page 123)
DAY 7		Ham and lettuce sandwich: 60 g/2½ oz lean ham, 60 g/2½ oz shredded lettuce, 1 tbsp low calorie mayonnaise and 75 g/3 oz wholewheat bread Fruit: 100 g/3½ oz grapes or cherries Tea: 1 slice wholewheat toast with butter and jam or honey NB Soak lentils for tomorrow.	Roast lamb: 150 g/5 oz lean roast lamb served with 2 tbsp **low fat gravy** (page 110) Vegetables: 100 g/3½ oz jacket baked potato, 100 g/3½ oz peas and 100 g/3½ oz carrots Apple crumble: 100 g/3½ oz serving with 2 tbsp single (light) cream

DAILY ALLOWANCE: 1.2 litres/1 pint (5 cups) whole milk

B

Lentil soup (page 109)
75 g/3 oz wholewheat toast with 15 g/½ oz low fat spread
Yogurt: 150 g/5 oz plain yogurt
Fruit: 100 g/3½ oz fresh orange segments

Cauliflower cheese: 300 g/10 oz serving
Vegetable: 150 g/5 oz boiled potato
Salad: 100 g/3½ oz sliced tomatoes with **low fat dressing** (page 110)
Fruit salad: 150 g/5 oz fresh fruit salad

DAY 8

A

Sardine and tomato sandwich: 100 g/3½ oz sardines, 100 g/3½ oz sliced tomatoes and 75 g/3 oz wholewheat bread with 15 g/½ oz low fat spread
Fruit: 1 pear

Kidneys in red wine (page 108). Use 200 g/7 oz kidney.
Brown rice: 60 g/2½ oz boiled
Salad: watercress and chicory (endive) with **low fat dressing** (page 110)
Rice pudding: 200 g/7 oz homemade or canned rice pudding with 30 g/1¼ oz rosehip syrup or 200 g/7 oz fresh fruit salad

DAY 9

Smoked mackerel: 100 g/3½ oz smoked mackerel served with 50 g/2 oz watercress, slices of lemon and 75 g/3 oz wholewheat bread with 15 g/½ oz low fat spread
Fruit: 200 g/7 oz grapes or cherries

Baked chicken: spread 1 chicken quarter with enough mustard and paprika to cover. Grill (broil), bake or barbecue for about 20-30 minutes until thoroughly cooked.
Vegetables: 150 g/5 oz jacket baked potato and 150 g/5 oz carrots
Rhubarb or prune fool: stew 150 g/5 oz rhubarb or stoned (pitted) prunes and blend with 100 g/3½ oz custard. Just before serving, add a swirl of single (light) cream.

DAY 10

A

Pickle and beef sandwich: 50 g/2 oz corned beef, 100 g/3½ oz sliced tomato, 40 g/1½ oz sweet pickle and 75 g/3 oz wholewheat bread
Fruit and nut yogurt: 150 g/5 oz plain yogurt mixed with 20 g/¾ oz raisins and 10 g/⅓ oz chopped mixed nuts

Fish pie (page 104)
Vegetables: 150 g/5 oz runner (string) beans
Fruit: 2 pears

DAY 11

B

Cheese and lettuce sandwich: 60 g/2½ oz Cheddar cheese, 60 g/2½ oz shredded lettuce, 1 tbsp low calorie mayonnaise and 75 g/3 oz wholewheat bread
Fruit: 2 apples

Chicken Véronique (page 100)
Vegetables: 150 g/5 oz boiled potato and 150 g/5 oz broccoli
Banana and ginger dessert: 50 g/2 oz chopped stem (preserved) ginger mixed with 100 g/3½ oz chopped banana and 150 g/5 oz plain yogurt. Serve chilled.

NB Soak apricots for tomorrow.

DAY 12

A

Baked beans on toast: 150 g/5 oz baked beans on 75 g/3 oz wholewheat toast with 15 g/½ oz low fat spread
Fruit: 2 apples

Veal escalope with ham (page 121)
Vegetables: 150 g/5 oz boiled potato and 150 g/5 oz peas
Apple and apricot dessert: 100 g/3½ oz apples stewed with 50 g/2 oz dried apricots

DAY 13

Salmon sandwich: 60 g/2½ oz canned or fresh salmon, 60 g/2½ oz shredded lettuce, 1 tbsp low calorie mayonnaise and 75 g/3 oz wholewheat bread
Fruit: 200 g/7 oz melon

Roast beef: 150 g/5 oz lean roast beef with 2 tbsp **low fat gravy** (page 110)
Vegetables: 100 g/3½ oz cauliflower with 150 g/5 oz carrots and 150 g/5 oz jacket baked potato
Fruit and honey yogurt: 150 g/5 oz plain yogurt mixed with 120 g/4 oz fresh fruit, 1 tsp honey and 1 tsp wheatgerm

DAY 14

Protein 21% ● Fat 39% ● Carbohydrate 50% ● Fibre 34 g ● Calcium 2149 mg (1200 mg) ● B1 1.97 mg (1.1 mg) ● B2 4.30 mg (1.8 mg) ● C 175 mg (60 mg) ● A (1,200 μg) ● Iron 16.45 mg (15 mg)

BREASTFEEDING

Breast milk is perfect for babies. It requires no preparation or sterilization and is always just the right temperature. Although its composition is largely controlled by the body in response to the baby's needs, it is also influenced by the mother's diet, which must therefore be extra nutritious.

This plan does not have to be followed exactly, but it does provide a good guide—incorporating plenty of dairy foods, including an extra pint of milk, for protein and calcium; fibre to offset constipation (a very common problem post-natally); and lots of fruit and vegetables, particularly carrots for vitamin A and dark green vegetables for folic acid.

Let yourself be guided by your hunger and keep meal times flexible, but try to eat and drink something when breastfeeding to help replace what you lose.

GETTING BACK INTO SHAPE… Attempting to slim in the first 6 weeks after the birth can reduce chances of producing milk and will certainly lower energy. Exercise is the more effective strategy. Start gently and build up gradually, giving yourself a full 9 months to get slim and fit again. It is important to start exercising as soon as you feel strong enough because the muscles are most responsive when they are healing.

Weight put on during pregnancy will tend to be lost quite slowly, but it will go as the baby's appetite increases. By the seventh week, when the baby starts taking more than you are putting in, weight should drop.

BE JUST AS CAREFUL about smoking, drinking and taking drugs as you were when pregnant. Harmful chemicals can still pass to the baby in the breast milk.

The new-born baby grows well on a low-salt, low-sugar diet. Breast milk, in particular, is low in salt. Yet intake is often raised dramatically after weaning – added either by the mother to suit her own taste or by food manufacturers to formulas and baby foods. The average salt intake of the weaned child may be more than 5 times its physiological requirement.

In some parts of the world, breastfeeding is reliably used as a method of family planning. The Kung! hunter/gatherer tribe in the Kalahari Desert, for example, manage to achieve an average space of four years between children in their families, not through any formal method of contraception but because the mother breastfeeds for three out of the four years.

In order to see whether the same protective effect might also apply to western-style breastfeeding, a research project was set up in Edinburgh with 12 nursing mothers. All of them, fortunately, wished to become pregnant again, and seven of them did – two before the return of their periods, indicating that menstruation cannot be relied upon as a mark of returned fertility.

These results do not rule out the contraceptive effectiveness of breastfeeding for western mothers, but they do show that the protective effects diminish with the western pattern of infrequent suckling, often supplemented with bottle or other type of infant food. In the study, there was a close correlation between conception and frequency and duration of breastfeeding. None of the women became pregnant until they were only feeding their child three times a day, or less, although two did actually ovulate (and so were potentially fertile) when breast feeding four times a day. This suggests that breastfeeding only becomes an effective contraceptive when taking place at least five times a day – preferably on demand – for periods of at least ten minutes a time.

BREAKFAST ALLOWANCE FOR DIET OVER THE PAGE:
A
1 egg (boiled, poached or scrambled); 50 g/2 oz wholewheat toast with 15 g/½ oz low fat spread and 25 g/1 oz marmalade; 150 ml/¼ pint (⅔ cup) unsweetened fruit juice
B
40 g/1½ oz Shredded Wheat, Weetaflakes, Weetabix or Allbran with 1 tsp sugar (if necessary); 150 ml/¼ pint (⅔ cup) unsweetened fruit juice

You don't need milk to make milk, but you do need a good intake of dairy foods to maintain optimum nutritional balance. Skimmed milk and low fat cheeses and yogurts cut down on calories, but not on calcium.

BREAKFASTS	LIGHT MEALS	MAIN MEALS

DAY 1

Lentil soup (page 109)
75 g/3 oz wholewheat toast with 15 g/½ oz low fat spread
Fruit: 1 banana

NB Soak lentils and make stock for tomorrow.

Lemon chicken escalope (see 10-day Blitz Diet, Day 10, page 63)
Vegetables: 150 g/5 oz boiled new potato and 150 g/5 oz broccoli served with 120 ml/4 fl oz (½ cup) **white sauce** (page 123)
Ice cream and apricots: 50 g/2 oz vanilla ice cream with 100 g/3½ oz fresh, canned or dried and soaked apricots

DAY 2

Meat and pickle sandwich: 60 g/2½ oz corned beef or cold lean meat, 40 g/1½ oz pickle, 50 g/2 oz watercress and 75 g/3 oz wholewheat bread with 15 g/½ oz low fat spread
Fruit: 1 pear

Cottage pie (page 102)
Vegetables: 100 g/3½ oz peas and 100 g/3½ oz carrots
Cheese and fruit: 25 g/1 oz crackers, 25 g/1 oz Edam cheese, 15 g/½ oz low fat spread and 100 g/3½ oz grapes

DAY 3

Cheese and tomato sandwich: 60 g/2½ oz Cheddar cheese, 100 g/3½ oz sliced tomatoes, 20 g/¾ oz low calorie mayonnaise and 75 g/3 oz wholewheat bread
Fruit: 1 orange

Lamb's liver (see Pregnancy Diet, Day 2, page 74)
Vegetables: 150 g/5 oz boiled new potatoes and 150 g/5 oz cabbage
Ginger dessert: 40 g/1½ oz stem (preserved) ginger with 3 tbsp single (light) cream

NB Soak prunes for tomorrow.

DAY 4

Herb omelette: prepare an omelette using 2 eggs, freshly chopped herbs and seasoning. Cook in a non-stick frying pan (skillet).
Salad: lettuce, watercress, cucumber and green pepper with **low fat dressing** (page 110).
75 g/3 oz wholewheat bread with 20 g/¾ oz low fat spread
Fruit: 100 g/3½ oz grapes

Pork fillet with prunes (page 114)
Vegetables: 150 g/5 oz boiled new potato and 100 g/3½ oz runner (string) beans
Apple meringue: peel, core and slice a large cooking apple and cook gently until soft. Transfer to an ovenproof dish and top with meringue. Place in a hot oven to brown the top and serve at once.

DAY 5

Sardines on toast: 60 g/2½ oz sardines and 100 g/3½ oz sliced tomatoes on 75 g/3 oz wholewheat toast with 15 g/½ oz low fat spread
Nut yogurt: 150 g/5 oz plain yogurt mixed with 25 g/1 oz chopped walnuts

Baked chicken with mushroom sauce: wrap 200 g/7 oz chicken breast in foil with 100 g/3½ oz mushrooms, 25 g/1 oz onion and seasoning. Bake in a moderately hot oven, 200°C (400°F) or Gas mark 6, for about 30 minutes. Prepare some **white sauce** (page 123), stir in the mushrooms and serve with the chicken.
Vegetables: 150 g/5 oz jacket baked potato and 150 g/5 oz spinach
Red fruit salad (page 115)

DAY 6

Pâté and tomato sandwich: 50 g/2 oz **liver pâté**, 100 g/3½ oz sliced tomatoes, 75 g/3 oz wholewheat bread and 15 g/½ oz low fat spread
Fruit: 1 apple
Tea: 2 Digestive biscuits (Graham crackers)

Whiting in lemon sauce
Vegetables: 150 g/5 oz boiled new potato and 150 g/5 oz peas
Fruit and cheese: 1 pear and 50 g/2 oz Camembert

DAY 7

Prawn sandwich: 50 g/2 oz prawns (shrimp), 25 g/1 oz shredded lettuce, 50 g/2 oz sliced tomatoes, 75 g/3 oz wholewheat bread and 20 g/¾ oz low calorie mayonnaise
Fruit: 2 Pears
Tea: 40 g/1½ oz scone with 10 g/⅓ oz low fat spread

Roast chicken: 150 g/5 oz roast chicken served with 50 g/2 oz bread sauce and 2 tbsp **low fat gravy** (page 110)
Vegetables: 150 g/5 oz boiled new potato, 100 g/3½ oz carrots and 100 g/3½ oz peas
Fruit yogurt: 150 g/5 oz plain yogurt mixed with fresh fruit

DAILY ALLOWANCE: 1.2 litres/2 pints (5 cups) whole milk

BREAKFASTS	LIGHT MEALS	MAIN MEALS	
	Lentil soup (page 109) 75 g/3 oz wholewheat toast with 15 g/½ oz low fat spread Cheese: 50 g/2 oz Edam Fruit: 1 apple	Beefburger: combine 200 g/7 oz minced (ground) lean chuck steak with a little minced onion, freshly chopped herbs and seasoning. Shape into patties and grill (broil) or barbecue. Serve with 50 g/2 oz sweet pickle. Vegetables: 150 g/5 oz boiled new potato and 100 g/3½ oz carrots Junket and fruit: 200 g/7 oz junket or 2 tbsp single (light) cream served with 100 g/3½ oz fresh or frozen blackberries or blueberries	DAY 8
	Poached egg and baked beans: 1 poached egg and 150 g/5 oz baked beans on 75 g/3 oz wholewheat toast with 15 g/½ oz low fat spread Fruit: 200 g/7 oz melon	Mixed grill: 200 g/7 oz lamb's kidneys grilled (broiled) with 15 g/½ oz lean bacon and 100 g/3½ oz tomatoes Brown rice: 50 g/2 oz boiled Vegetables: 150 g/5 oz cabbage and 100 g/3½ oz poached mushrooms **Baked apple with plums and red wine** (page 96)	DAY 9
	Ham sandwich: 60 g/2½ oz lean ham, 50 g/2 oz shredded lettuce, 15 g/½ oz low calorie mayonnaise and 75 g/3 oz wholewheat bread Fruit: 2 apples Tea: 40 g/1½ oz scone with 10 g/⅓ oz low fat spread	Baked fish: place 200 g/7 oz white fish in foil with 100 g/3½ oz sliced tomatoes, 100 g/3½ oz sweetcorn (kernel corn) and seasoning. Seal the foil and bake in a moderately hot oven, 200°C (400°F) or Gas Mark 6, for 15 minutes. Vegetables: 150 g/5 oz boiled new potato and 100 g/3½ oz peas Cheese and fruit: 50 g/2 oz Cheddar cheese and 100 g/3½ oz grapes	DAY 10
	Egg sandwich: 2 chopped hard-boiled eggs mixed with 15 g/½ oz low calorie mayonnaise, seasoning and 50 g/2 oz cress with 75 g/3 oz wholewheat bread Banana yogurt: 150 g/5 oz plain yogurt mixed with 100 g/3½ oz chopped banana	Avocado vinaigrette: 100 g/3½ oz sliced avocado served with **low fat dressing** (page 110) Lamb chops: 100 g/3½ oz lamb chop grilled (broiled) with fresh rosemary and garlic Vegetables: 150 g/5 oz jacket baked potato and 100 g/3½ oz carrots Rice pudding: 150 g/5 oz homemade or canned rice pudding with 2 tsp jam (jelly)	DAY 11
	Smoked mackerel pâté: blend together 100 g/3½ oz smoked mackerel, 50 g/2 oz cottage cheese, lemon juice and black pepper. Chill well and serve with 50 g/2 oz watercress and 75 g/3 oz wholewheat toast. Fruit: 2 pears	**Cheese pie** **Ratatouille** (page 114) Fruit yogurt: 150 g/5 oz plain yogurt mixed with 100 g/3½ oz orange slices and 100 g/3½ oz canned or fresh lychees	DAY 12
(image)	Carrot, cheese and nut sandwich: 50 g/2 oz grated carrot, 25 g/1 oz Cheddar cheese, 15 g/½ oz chopped walnuts, seasoning and 75 g/3 oz wholewheat bread Fruit: 1 apple	Poached chicken: 150 g/5 oz poached chicken with 2 tbsp **low fat gravy** (page 110) Vegetables: 100 g/3½ oz broccoli and 50 g/2 oz poached mushrooms Fruit: 1 peach or banana	DAY 13
	Tongue and tomato sandwich: 60 g/2½ oz tongue or lean meat, 25 g/1 oz chopped celery, 50 g/2 oz sliced tomato, 15 g/½ oz low calorie mayonnaise and 75 g/3 oz wholewheat bread Fruit: 200 g/7 oz melon Tea: 50 g/2 oz fruit cake	Roast meat: 125 g/4 oz lean roast meat with 2 tbsp **low fat gravy** (page 110) Vegetables: 150 g/5 oz jacket baked potato, 100 g/3½ oz carrots and 100 g/3½ oz cauliflower Rhubarb or prune fool: (See Pregnancy Diet, Day 10, page 75).	DAY 14

Entertaining

Eating less does not have to mean eating alone. Share a deliciously light meal using these menus, devised on a seasonal basis, and you will find that you can eat surprisingly well without breaking your diet. Friends will find the focus on fresh fruits, vegetables, fish and meat a refreshing change from the excesses too often associated with dining out.

Suitable wines, suggested at the beginning of each menu, should be served with the main course only – the first courses and desserts, being mainly composed of salads and fruits, are rather too acid to be accompanied with wine. Serve a sparkling mineral water instead and keep it on the table throughout the meal. The total calorie count given for each menu does not include any allowance for wine, so calculate this separately and add it on.

Ginger soup .... 10 Cal.
Tomato and mozzarella salad .... 140 Cal.
Poached goujons of sole .... 200 Cal.
Grapes in orange jelly .... 90-125 Cal.
Total Calories (approx): 440-475
Wines: Vouvray or Sancerre, chilled

Ginger Soup
This recipe needs to be started a day in advance.

METRIC/IMPERIAL	AMERICAN
1 pheasant, duck or chicken (or 1 carcase and 500 g/1 lb raw chicken joints)	1 pheasant, duck or chicken (or 1 carcase and 1 lb raw chicken joints)
1 onion, quartered	1 onion, quartered
1 leek, quartered	1 leek, quartered
1 large carrot, quartered	1 large carrot, quartered
2 sticks celery, halved	2 celery stalks, halved
3 stalks parsley	3 stalks parsley
1 small bay leaf	1 small bay leaf
salt and freshly ground black pepper	salt and freshly ground black pepper

Garnish:

1½ tbsp finely chopped ginger	1½ tbsp finely chopped ginger
12 sprigs watercress	12 sprigs watercress

Put the bird in a pressure cooker – a tough old game bird will do very well. Alternatively, you can use the carcase of a bird, adding some raw chicken joints for flavour. Add flavouring vegetables, herbs, salt and pepper. Cover with cold water and bring to the boil. Remove any scum that floats to the surface, then cover and cook on high pressure for 20 minutes. (If using an ordinary pan, allow 1 hour.) Reduce the pressure by running under cold water, and remove the bird. Remove the breasts and wings combined from the bird. (These can be eaten the same day, either hot or cold, with salad.) Put the bird back in the pot, cover and cook for another 40 minutes under high pressure (or 2 hours in an ordinary saucepan). Strain the stock and leave to cool, then chill overnight.

Next day, remove every scrap of fat from the surface and measure the stock. You only need 1.2 litres/2 pints (5 cups), so if you have more, reduce by fast boiling. Reheat and adjust the seasoning. Just before serving, bring back to the boil and drop in the chopped ginger. Simmer for 30 seconds, then add the watercress and turn off the heat. Stand, covered, for 5 minutes before serving in small cups.

Total Calories: 60
Calories per serving: 10

Tomato and Mozzarella Salad

METRIC/IMPERIAL	AMERICAN
1 kg/2 lb tomatoes, skinned and sliced	2 lb tomatoes, skinned and sliced
1 mozzarella, cut in 5 mm/¼ in cubes	1 mozzarella cut in ¼ in cubes
2 tbsp olive oil	2 tbsp olive oil
1 tbsp lemon juice	1 tbsp lemon juice
freshly ground black pepper	freshly ground black pepper

Lay the sliced tomatoes on a flat dish and scatter the little cubes of mozzarella over them. Dribble over the oil and lemon juice, and sprinkle with black pepper.

Total Calories: 840
Calories per serving: 140

Poached Goujons of Sole with Tarragon

METRIC/IMPERIAL	AMERICAN
1 kg/2 lb fillets of Dover sole, skinned, with bones, etc.	2 lb fillets of sole, skinned, with bones, etc.
½ small onion	½ small onion
½ small carrot	½ small carrot
ends of leek and celery	ends of leek and celery
¼ tsp sea salt and 6 black peppercorns	¼ tsp coarse salt and 6 black peppercorns
15 g/½ oz butter	1 tbsp butter
1 tbsp sunflower seed oil	1 tbsp sunflower seed oil
3 shallots, finely chopped	3 shallots, finely chopped
150 ml/¼ pint dry white wine	⅔ cup dry white wine
5 tbsp single cream	⅓ cup light cream
4 tbsp chopped tarragon	¼ cup chopped tarragon

Cut the fish fillets into strips diagonally, about 6 cm × 1 cm (2½ ins × ½ in). Put the fish bones, skins, etc, in a pan with the onion, carrot, leek and celery, salt and peppercorns. Add 450 ml/¾ pint (2 cups) cold water, bring to the boil and simmer for 25 minutes. Strain, then reduce to 200 ml/⅓ pint (⅞ cup) by fast boiling.

Melt the butter and oil in a saucepan and cook the shallot until it softens and starts to change colour. Add the fish stock and the wine and bring to the boil, stirring. Drop in the strips of fish, a few at a time, and

From the left: Poached Goujons of Sole with Tarragon, Ginger Soup, Tomato and Mozzarella Salad, Grapes in Orange Jelly

adjust the heat so that the liquid barely simmers. Poach the fish for 1-2 minutes, then transfer to a dish, using a slotted spoon, and keep warm. When all are cooked, measure the liquid; if much more than 200 ml/ ⅓ pint (⅞ cup), reduce by fast boiling, then stir in the cream, adding salt and pepper to taste. Put the strips of fish back into the sauce, folding them in gently, with most of the tarragon, reserving a little for the garnish. Remove from the heat and stand, covered, for a couple of minutes to infuse the sauce with the flavour of tarragon, then pour into a clean dish and scatter the reserved tarragon over the top. Accompany with a lettuce salad dressed with lemon juice, and boiled or steamed potatoes for those who can afford the extra calories.

Total Calories: 1200 (without potatoes)
Calories per serving: 200

Grapes in Orange Jelly

METRIC/IMPERIAL
8 large oranges or 12 small ones
25 g/1 oz sugar
1½ packets gelatine (¾ oz)
350 g/12 oz white grapes, peeled and seeded

AMERICAN
8 large oranges or 12 small ones
2 tbsp sugar
3 envelopes gelatine
¾ lb white grapes, peeled and pitted

Start a day, or several hours, in advance. Pare the rind of 3 of the oranges, and put in a bowl. Squeeze the juice of all the oranges. Measure the juice and pour it over the rind. Measure the amount of water needed to make the orange juice up to 900 ml/1½ pints (3¾ cups) and put it in a saucepan with the sugar. Bring to the boil and stir until all the sugar has dissolved, then add the fruit juice and rind. Bring back to the boil and skim until the surface is clear. Add 1 tablespoon cold water, bring back to the boil, and skim again. Remove from the heat and shake in the gelatine. Whisk with a fork until it has dissolved, then leave until cool.

When the liquid is cold, pour through a strainer and fill a 900 ml/1½ pint (3¾ cup) ring mould. Chill in the refrigerator overnight. Next day, turn out onto a flat plate and fill the centre with the grapes. (If you don't have a ring mould, make in a dish and serve without turning out. The grapes may be put in the bottom of the dish or omitted.)

Total Calories: 750, or 540 (without grapes)
Calories per serving: 125 or 90

Total Calories (approx): 500–520
Wines: Muscadet or Pouilly Fumé, chilled

Artichokes with Herb Sauce

METRIC/IMPERIAL	AMERICAN
6 globe artichokes, as fresh as possible	6 globe artichokes, as fresh as possible
Sauce:	*Sauce:*
40 g/1½ oz tofu (bean curd from health food stores)	1½ oz tofu (bean curd from health food stores)
150 ml/¼ pint plain yogurt	⅔ cup plain yogurt
3 tbsp sunflower seed oil	3 tbsp sunflower seed oil
3 tsp Dijon mustard	3 tsp Dijon-style mustard
6 tbsp freshly chopped herbs (chives, chervil, dill, tarragon, etc)	6 tbsp freshly chopped herbs (chives, chervil, dill, tarragon, etc)

Use the very freshest artichokes you can find, for their calorie content increases daily during storage, as the inulin is converted into sugar. Boil as usual; drain and leave to cool. Serve within 2 hours of cooking.

To make the sauce, put the tofu, yogurt, oil and mustard into a food processor and process until blended. Tip into a bowl and stir in the chopped herbs. Serve either in the centre of the artichokes, after removing the inner core of leaves and the choke, or in a separate bowl.

Total Calories: 550
Calories per serving: 90

Poached Trout with Watercress Sauce

METRIC/IMPERIAL	AMERICAN
6 rainbow trout (smallish)	6 rainbow trout (smallish)
few plaice bones, fish heads, etc.	few fish bones, heads, etc.
1 onion, halved	1 onion, halved
1 carrot, halved	1 carrot, halved
ends of leek and celery	ends of leek and celery
1 bay leaf	1 bay leaf
3 stalks parsley	3 stalks parsley
1 tsp salt	1 tsp salt
6 black peppercorns	6 black peppercorns
150 ml/¼ pint white wine	⅔ cup white wine
Watercress Sauce (optional):	*Watercress Sauce (optional):*
25 g/1 oz butter	2 tbsp butter
1½ tbsp flour	1½ tbsp flour
300 ml/½ pint fish stock (from poaching trout)	1¼ cups fish stock (from poaching trout)
5 tbsp single cream (for a hot sauce)	⅓ cup light cream (for a hot sauce)
2 tsp grated horseradish	2 tsp grated horseradish
2 tsp Dijon mustard	2 tsp Dijon-style mustard
1 tbsp orange juice	1 tbsp orange juice
salt and freshly ground black pepper	salt and freshly ground black pepper
1 tbsp finely chopped watercress, leaves only	1 tbsp finely chopped watercress, leaves only
5 tbsp plain yogurt (for a cold sauce)	⅓ cup plain yogurt (for a cold sauce)

Put the fish bones into a fish kettle with the flavouring vegetables, herbs and seasonings. Cover with cold water, add the white wine and bring slowly to the boil. Half cover the pot and simmer for 25 minutes, then remove the fish bones, vegetables and herbs. Bring back to the boil and drop in the trout. Adjust the heat so that it barely simmers, and poach for 5–7 minutes, depending on the size of the trout. Remove them and keep hot, or leave to cool. To avoid extra calories, simply boil up the stock until reduced slightly. Pour into a sauceboat and serve with the fish.

To serve with a hot sauce, boil up the stock till reduced to a good flavour, then strain and measure 300 ml/½ pint (1¼ cups). Melt the butter in a saucepan, stir in the flour and cook for 1 minute, stirring. Pour on the hot stock, stirring till smooth, and simmer for 3 minutes. Then add the cream, horseradish, mustard, orange juice, salt and pepper. Simmer for another minute, then stir in the chopped watercress. Pour into a sauceboat and serve with the trout. Accompany with steamed mange-touts and new potatoes for those who are not on a diet.

For a cold dish, make the sauce as above but omit the cream and watercress. Pour into a bowl and cool quickly in a sink half full of cold water, stirring to prevent a skin forming. When it is cold, stir in the yogurt, beating until smooth, and the chopped watercress. Pour into a sauceboat and serve with the cold trout, after removing the top skin. Accompany with a lettuce salad and steamed new potatoes, served warm, for those who are not dieting.

Calories per serving (with hot sauce): 220 (with cold sauce): 200
Total Calories (approx) (with hot sauce): 1320 (with cold sauce): 1200

Mixed Red and Green Salad

METRIC/IMPERIAL	AMERICAN
1 round lettuce, inner leaves only	1 round lettuce, inner leaves only
25 g (1 oz) tender spinach, cut in thinnest possible strips	1 oz tender spinach, cut in thinnest possible strips
1 small head radicchio, when available, cut in squares	1 small head radicchio, when available, cut in squares
25 g (1 oz) mâche (corn salad, lambs lettuce), trimmed	1 oz corn salad, trimmed
Dressing:	*Dressing:*
1 tbsp white wine vinegar	1 tbsp white wine vinegar
½ tbsp lemon juice	½ tbsp lemon juice
3 tbsp sunflower seed oil	3 tbsp sunflower seed oil
sea salt and freshly ground black pepper	sea salt and freshly ground black pepper

Lay the lettuce leaves in a salad bowl and scatter the strips of spinach over them. Lay the red squares of radicchio over the spinach, and the individual leaves of mâche (corn salad) over all. Mix the dressing in a small bowl. Before serving, mix the dressing again, pour over the salad, and toss lightly.

Total Calories: 400
Calories per serving: 70

Raspberry Jelly

METRIC/IMPERIAL	AMERICAN
500 g/1 lb raspberries, fresh or frozen	3 cups American raspberries, fresh or frozen
50 g/2 oz sugar	¼ cup sugar
1½ packets gelatine (¾ oz)	3 envelopes gelatine
2 ripe peaches	2 ripe peaches

Put the raspberries in a pan with the sugar. (If using frozen raspberries, thaw first.) Heat slowly until the juice runs, then increase the heat until it

From the front: Raspberry Jellies with Foamy Almond Sauce, Artichokes with Herb Sauce, Mixed Red and Green Salad, Poached Trout

boils. Cook for 10 minutes, watching to see that the berries don't stick. Push through a coarse sieve (strainer) or fine food mill, pressing through everything except the seeds. Measure the juice and make up to 500 ml/ 18 fl oz (12¼ cups) with water. Soak the gelatine in a cup in 4 tablespoons water for 10 minutes, then stand in a small pan of very hot water until dissolved. Mix the gelatine with the juice, strain again, and cool.

Chill 6 small moulds in the freezer. Oval *oeuf en gelée* moulds are ideal. Peel the peaches and remove the stones (pits); cut them in quarters, then across in small slices. Pour a thin layer of liquid jelly into each mould and chill again until set. Arrange a layer of sliced peaches over the jelly, then add more liquid jelly to come level. Chill again and, when the second layer has set, fill up the moulds with remaining sliced peaches and liquid jelly. Chill in the refrigerator until completely set. Unmould onto small flat plates and serve with cream for those who are not on a diet.

Total Calories: 325
Calories per serving: 55

Foamy Almond Sauce

METRIC/IMPERIAL	AMERICAN
2 egg yolks	*2 egg yolks*
5 tbsp milk	*⅓ cup milk*
2 tbsp caster sugar	*2 tbsp sugar*
1 tbsp ground almonds	*1 tbsp ground almonds*

Have a china bowl standing over a saucepan of simmering water. Break the egg yolks into the bowl and beat with a wire whisk. After 2 minutes, start adding the milk, sugar and ground almonds, continuing to whisk steadily. Continue beating for about 5 minutes, until the sauce is light and foamy, and very slightly thickened. (It should just coat the back of a wooden spoon lightly.) Transfer the bowl to a sink half full of cold water and cool to luke-warm, stirring frequently to prevent a skin forming.

When the sauce has cooled sufficiently pour a little of it around each jelly on its plate, just before serving.

Total Calories: 500
Calories per serving: 85

Tomatoes stuffed with cucumber .... 40 Cal.
Grilled pepper salad .... 55 Cal.
Steamed bass, or salmon trout .... 175–260 Cal.
Sliced peaches, with yogurt cream .... 90 Cal.

Total Calories (approx): 360–445
Wine: Chablis, chilled

Tomatoes Stuffed with Cucumber

METRIC/IMPERIAL	AMERICAN
6 medium tomatoes	6 medium tomatoes
½ cucumber, peeled	½ cucumber, peeled
300 ml/½ pint plain yogurt	1¼ cups plain yogurt
1 clove garlic, crushed	1 clove garlic, crushed
sea salt and freshly ground black pepper	coarse salt and freshly ground black pepper
1–2 dashes Tabasco	1–2 dashes hot pepper sauce
2 tbsp chopped mint	2 tbsp chopped mint
1 bunch watercress	1 bunch watercress

Cut a slice off the tops of the tomatoes and scoop out the insides with a sharp-edged teaspoon. Drain away the seeds and juice and chop the flesh. Stand the tomatoes upside-down to drain for 30 minutes, then pat dry with absorbent kitchen paper towels. Grate the cucumber coarsely and mix into the yogurt with the garlic. Add the chopped tomato flesh, salt and pepper, and a couple of dashes of Tabasco (hot pepper sauce). Stir in the chopped mint and pile into the tomato cases. Serve on a bed of watercress, as a first course.

Total Calories: 240
Calories per serving: 40
NOTE: *A grilled (broiled) pepper salad may be added, as another hors d'oeuvre. In this case omit the watercress.*

Grilled Pepper Salad

METRIC/IMPERIAL	AMERICAN
6 medium peppers, preferably red, yellow and green, or just red and green	6 medium peppers, preferably red, yellow and green, or just red and green
2 tbsp olive oil	2 tbsp olive oil
sea salt and freshly ground black pepper	coarse salt and freshly ground black pepper

Preheat the grill (broiler), lay the peppers on the grill pan and cook as close to the heat as possible. Turn them over as the skin blisters, until they are evenly charred and blackened all over. Remove from the heat and leave to cool. Later, scrape away the skin with a small knife, and cut away the stalk and inner membrane, washing away the seeds under cold running water. Cut the flesh into petal shapes and lay on a flat dish. Sprinkle with olive oil, sea salt and black pepper. Serve as an hors d'oeuvre with stuffed tomatoes. A dish of hard-boiled eggs in mayonnaise may be added for those who are not dieting.

Total Calories: 340
Calories per serving: 55

Steamed Bass or Salmon Trout, Chinese Style

METRIC/IMPERIAL	AMERICAN
1 bass, or salmon trout, weighing 1.5 kg/3–3½ lb	1 bass, or salmon trout, weighing 1.5 kg/3–3½ lb
1 tsp sea salt	1 tsp coarse salt
1 tsp sugar	1 tsp sugar
½ tbsp sesame oil (from Chinese supermarket)	½ tbsp sesame oil (from Chinese supermarket)
½ tbsp soy sauce	½ tbsp soy sauce
8 thin slices root ginger	8 thin slices root ginger
2 large cloves garlic, peeled and thinly sliced	2 large cloves garlic, peeled and thinly sliced
4 spring onions, sliced lengthwise	4 scallions, sliced lengthwise
Sauce:	*Sauce:*
2 tbsp dry vermouth	2 tbsp dry vermouth
2 tbsp sunflower seed oil	2 tbsp sunflower seed oil
1 tbsp sesame oil	1 tbsp sesame oil
1 tbsp soy sauce	1 tbsp soy sauce
Garnish:	*Garnish:*
4 spring onions	4 scallions

Rub the fish inside and out with the salt, sugar, sesame oil and soy sauce. Lay a large piece of foil on a table and scatter half the sliced ginger, garlic and spring onions (scallions) over it. Lay the fish on them and scatter the remainder on top of it. Wrap the foil round the fish so that it is totally enclosed, and lay on the rack of a fish kettle. Bring about 1.5 cm/¾ in water to the boil in the kettle, then lower the rack into it and cover. Boil steadily for 30 minutes, then look to see if the fish is cooked. If the flesh comes away easily from the central bone, it is ready to serve.

While the fish cooks, make the sauce and prepare the garnish. Mix the sauce ingredients in a small bowl. Cut the spring onions (scallions) across into 3.5–5 cm (1½–2 in) lengths, then cut each piece into thin slivers. When the fish is ready, unwrap it and slide onto a platter. Strain the juices into the sauce and discard the garlic, ginger and spring onions (scallions). Remove the top skin from the fish, give the sauce a final whisk, and pour it over. Scatter with the slivers of spring onion (scallion) and serve. No vegetable is necessary, but you can accompany the fish with steamed mangetout if you like, and boiled or steamed new potatoes for those who can afford to eat them.

Total Calories: 1050
Calories per serving: 175 with mangetout

Sliced Peaches with Yogurt Cream

METRIC/IMPERIAL	AMERICAN
4 large peaches or 6 apricots	4 large peaches or 6 apricots
65 ml/2½ fl oz carton plain yogurt	¼ cup + 1 tbsp plain yogurt
2 tbsp whipped cream	2 tbsp whipped cream
1 egg white, beaten	1 egg white, beaten
½ tbsp vanilla sugar	½ tbsp vanilla sugar

Remove the stones (pits) from the peaches, skin them and slice. (Stone and slice apricots, if used.) Divide the slices between 6 glass bowls. Beat the yogurt until smooth, then fold in the whipped cream and the beaten egg white. Finally, fold in the vanilla sugar. Put a spoonful on the sliced fruit in each of the bowls.

Total Calories: 450
Calories per serving: 90

From the front: Grilled Pepper Salad, Tomatoes with Cucumber, Sliced Peaches with Yogurt Cream, Steamed Bass or Salmon Trout, Chinese Style

MENU IV SPRING/SUMMER

Ceviche of scallops .... 100 Cal.
(or Prawn, spinach & mushroom salad) .... 125 Cal.
Grilled chicken breasts with watercress .... 230–280 Cal.
Fresh fruit salad .... 70–90 Cal.

Total Calories (approx): 525–595
Wines: Beaujolais Villages or a dry rosé, lightly chilled

Ceviche of Scallops
This recipe must be started a day in advance.

METRIC/IMPERIAL	AMERICAN
12 large scallops, with 6 flat shells	*12 large scallops, with 6 flat shells*
250 ml/8 fl oz fresh lime or lemon juice or a mixture of the two	*1 cup fresh lime or lemon juice or a mixture of the two*
1½ tbsp finely chopped shallot	*1½ tbsp finely chopped shallot*
1½ tbsp finely chopped parsley	*1½ tbsp finely chopped parsley*
1½ tbsp olive oil	*1½ tbsp olive oil*

Start a day in advance. Clean the scallops, wash them and pat dry.. Cut away the orange part and slice the white part into 1 cm/½ in slices. Put them in a bowl and pour the lime or lemon juice over them; chill for 24 hours. Just before serving, pour off the fruit juice and discard. Stir in the shallot, parsley and oil. Serve on the scallop shells.

Total Calories: 600
Calories per serving: 100

Prawn, Spinach & Mushroom Salad

METRIC/IMPERIAL	AMERICAN
250 g/8 oz tender spinach	*½ lb tender spinach*
250 g/8 oz button mushrooms	*½ lb button mushrooms*
250 g/8 oz peeled prawns	*½ lb shelled shrimp*
3 tbsp sunflower seed oil	*3 tbsp sunflower seed oil*
3 tbsp lemon juice	*3 tbsp lemon juice*
freshly ground black pepper	*freshly ground black pepper*

Pick the leaves off the washed spinach, discarding the stalks and pile loosely in a bowl. Wipe the mushrooms, trim the stalks level with the caps, and cut in halves or quarters, according to size. Scatter over the spinach. Lay the prawns (shrimp) over the mushrooms. Pour over the oil and lemon juice and toss well, sprinkling with freshly ground black pepper. Salt is not necessary.

Total Calories: 740
Calories per serving: 125

From the left: Prawn, Spinach & Mushroom Salad, Fresh Fruit Salad, Ceviche of Scallops, Grilled Chicken Breasts with Watercress

Grilled Chicken Breasts with Watercress

METRIC/IMPERIAL	AMERICAN
6 chicken breasts (skinned, optional)	6 chicken breasts (skinned, optional)
2 tbsp Dijon mustard	2 tbsp Dijon-style mustard
2 tbsp sunflower seed oil	2 tbsp sunflower seed oil
juice of 1 lemon	juice of 1 lemon
freshly ground black pepper	freshly ground black pepper
2 lemons, cut in quarters	2 lemons, cut in quarters

Watercress Salad:

2 bunches watercress	2 bunches watercress
1 tbsp olive oil	1 tbsp olive oil
juice of 1 lemon	juice of 1 lemon

Start 2 hours before serving. Paint the chicken joints with mustard. Lay them in a shallow dish and spoon over the oil and lemon juice. Grind some black pepper over them and leave for about 1 hour.

Later, heat the grill (broiler). Cook the chicken pieces until they are golden brown, allowing 8–10 minutes each side and basting with any oil and lemon juice in the pan. (Don't add more.) While they cook, trim the watercress using only the tender sprigs. Wash and shake dry, then pile in a bowl. Add oil and lemon juice and toss. Make a bed of watercress on a flat dish and serve the chicken joints on it, or serve the watercress in the bowl. Garnish the chicken with extra lemon quarters.

Total Calories: 1400
Calories per serving: 230 (without skin)

Fresh Fruit Salad

METRIC/IMPERIAL	AMERICAN
2 peaches, skinned and stoned	2 peaches, skinned and pitted
1 small melon, ogen or honeydew, or 1 wedge watermelon	1 small melon, ogen or honeydew, or 1 wedge watermelon
3 apricots or plums, stoned	3 apricots or plums, pitted
250 g/8 oz strawberries	1¾ cups strawberries
250 g/8 oz cherries, stoned, or grapes, seeded	2 cups pitted cherries or grapes
2 tbsp caster sugar	2 tbsp sugar
3 tbsp orange juice	3 tbsp orange juice
3 tbsp lime juice	3 tbsp lime juice

Cut the peaches, melon and apricots (or plums) into pieces about 1 cm/½ in square and pile in a glass bowl. Add the strawberries, halved, quartered or chopped, according to size, and the halved cherries (if using grapes, peel them if you have the time). Sprinkle with sugar and pour over the fruit juices. (When fresh limes are not available, use 4 tablespoons orange juice and 2 tablespoons lemon juice.) Serve with cream for those who are not dieting, or plain yogurt as an optional extra for those who are.

Total Calories: 420 (550 with yogurt)
Calories per serving: 70 (90 with 2 tbsp plain yogurt)

Smoked trout salad .... 175 Cal.
Boiled beef with horseradish sauce .... 495 Cal.
Sliced pink grapefruit with orange juice .... 75 Cal.

Total Calories: 745

Wines: Madiran or Cahors, at room temperature

Smoked Trout Salad

METRIC/IMPERIAL	AMERICAN
12 inner leaves batavia or curly endive	12 leaves chicory
12–14 leaves radicchio, when available	12–14 leaves radicchio, when available
18 tiny sprigs watercress or rosettes mâche	18 tiny sprigs watercress or lambs' lettuce (corn salad)
75 g/3 oz leek, or spring onions, white parts only	3 oz leek, or scallions, white parts only
75 g/3 oz carrot	3 oz carrot
75 g/3 oz fennel, when available	3 oz fennel, when available
2 × 6 oz smoked trout, skinned and filleted	2 × 6 oz smoked trout, skinned and filleted
75 g/3 oz button mushrooms, caps only, sliced	1 cup sliced button mushrooms

Dressing:

METRIC/IMPERIAL	AMERICAN
1 tbsp lemon juice	1 tbsp lemon juice
1 tbsp white wine vinegar	1 tbsp white wine vinegar
2 tbsp olive oil	2 tbsp olive oil
2 tbsp sunflower seed oil	2 tbsp sunflower seed oil
sea salt and freshly ground black pepper	sea salt and freshly ground black pepper

Wash all the leaves and shake dry. Cut the leek (or spring onions/scallions), carrot and fennel into the thinnest possible slivers, like split matchsticks, about 3.5 cm/1½ in long. Put them in a small strainer and suspend in boiling water for exactly 1 minute, then drain and hold under cold running water. Drain again.

Cut each trout fillet across into 3 or 4 pieces. Using kitchen scissors, cut the salad leaves in pieces about 2.5 cm/1 in square and mix together. Divide them between 6 plates and scatter the sliced mushrooms over and among them. Lay the slivers of poached vegetables over all. Mix all the dressing ingredients together. Arrange the pieces of smoked trout round the edges of the plates. Just before serving, spoon a little of the dressing over each salad. Do not toss. Serve as a first course or as a very light main dish.

Total Calories: 1050
Calories per serving: 175

Boiled Beef with Horseradish Sauce

METRIC/IMPERIAL	AMERICAN
1.5 kg/3½ lb (unsalted) silverside of beef	3½ lb boneless rump
1 tsp sea salt	1 tsp coarse salt
12 black peppercorns	12 black peppercorns
1 large onion, halved	1 large onion, halved
1 large carrot, halved	1 large carrot, halved
1 leek, halved	1 leek, halved
1 stick celery, halved	1 celery stalk, halved
1 bay leaf	1 bay leaf
3 stalks parsley	3 stalks parsley

Horseradish sauce:

METRIC/IMPERIAL	AMERICAN
150 ml/¼ pint plain yogurt	2/3 cup plain yogurt
2 tbsp grated horseradish	2 tbsp grated fresh horseradish
2 tsp lemon juice	2 tsp lemon juice

From the left: Boiled Beef with Horseradish Sauce, Sliced Grapefruit with Orange Juice, Smoked Trout Salad

Put the beef in a casserole and cover with cold water. Bring to the boil, removing any scum that rises to the surface. When it is quite clear, add salt and black peppercorns, onion, carrot, leek, celery, bay leaf and parsley. Simmer gently for 1½ hours, or 30 minutes per 500 g/lb if cooking a larger piece.

While the beef is cooking, make the sauce. Beat the yogurt until smooth, then stir in the grated horseradish and lemon juice. When the beef is cooked, carve it in thin slices and lay on a platter. Strain the stock into a bowl; allow it to settle for a few moments, then extract some of it from below the surface, using a bulb baster. Pour into a small jug. Serve the sliced beef with its stock accompanied by horseradish sauce and a dish of boiled carrots. (Boiled potatoes or even dumplings can be added for those who are not dieting.) The rest of the beef stock can be made into a delicious consommé for another meal. (See recipe for Ginger Soup p. 82 and substitute beef stock for game or poultry.) Any leftover beef can be eaten cold the following day with a salad.

Total Calories: 2780
Calories per serving: 495

Sliced Grapefruit with Orange Juice

METRIC/IMPERIAL	AMERICAN
3 pink grapefruit	*3 pink grapefruit*
juice of 2 oranges	*juice of 2 oranges*
1 tbsp caster sugar	*1 tbsp sugar*

Cut the peel off the grapefruit, taking the white pith with it, and cut in slices. Lay the grapefruit slices on a dish and sprinkle the sugar over them. Pour the fresh orange juice over and chill for an hour or two before serving.

Total Calories: 450
Calories per serving: 75

Vegetable terrine .... 50 Cal.
(or Prawn, spinach & mushroom salad) .... 90 Cal.
Calves' liver with orange juice .... 250–355 Cal.
Ricotta with herbs .... 60 Cal.

Total Calories: 360–505

Wines: Bourgeuil or Chinon, lightly chilled

Vegetable Terrine
This recipe needs to be started a day or two in advance.

METRIC/IMPERIAL	AMERICAN
Aspic:	**Aspic:**
750 g/1½ lb raw chicken joints or ½ raw chicken	*1½ lb raw chicken joints or ½ raw chicken*
½ calf's foot, or a pig's trotter, split	*½ calf's foot, or a pig's foot, split*
2 onions, halved, with extra onion skins	*2 onions, halved, with extra onion skins*
2 leeks, halved	*2 leeks, halved*
2 sticks celery, halved	*2 celery stalks, halved*
½ bay leaf	*½ bay leaf*
½ tsp salt	*½ tsp salt*
6 black peppercorns	*6 black peppercorns*
1 egg white, plus shell	*1 egg white, plus shell*
Vegetables:	**Vegetables:**
125 g/4 oz French beans	*¼ lb green beans*
125 g/4 oz carrots	*¼ lb carrots*
125 g/4 oz courgettes, unpeeled	*¼ lb zucchini, unpeeled*
125 g/4 oz broccoli	*¼ lb broccoli*
1 large bunch spring onions	*1 large bunch scallions*
Tomato Purée:	**Tomato Purée:**
500 g/1 lb ripe tomatoes, skinned and quartered	*1 lb ripe tomatoes, skinned and quartered*
1 tbsp orange juice	*1 tbsp orange juice*

Start 1–2 days in advance. Put the chicken and the calf's foot (or pig's trotter) in a deep pan and cover with cold water. Bring very slowly to the boil, skimming often as it approaches boiling point. When the surface is clear, add the halved vegetables, bay leaf, salt and peppercorns. Half cover the pan and simmer for 3 hours, skimming now and then. When the time is up, strain and cool. Throw away the meat and vegetables. Chill the stock overnight.

Next day, measure the stock. You only need about 1 litre/1¾ pints (4¼ cups), so if there is much more, reduce by fast boiling. Beat the egg white until foamy, but not stiff, and mix the crushed shell with it. Stir into the stock and reheat, beating with a whisk as it approaches boiling point. Let it boil up to the top of the pan, then remove from the heat and allow to settle. Replace over the heat and boil up once more, then pour through a strainer lined with a piece of muslin (cheesecloth). The strained aspic should be crystal clear. (If not, pour back into the pan, add the egg whites and boil up and strain once more.) Leave to cool, while you prepare the vegetables.

Trim the beans, cutting them in pieces about 3.5 cm/1½ in long. Cut the carrots and courgettes (zucchini) into similar strips. Divide the broccoli into sprigs. Trim the spring onions (scallions), leaving on the best part of the green leaves. Poach the vegetables separately in lightly salted water, keeping them quite crisp. Drain and cool in separate piles. To make the tomato purée, blend the tomatoes in a food processor, stir in the orange juice and chill.

Have 6 moulds chilling in the refrigerator. Oval *oeuf en gelée* tins are ideal, or small china dishes. (If you don't have 6 individual dishes, you can use a small loaf tin.) Pour a thin layer of aspic into each mould and put in the freezer for a few minutes to set. Then lay a few spring onions

(scallions) diagonally across each one. Pour in enough aspic to half cover them, and chill again. Once the second layer is set, you can fill the moulds with layers of different vegetables, pouring in the aspic to come level with the top. Chill in the refrigerator for 2–3 hours, until set, or overnight if more convenient. To serve, unmould onto small flat plates, and pour a little tomato purée around each one. Serve as a first course.

Total Calories: 300
Calories per serving: 50

Calves' Liver with Orange Juice

METRIC/IMPERIAL	AMERICAN
15 g/½ oz butter	*1 tbsp butter*
2 tbsp sunflower seed oil	*2 tbsp sunflower seed oil*
6 thin slices calves' liver (400 g/ 14 oz)	*6 thin slices calf liver (14 oz)*
4 shallots, chopped	*4 small onions, chopped*
8 tbsp freshly chopped parsley	*½ cup freshly chopped parsley*
sea salt and freshly ground black pepper	*coarse salt and freshly ground black pepper*
120 ml/4 fl oz orange juice	*½ cup orange juice*

Heat the butter with half the oil in a frying pan and cook the liver very briefly; 2 minutes on each side should be enough. Remove to a warm dish and put the remaining oil in the pan. Add the chopped shallots and cook for 1½–2 minutes, until golden. Add the parsley, sea salt and black pepper, and stir round until well mixed. Pour in the orange juice, swirl round once or twice, and pour over the liver. Serve with steamed broccoli and 150 g/5 oz new potatoes, or rice for those not on a diet.

Total Calories: 1500

Calories per serving: 250 with broccoli; 355 with potatoes

Ricotta with Herbs, Celery, and Water Biscuits

METRIC/IMPERIAL	AMERICAN
2 tbsp freshly chopped herbs (chives, dill, parsley, etc)	*2 tbsp freshly chopped herbs (chives, dill, parsley, etc)*
175 g/6 oz ricotta or low-fat curd cheese	*¾ cup ricotta or low-fat curd cheese*
sea salt and freshly ground black pepper	*coarse salt and freshly ground black pepper*
1 head celery, inner stalks only	*1 bunch celery, inner stalks only*
water biscuits	*crackers*

Stir a quarter of the chopped herbs into the ricotta, adding a little salt and freshly ground black pepper. Form the ricotta into a round and flatten the top. Sprinkle the remaining herbs over the disc, and press into a ramekin to shape it. Turn out on to a flat dish and serve, with the celery and water biscuits (crackers).

Total Calories: 350

Calories per serving: 60 with 2 biscuits (crackers).

From the front: Ricotta with Herbs, Celery and Water Biscuits, Vegetable Terrine, Calves' Liver with Orange Juice

Recipe index

Use this alphabetical recipe reference section while following the diet, and afterwards too as a guide to a healthier style of eating – for these recipes not only save on calories but also on fat and sugar. The emphasis is on fresh, lightly cooked foods, fibre, wholegrains and an adventurous range of seasonings that helps make food appetizing while cutting down on salt. These are fundamental principles of good nutrition and worth carrying into your everyday diet whether you want to lose weight or not.

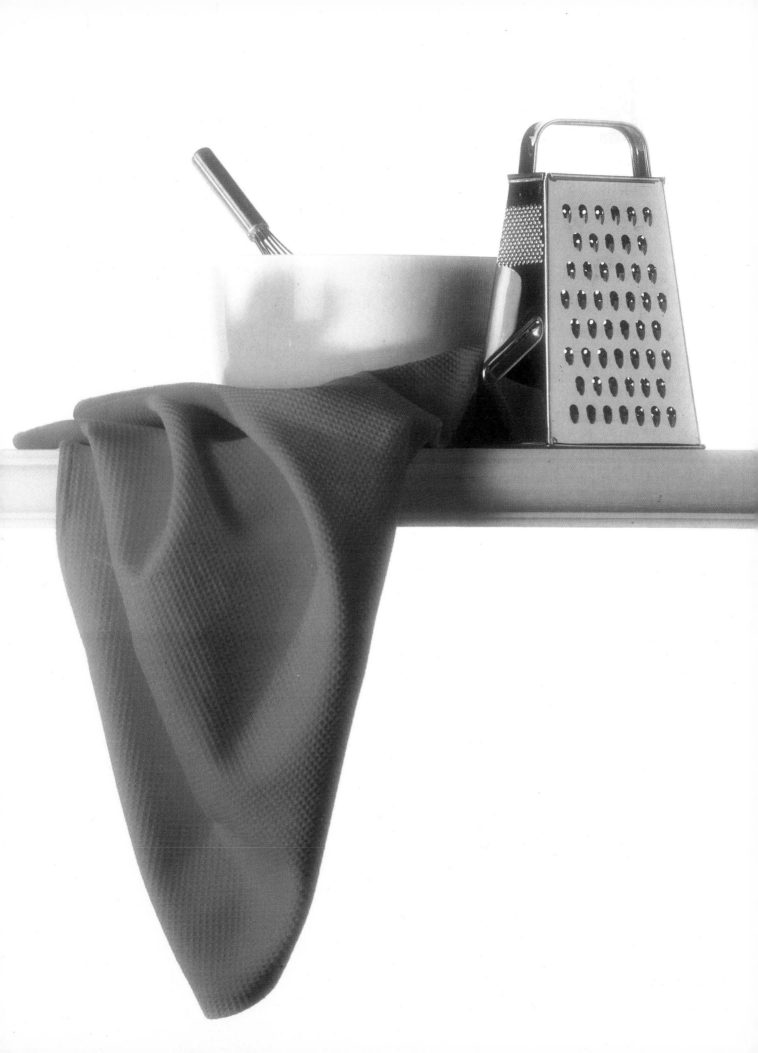

Americana Sauce

Metric/Imperial
1 tbsp olive oil
1 medium onion, chopped
1 clove garlic, crushed
1 tsp tomato purée
250 g/8 oz tomatoes, skinned,
    seeded and chopped (or canned)
salt and freshly ground black pepper
2 tbsp freshly chopped parsley

American
1 tbsp olive oil
1 medium onion, chopped
1 clove garlic, crushed
1 tsp tomato paste
1 cup skinned, seeded and chopped
    tomatoes (or canned)
salt and freshly ground black pepper
2 tbsp freshly chopped parsley

Heat the oil in a saucepan and lightly brown the onion with the garlic. Add the tomato purée (paste), tomatoes and seasoning. Simmer gently for about 15 minutes, stirring occasionally. Sprinkle with parsley before serving with pasta.
TOTAL CALORIES: 190
CALORIES PER SERVING: 95
SERVES 2

Artichoke Salad

Metric/Imperial
3 canned artichoke hearts, drained
    and sliced in half
1 tomato, sliced
few crisp lettuce leaves. shredded
1 tbsp Low Fat Dressing (page 110)
freshly chopped parsley

American
3 canned artichoke hearts, drained
    and sliced in half
1 tomato, sliced
few crisp lettuce leaves. shredded
1 tbsp Low Fat Dressing (page 110)
freshly chopped parsley

Arrange the artichoke hearts and the tomato slices on a bed of lettuce. Pour over the vinaigrette and toss lightly. Sprinkle with parsley.
TOTAL CALORIES: 65
SERVES 1

Variation
For a more substantial salad, add the following:
25 g/ 1 oz fresh green beans,
    blanched
50 g/2 oz tuna, drained
50 g/2 oz new potatoes, boiled in
    their skins and diced

Arrange these ingredients with the artichokes and tomatoes on the lettuce. Serve this salad as a light supper or lunch dish.
TOTAL CALORIES: 150

Aubergine Pie

Metric/Imperial
350 g/12 oz aubergines, trimmed and
    sliced
salt
Sauce:
500 g/1 lb tomatoes, skinned, seeded
    and chopped
1 bouquet garni
3 tbsp dry white wine
dash of Worcestershire sauce
1 clove garlic, crushed
1 large onion, finely chopped
salt and freshly ground black pepper
1 tbsp tomato purée
100 g/3½ oz Edam cheese, thinly
    sliced
25 g/1 oz fresh wholewheat
    breadcrumbs

American
¾ lb eggplant, trimmed and sliced
salt
Sauce:
2 cups skinned, seeded and chopped
    tomatoes
1 bouquet garni
3 tbsp dry white wine
dash of Worcestershire sauce
1 clove garlic, crushed
1 large onion, minced
salt and freshly ground black pepper
1 tbsp tomato paste
½ cup thinly sliced Edam cheese
½ cup soft wholewheat
    breadcrumbs

Arrange the aubergine (eggplant) in a colander, sprinkle with salt and leave for 1 hour. Rinse in cold water and dry on kitchen paper towels.

Put the tomatoes, bouquet garni, wine, Worcestershire sauce, garlic and onion into a saucepan and season well. Bring to the boil and simmer, uncovered, for 30–35 minutes. Remove the bouquet garni and stir in the tomato purée (paste). Adjust the seasoning, if necessary. Arrange a layer of aubergine (eggplant) in the bottom of an ovenproof dish. Spoon over a little tomato sauce, then arrange a little sliced cheese on top. Continue layering, finishing with cheese and breadcrumbs.

Bake in a preheated moderately hot oven, 200°C (400°F) or Gas Mark 6, for 35–40 minutes or until the aubergine (eggplant) is tender and the cheese topping golden brown.
TOTAL CALORIES: 360
CALORIES PER SERVING: 90
SERVES 4

Variation
Replace the aubergines (eggplant) with courgettes (zucchini).

TOTAL CALORIES: 300
CALORIES PER SERVING: 75

Baked Apple with Blackcurrant Sauce

Metric/Imperial
50 g/2 oz fresh blackcurrants
2 tbsp natural unsweetened apple
    juice
2 tsp thin honey
1 × 175 g/6 oz Bramley cooking
    apple, cored

American
½ cup fresh blackcurrants
2 tbsp natural unsweetened apple
    juice
2 tsp thin honey
1 × 6 oz tart apple, cored

Place the blackcurrants, apple juice and honey in a saucepan. Bring to the boil then simmer gently for 5 minutes until the currants are tender. Leave to cool, then purée.

Make a shallow cut around the middle of the apple. Place the apple in an ovenproof dish, pour the blackcurrant sauce into the centre and around the apple. Cover with a lid or foil and bake in a preheated moderate oven, 180°C (350°F) or Gas Mark 4, for 40–50 minutes until tender.
TOTAL CALORIES: 130
SERVES 1

Baked Apple with Plums and Red Wine

Metric/Imperial
1 × 175 g/6 oz Bramley cooking
    apple, cored
2 medium ripe plums, stoned
2 tsp thin honey
pinch of cinnamon
small pinch of ground cloves
1 tbsp dry red wine

American
1 × 6 oz tart apple, cored
2 medium ripe plums, pitted
2 tsp thin honey
pinch of cinnamon
small pinch of ground cloves
1 tbsp dry red wine

Make a shallow cut around the middle of the apple and place in an ovenproof dish. Chop the plums and mix with the honey, cinnamon and cloves. Fill the cavity in the apple with the mixture and pour over the wine. Cover with a lid or foil and bake in a preheated moderate oven, 180°C (350°F) or Gas Mark 4, for 40–50 minutes until the apple is tender. Serve hot or cold.
TOTAL CALORIES: 120
SERVES 1

From the front: Artichoke Salad,
Baked Fish with Ginger

Barbecue Lamb

Metric/Imperial
pinch of garlic salt
pinch of dry mustard
pinch of sugar
pinch of ground ginger
freshly ground black pepper
1 × 175 g/6 oz lamb chop, fat removed
150 ml/¼ pint stock
2 tsp cornflour
1 tbsp water
freshly chopped parsley
Sauce:
2 tsp tomato ketchup
2 tsp Worcestershire sauce
1 tsp fruit sauce
½ tsp vinegar
dash of Tabasco

American
pinch of garlic salt
pinch of dry mustard
pinch of sugar
pinch of ground ginger
freshly ground black pepper
1 × 6 oz lamb chop, fat removed
⅔ cup stock
2 tsp cornstarch
1 tbsp water
freshly chopped parsley
Sauce:
2 tsp ketchup
2 tsp Worcestershire sauce
1 tsp fruit chutney
½ tsp vinegar
dash of hot pepper sauce

Mix the dry seasonings together and rub on both sides of the lamb. Cover and allow to stand for several hours.

Place in a non-stick frying pan (skillet) and fry quickly to brown both sides. Pour over the stock, bring to the boil and simmer gently for 30 minutes. Remove chop and keep warm. Blend the cornflour (cornstarch) with the water and pour into the hot cooking liquor. Bring to the boil stirring, until thickened. Mix the tomato ketchup and sauce ingredients together, stir into the cooking liquid. Boil to reduce slightly and return the chop to the pan. Cook for 20 minutes or until the meat is tender. Serve with parsley.
TOTAL CALORIES: 330
SERVES 1
Note: To barbecue the lamb chop, spread the chop with the dry seasoning and sprinkle with 1 tablespoon lemon or lime juice. Leave to stand (see recipe above). Place the chop on a barbecue and cook for 7–10 minutes each side, until browned and cooked through. Cook the sauce as directed.

Baked Egg

Metric/Imperial
1 tbsp cooked mixed vegetables
1 egg
salt and freshly ground black pepper
1 tbsp whipping cream

American
1 tbsp cooked mixed vegetables
1 egg
salt and freshly ground black pepper
1 tbsp whipping cream

Put the cooked vegetables into a small cocotte dish. Break in the egg and sprinkle with seasoning. Pour the whipping cream onto the egg. Bake in a preheated moderate oven, 180°C (350°F) or Gas Mark 4, for 7 minutes. Serve at once.
TOTAL CALORIES: 180
SERVES 1

Variations
Replace the mixed vegetables with:
25 g/1 oz peeled prawns (shrimp) or *25 g/1 oz (2 tbsp) cooked ham, diced,* or *25 g/1 oz smoked salmon, diced*
TOTAL CALORIES:
with prawns (shrimp): 185
with ham: 230
with smoked salmon: 195

Baked Fish with Ginger

Metric/Imperial
1 × 175 g/6 oz cod cutlet
2 spring onions, finely chopped
small piece root ginger, finely chopped
grated rind of ½ lemon
1 tbsp dry sherry
spring onion and lemon slices

American
1 × 6 oz cod steak
2 scallions, minced
small piece ginger root, finely chopped
grated rind ½ lemon
1 tbsp dry sherry
scallion and lemon slices

Place the fish in an ovenproof dish. Sprinkle with the spring onion (scallion), ginger and lemon rind, then spoon over the sherry. Cover and chill for 2–3 hours.

Cook, covered, in a preheated moderate oven, 180°C (350°F) or Gas Mark 4, for 15 minutes or until the fish is tender and flakes easily. Serve garnished with the spring onion (scallion) and lemon slices.
TOTAL CALORIES: 150
SERVES 1

Banana, Honey and Nut Fool

Metric/Imperial
2 medium bananas (total weight 175 g/6 oz)
2 tsp thin honey
grated rind and juice of ½ lemon
15 g/½ oz hazelnuts, chopped and toasted
150 ml/¼ pint plain yogurt

American
2 medium bananas (total weight 6 oz)
2 tsp thin honey
grated rind and juice of ½ lemon
2 tbsp chopped hazelnuts, toasted
⅔ cup plain yogurt

Mash the bananas with the honey, lemon rind and juice. Stir in the hazelnuts and yogurt and mix well. Spoon the mixture into 2 individual glasses and serve at once.
TOTAL CALORIES: 320
CALORIES PER SERVING: 160
SERVES 2

Beef Carbonnade

Metric/Imperial
250 g/8 oz lean stewing steak, cubed
1 onion, chopped
pinch of grated nutmeg
pinch of sugar
freshly chopped mixed herbs or
    1 bouquet garni
150 ml/¼ pint brown ale
150 ml/¼ pint beef stock
salt and freshly ground black pepper
2 tsp cornflour
1 tbsp water
freshly chopped parsley

American
½ lb lean stewing steak, cubed
1 onion, chopped
pinch of grated nutmeg
pinch of sugar
freshly chopped mixed herbs or
    1 bouquet garni
⅔ cup brown ale
⅔ cup beef stock
salt and freshly ground black pepper
2 tsp cornstarch
1 tbsp water
freshly chopped parsley

Put the steak, onion, nutmeg, sugar, freshly chopped herbs or bouquet garni, ale and stock into a saucepan. Season and cover the pan, simmer gently for 1½–2 hours until the meat is tender. Mix the cornflour (cornstarch) with water. Stir into the casserole and bring to the boil, stirring constantly. Remove the bouquet garni, if using, and adjust the seasoning. Sprinkle with parsley before serving.
TOTAL CALORIES: 600
CALORIES PER SERVING: 300
SERVES 2

Variation
Substitute the brown ale with red wine and add 100 g/4 oz (1 cup) sliced mushrooms 30 minutes before the end of cooking time.
TOTAL CALORIES: 660
CALORIES PER SERVING: 330

Beef Goulash

Metric/Imperial
1 tsp oil
250 g/8 oz lean stewing beef, diced
1 medium onion, sliced
1 clove garlic, crushed
1 tbsp tomato purée
2 tsp paprika
1 tbsp flour
300 ml/½ pint beef stock
salt and freshly ground black pepper
1 bouquet garni
½ red pepper, seeded and sliced
3 tbsp plain yogurt

American
1 tsp oil
½ lb lean stewing beef, diced
1 medium onion, sliced
1 clove garlic, crushed
1 tbsp tomato paste
2 tsp paprika
1 tbsp flour
1¼ cups beef stock
salt and freshly ground black pepper
1 bouquet garni
½ red pepper, seeded and sliced
3 tbsp plain yogurt

Heat the oil in a heavy-based saucepan and brown the meat on all sides. Remove and keep warm. Fry (sauté) the onion and garlic until lightly browned. Add the tomato purée (paste), paprika and flour and cook for 1 minute, stirring. Add the stock and bring to the boil. Stir in the meat, seasoning, bouquet garni and red pepper. Cover and simmer gently for 1–1½ hours, stirring occasionally.

Discard the bouquet garni, adjust the seasoning and stir in the yogurt. Serve at once.
TOTAL CALORIES: 600
CALORIES PER SERVING: 300
SERVES 2
Note: If freezing, omit yogurt and add when re-heated, just before serving.

Left: Brown Rice and Nut Salad
Right: Carrot Soup

Bitkis

Metric/Imperial
250 g/8 oz lean minced beef
1 small onion, finely chopped
1 tbsp freshly chopped parsley
50 g/2 oz fresh wholewheat
   breadcrumbs
salt and freshly ground black pepper
flour
2 tsp oil
150 ml/¼ pint tomato sauce (see
   Gnocchi and Tomato Sauce recipe
   page 105)
4 tbsp plain yogurt

American
1 cup firmly packed lean ground beef
1 small onion, minced
1 tbsp freshly chopped parsley
1 cup soft fresh wholewheat bread
   crumbs
salt and freshly ground black pepper
flour
2 tsp oil
⅔ cup tomato sauce (see Gnocchi
   and Tomato Sauce page 105)
4 tbsp plain yogurt

Mix together the meat, onion, parsley, breadcrumbs and seasoning. Shape into 8 flat cakes, adding a little water if necessary to make the mixture hold together. Heat the oil in a non-stick frying pan until hot. Roll the cakes in flour and fry until brown on both sides. Arrange in a shallow ovenproof dish and pour over the tomato sauce. Bake in a preheated moderate oven, 180°C (350°F) or Gas Mark 4, for about 30 minutes. Heat the yogurt and pour over the Bitkis.
TOTAL CALORIES: 600
CALORIES PER SERVING: 150
SERVES 4

Braised Kidneys

Metric/Imperial
5 lambs' kidneys, halved, skinned
   and cored
1 small onion, chopped
1 carrot, sliced
1 tsp oil
2 tsp flour
175 ml/6 fl oz stock
1 tsp tomato purée
freshly chopped herbs (rosemary,
   sage, thyme)
salt and freshly ground black pepper
75 g/3 oz button mushrooms, sliced
freshly chopped parsley
25 g/1 oz brown rice, boiled, to serve

American
5 lamb kidneys, halved, skinned and
   cored
1 small onion, chopped
1 carrot, sliced
1 tsp oil

2 tsp flour
¾ cup stock
1 tsp tomato paste
freshly chopped herbs (rosemary,
   sage, thyme)
salt and freshly ground black pepper
¾ cup sliced button mushrooms
freshly chopped parsley
2 tbsp brown rice, boiled, to serve

Place the kidneys in a saucepan with the onion, carrot and oil. Cook gently for 5 minutes, then sprinkle in the flour and cook, stirring, for 1 minute. Add the stock, tomato purée (paste), herbs and seasoning. Simmer for a further 10 minutes, stirring in the mushrooms 5 minutes before the end of the cooking time. Serve at once, sprinkled with parsley and on a bed of brown rice.
TOTAL CALORIES: 420
CALORIES PER SERVING: 210
SERVES 2

Brown Rice and Nut Salad

Metric/Imperial
75 g/3 oz brown rice
salt and freshly ground black pepper
50 g/2 oz peeled prawns
2 spring onions, finely chopped
25 g/1 oz green pepper, seeded and
   thinly sliced
25 g/1 oz red pepper, seeded and
   thinly sliced
half quantity Lemon and Mustard
   Dressing (page 115)
15 g/½ oz cashew nuts
15 g/½ oz flaked almonds, toasted
2 tbsp freshly chopped parsley

American
⅓ cup brown rice
salt and freshly ground black pepper
⅓ cup shelled shrimp
2 scallions, finely chopped
1 oz green pepper, seeded and thinly
   sliced (about 1 tbsp)
1 oz red pepper, seeded and thinly
   sliced (about 1 tbsp)
half quantity Lemon and Mustard
   Dressing (page 115)
2 tbsp sliced almonds, toasted
1 tbsp cashew nuts
2 tbsp freshly chopped parsley

Cook the rice in boiling salted water for 30–35 minutes until tender, but still 'al dente'. Drain and cool.
   Place the rice in a bowl and season. Add the prawns (shrimp), spring onions (scallions) and peppers. Pour over the dressing and stir in the nuts and parsley. Mix well until the rice, vegetables and nuts are coated in the dressing.
TOTAL CALORIES: 500
CALORIES PER SERVING: 250
SERVES 2

Cannelloni

Metric/Imperial
4 cannelloni
oil
350 g/12 oz spinach, chopped
salt and freshly ground black pepper
125 g/4 oz low fat curd cheese
pinch of grated nutmeg
Sauce:
150 ml/¼ pint stock
1 carrot, sliced
1 medium onion, sliced
1 stick celery, sliced
1 × 200 g/7 oz can tomatoes,
   chopped
1 bay leaf
1 tsp vinegar

American
4 cannelloni
oil
¾ lb spinach, chopped
salt and freshly ground black pepper
½ cup low fat small curd cottage
   cheese
pinch of grated nutmeg
Sauce:
⅔ cup stock
1 carrot, sliced
1 medium onion, sliced
1 celery stalk, sliced
1 can (8 oz) tomatoes, chopped
1 bay leaf
1 tsp vinegar

Place the cannelloni in boiling water with a few drops of oil and cook for 5 minutes until partially cooked. Drain and keep warm. Meanwhile, place the spinach in a saucepan with a little water and boil for 2–3 minutes. Drain very thoroughly. Mix with the seasoning, cheese and nutmeg, and fill the cannelloni. Set aside.
   To make the sauce, place all the ingredients with seasoning in a saucepan and simmer for 10 minutes. Cool slightly, remove the bay leaf, and purée in a blender. Place the cannelloni in a shallow ovenproof dish and pour over the sauce. Bake in a preheated moderately hot oven, 200°C (400°F) or Gas Mark 6, for 5–10 minutes until the pasta is cooked. Serve at once.
TOTAL CALORIES: 645
CALORIES PER SERVING: 325
SERVES 2

Variation
Replace the spinach filling with the meat sauce in Lasagne and use to fill the cannelloni as above.
TOTAL CALORIES: 900
CALORIES PER SERVING: 450

Carrot Soup

Metric/Imperial
1 small onion, chopped
2 carrots, chopped
2 tsp flour
200 ml/⅓ pint stock
salt and freshly ground black pepper
5 tbsp skimmed milk
little crushed garlic (optional)
freshly chopped mint

American
1 small onion, chopped
2 carrots, chopped
2 tsp flour
⅞ cup stock
salt and freshly ground black pepper
⅓ cup skimmed milk
little crushed garlic (optional)
freshly chopped mint

Place the onion and carrots in a non-stick saucepan. Sprinkle on the flour and cook, stirring, for 1 minute. Pour on the stock, and adjust the seasoning. Bring to the boil and simmer for 30 minutes. Cool slightly, then purée the soup in a blender. Return the soup to the clean pan, add the milk and garlic (if using) and return to the boil. Serve sprinkled with freshly chopped mint.
TOTAL CALORIES: 190
SERVES 1

Celery Soup

Metric/Imperial
4 sticks celery, chopped
1 onion, chopped
150 ml/¼ pint stock
5 tbsp skimmed milk
salt and freshly ground black pepper
freshly chopped parsley
1 tsp cornflour

American
4 celery stalks, chopped
1 onion, chopped
⅔ cup stock
⅓ cup skimmed milk
salt and freshly ground black pepper
freshly chopped parsley
1 tsp cornstarch

Place the celery, onion, stock, milk and seasoning in a saucepan, bring to the boil and simmer for about 20 minutes. Cool slightly, then purée in a blender. Return to the clean saucepan and stir in the cornflour (cornstarch) mixed with 1 tablespoon of cold water. Bring to the boil, stirring constantly, until thickened. Sprinkle with parsley and serve with 40 g/1½ oz (1 slice) wholewheat bread and 25 g/1 oz Edam cheese.
TOTAL CALORIES: 80
SERVES 1

Chicken Florentine

Metric/Imperial

4 chicken breasts
450 ml/¾ pint chicken stock
1 bay leaf
salt and freshly ground black pepper
Spinach sauce:
100 g/4 oz frozen chopped spinach
1 bunch watercress, blanched
150 ml/¼ pint thin cream
1½ tbsp freshly chopped tarragon
1½ tbsp freshly chopped parsley

American

4 chicken breasts
2 cups chicken stock
1 bay leaf
salt and freshly ground black pepper
Spinach sauce:
¼ lb frozen chopped spinach
1 bunch watercress, blanched
⅔ cup light cream
1½ tbsp freshly chopped tarragon
1½ tbsp freshly chopped parsley

Bring the stock to the boil, add the chicken breasts, bay leaf and seasoning and simmer, covered, for 35 minutes. Remove the skin from the breasts, and keep them warm. Strain and reserve 150 ml/¼ pint (¾ cup) stock.   Cook the spinach and drain well, then purée in a blender with the watercress, stock, cream and herbs. Pour into a saucepan and simmer for 3 minutes. Season, then pour the sauce over the chicken and serve at once.
TOTAL CALORIES: 1600
CALORIES PER SERVING: 400
SERVES 4

Chicken Salad with Curry Sauce

Metric/Imperial

250 g/8 oz boneless cooked chicken,
    skinned and diced
125 g/4 oz avocado flesh, diced
2 spring onions, chopped
curly endive leaves
25 g/1 oz cashew nuts or peanuts
Sauce:
1 tsp curry powder
1 clove garlic, crushed
3 tbsp plain yogurt
1 tbsp low calorie mayonnaise
2 tsp freshly chopped coriander or
    parsley

American

½ lb boneless cooked chicken,
    skinned and diced
¼ lb avocado flesh, diced
2 scallions, chopped
chicory leaves
2 tbsp cashew nuts or peanuts
Sauce:
1 tsp curry powder
1 clove garlic, crushed
3 tbsp plain yogurt
1 tbsp low calorie mayonnaise
2 tsp freshly chopped coriander or
    parsley

To make the sauce, put the curry powder and garlic into a bowl; gradually add the yogurt and mayonnaise, and mix well. Cover and refrigerate for 2–3 hours, then stir in the coriander or parsley.
Put the chicken, avocado and spring onion (scallion) into a bowl. Spoon over the sauce and mix well, until all the ingredients are coated in the sauce. Arrange the endive (chicory) leaves on a serving plate, pile the chicken mixture on top and sprinkle the cashew nuts or peanuts. Serve at once.
TOTAL CALORIES: 840
CALORIES PER SERVING: 420
SERVES 2

Chicken Veronique

Metric/Imperial

250 g/8 oz chicken joint
salt and freshly ground black pepper
sprig of fresh tarragon
stock (see method)
1 tsp cornflour
1 tbsp water
2 tsp lemon juice
8 grapes, pips removed and skinned

American

½ lb chicken joint
salt and freshly ground black pepper
sprig of fresh tarragon
stock (see method)
1 tsp cornstarch
1 tbsp water
2 tsp lemon juice
8 grapes, pitted and skinned

Skin the chicken joint and sprinkle with seasoning. Place on a piece of foil large enough to enclose it, lay the tarragon on top and fold up. Bake in a preheated moderate oven, 180°C (350°F) or Gas Mark 4, for about 1 hour. Remove the chicken and keep warm. Keep the juices and make up to 150 ml/¼ pint (⅔ cup) with stock, then pour into a saucepan. Mix the cornflour (cornstarch) with the water and stir into the stock. Bring to the boil, stirring, and add the lemon juice and seasoning. When the sauce is thickened, add the grapes and continue to cook for 5 minutes. Pour the sauce over the chicken before serving.
TOTAL CALORIES: 260
SERVES 1

Chicken with Almonds

Metric/Imperial

250 g/8 oz chicken joint
1 tsp oil
1 small onion, sliced
pinch of mixed dried herbs
salt and freshly ground black pepper
2 tbsp blanched almonds

American

½ lb chicken joint
1 tsp oil
1 small onion, sliced
pinch of mixed dried herbs
salt and freshly ground black pepper
2 tbsp blanched almonds

Remove the skin from the chicken and discard. Heat the oil in a nonstick frying pan (skillet) and add the onion, chicken, herbs and seasoning. Cook gently for 20–25 minutes, turning occasionally, until chicken is cooked through. Add the almonds and cook until golden brown.
TOTAL CALORIES: 350
SERVES 1

Chicken with Peach and Ginger

Metric/Imperial

250 g/8 oz chicken joint
salt and freshly ground black pepper
½ ripe peach, peeled
1 tsp ground ginger
1 tsp redcurrant jelly
watercress

American

½ lb chicken joint
salt and freshly ground black pepper
½ ripe peach, peeled
1 tsp ground ginger
1 tsp red currant jelly
watercress

Sprinkle the chicken with seasoning. Place in an ovenproof dish and bake in a preheated moderate oven, 180°C (350°F) or Gas Mark 4, for 30–35 minutes. About 10 minutes before the chicken is cooked, sprinkle the peach half with ginger and put in the oven to warm through. Spoon the redcurrant jelly into the hollow of the peach and serve at once with the

chicken and watercress. (Do not eat the skin.)
TOTAL CALORIES: 240
SERVES 1

Chilli con Carne

Metric/Imperial
200 g/7 oz very lean minced beef
1 large onion, finely chopped
1 tsp chilli powder
1 tsp paprika
salt and freshly ground black pepper
150 ml/¼ pint tomato juice
250 g/8 oz canned red kidney beans
. freshly chopped parsley

American
1 cup very lean ground beef
1 large onion, finely chopped
1 tsp chili powder
1 tsp paprika
salt and freshly ground black pepper
⅔ cup tomato juice
¾ cup canned red kidney beans
freshly chopped parsley

From the left: Chinese Cabbage and Chicken Salad, Chicken with Peach and Ginger

Place the meat in a non-stick saucepan and fry (sauté) quickly, stirring constantly, until browned. Drain off excess fat and pat the meat with kitchen paper towel. Add the onion to the meat in the pan, sprinkle over the spices and seasoning and cook for 1 minute before pouring in the tomato juice. Bring to the boil, cover and simmer gently for 1 hour or until the beef is tender. Moisten with a little water during cooking if necessary. Add the beans, adjust the seasoning and heat through before serving. Garnish with the parsley.
TOTAL CALORIES: 700
CALORIES PER SERVING: 350
SERVES 2

Chinese Cabbage and Chicken Salad

Metric/Imperial
50 g/2 oz Chinese cabbage, thinly sliced
50 g/2 oz red cabbage, thinly sliced
2 spring onions
50 g/2 oz fresh beansprouts
25 g/1 oz button mushrooms, sliced
2 tsp soy sauce
juice and grated rind of 2 limes
25 g/1 oz cucumber, cut into julienne strips
2 medium carrots, cut into julienne strips
250 g/8 oz lean boneless chicken, cooked and cut into julienne strips
2 sticks celery, cut into julienne strips

American
¾ cup thinly sliced Chinese cabbage
¾ cup thinly sliced red cabbage
2 scallions
1 cup fresh beansprouts
¼ cup sliced button mushrooms
2 tsp soy sauce
juice and grated rind of 2 limes
1 oz cucumber, cut into matchstick strips
2 medium carrots, cut into matchstick strips
½ lb lean boneless chicken, cooked and cut into matchstick strips
2 celery stalks, cut into matchstick strips

Place the cabbage in a bowl and add the spring onions (scallions), beansprouts and mushrooms. Mix together the soy sauce, lime juice and rind, pour over the cabbage mixture and toss well. Pile onto a serving dish and arrange the strips of cucumber, carrot, chicken and celery in a lattice pattern on top.
TOTAL CALORIES: 420
CALORIES PER SERVING: 210
SERVES 2

Chinese Stuffed Pepper

Metric/Imperial
1 large green or red pepper
Filling:
25 g/1 oz brown rice
1 stick celery, finely chopped
1 clove garlic, crushed
25 g/1 oz flat mushrooms, chopped
1 tomato, skinned, seeded and chopped
1 small leek, finely chopped
150 ml/¼ pint dry white wine
½ tsp mixed dried herbs
little salt
freshly ground black pepper
little stock (see method)
25 g/1 oz sweetcorn
2 tsp soy sauce
chopped fresh coriander

American
1 large green or red pepper
Filling:
2 tbsp brown rice
1 celery stalk, finely chopped
1 clove garlic, crushed
¼ cup chopped flat mushrooms
1 tomato, skinned, seeded and chopped
1 small leek, finely chopped
⅔ cup dry white wine
½ tsp mixed dried herbs
little salt
freshly ground black pepper
little stock (see method)
1 tbsp whole kernel corn
2 tsp soy sauce
chopped fresh coriander

Remove the top of the pepper by cutting through just below the stem. Discard the seeds and white pith and blanch in boiling water for 2 minutes. Drain well.

Place the rice, celery, garlic, mushrooms, tomato and leek in a saucepan. Pour over the wine and add the herbs and seasoning. Bring to the boil, half cover, and simmer gently for 25 minutes or until the rice is almost tender. Add a little stock if the mixture becomes too dry, stirring occasionally. Mix in the corn and soy sauce.

Stand the pepper in an ovenproof dish and spoon the rice mixture into the centre. Spoon any remaining mixture around the pepper. Cover with foil and cook in a preheated moderate oven, 180°C (350°F) or Gas Mark 4, for 15–20 minutes or until the pepper is tender. Serve hot, sprinkled with chopped coriander.
TOTAL CALORIES: 170
SERVES 1
Note: If liked, the pepper can be sprinkled with toasted sesame seeds.

Corn and Fish Chowder

Metric/Imperial
25 g/1 oz lean bacon, diced
½ onion, chopped
1 stick celery, sliced
½ green pepper, chopped
2 tsp flour
150 ml/¼ pint light stock
salt and freshly ground black pepper
75 g/3 oz cooked white fish, diced
50 g/2 oz cooked sweetcorn
150 ml/¼ pint skimmed milk

American
1 tbsp diced lean bacon
½ onion, chopped
1 celery stalk, sliced
½ green pepper, chopped
2 tsp flour
⅔ cup light stock
salt and freshly ground black pepper
3 oz cooked white fish, diced
⅓ cup cooked kernel corn
⅔ cup skimmed milk

Brown the bacon in a non-stick pan, then add the onion, celery and pepper. Cook for 2–3 minutes, stirring. Sprinkle over the flour and continue stirring for 1 minute. Add the stock and seasoning, bring to the boil and simmer for 5 minutes. Stir in the fish, sweetcorn (kernel corn) and milk. Simmer for 4 minutes and serve.
TOTAL CALORIES: 250
SERVES 1

Cottage Pie

Metric/Imperial
125 g/4 oz very lean minced beef or veal
1 small onion, chopped
1 small carrot, diced
2 tomatoes, chopped
pinch of mixed dried herbs
1 tsp tomato purée
salt and freshly ground black pepper
1–2 tbsp stock
150 g/5 oz freshly mashed potato

American
½ cup very lean ground beef or veal
1 small onion, chopped
1 small carrot, diced
2 tomatoes, chopped
pinch of mixed dried herbs
1 tsp tomato paste
salt and freshly ground black pepper
1–2 tbsp stock
⅔ cup freshly mashed potato

Put the meat, onion, carrot, tomatoes, herbs, tomato purée (paste) and seasoning into a non-stick frying pan (skillet). Pour over the stock, bring to the boil and then simmer gently, stirring often, until the meat is cooked. Pour off any fat and transfer the meat mixture to an ovenproof

dish. Cover with the potato; place in a moderate oven, 180°C (350°F) or Gas Mark 4, for about 20 minutes.
TOTAL CALORIES: 390
SERVES 1

Courgette and Tomato Pie

Metric/Imperial
1 × 397 g/14 oz can tomatoes
50 g/2 oz onions, sliced
1 or 2 cloves garlic, crushed
1 tsp mixed dried herbs
salt and freshly ground black pepper
2 tsp freshly chopped basil
2 tbsp dry white wine
500 g/1 lb courgettes, sliced diagonally
Topping:
500 g/1 lb potatoes
50 g/2 oz low fat cream cheese with herbs
2 tbsp skimmed milk
2 spring onions, chopped
freshly ground black pepper
grated nutmeg
25 g/1 oz Edam cheese, grated

American
1 can (16 oz) tomatoes
½ cup sliced onions
1 or 2 cloves garlic, crushed
1 tsp mixed dried herbs
salt and freshly ground black pepper
2 tsp freshly chopped basil
2 tbsp dry white wine
1 lb zucchini, sliced diagonally
Topping:
1 lb potatoes
¼ cup low fat cream cheese with herbs
2 tbsp skimmed milk
2 scallions, chopped
freshly ground black pepper
grated nutmeg
¼ cup grated Edam cheese

Place the tomatoes and juice in a saucepan. Add the onions, garlic, herbs, and season well. Bring to the boil and add the wine. Cook, uncovered, for 20 minutes, then add the courgettes (zucchini). Reduce the heat and cook for a further 2–3 minutes. Spoon the mixture into 4 individual ovenproof dishes.
Boil the potatoes until soft, then drain and mash until smooth. Mix in the cream cheese, skimmed milk, spring onions (scallions), black pepper and a little nutmeg. Spoon on top of the courgettes (zucchini) mixture and press the top with a fork. Sprinkle over the grated cheese. Place in a preheated moderately hot oven, 200°C (400°F) or Gas Mark 6, for 20–25 minutes or until brown.
TOTAL CALORIES: 860
CALORIES PER SERVING: 215
SERVES 4

Cream of Onion Soup

Metric/Imperial
600 ml/1 pint skimmed milk
1 bay leaf
15 g/½ oz butter
2 onions, sliced
2 tsp flour
salt and freshly ground black pepper
1 egg, beaten

American
2½ cups skimmed milk
1 bay leaf
1 tbsp butter
2 onions, sliced
2 tsp flour
salt and freshly ground black pepper
1 egg, beaten

Heat the milk and bay leaf until scalded, then set aside. Melt the butter in a saucepan and add the onion. Cook without browning until the onion is soft, then stir in the flour. Continue cooking for 1 minute, stirring well. Strain the milk onto the mixture and bring to the boil, stirring constantly. Simmer for 10 minutes and add seasoning. Cool the soup slightly, then purée in a blender until smooth. Return the soup to the clean pan and gradually stir in the beaten egg – do not allow to boil. Sprinkle with parsley and serve.
TOTAL CALORIES: 445
CALORIES PER SERVING: 225
SERVES 2

Crêpes
Makes 8

Metric/Imperial
125 g/4 oz plain flour
pinch of salt
1 egg
300 ml/½ pint skimmed milk

American
1 cup all-purpose flour
pinch of salt
1 egg
1¼ cups skimmed milk

Sift the flour and salt into a mixing bowl and make a well in the centre. Beat the egg and half the milk together and pour into the well. Using a wooden spoon, gradually stir the mixture until all the flour has been drawn in from the sides. Then beat well until the mixture is smooth. Stir in the remaining milk and set aside in a cool place for several hours before using.
Wipe a little oil around a non-stick frying pan (skillet). Heat the pan and when the oil is almost smoking, pour in a little crêpe mixture to cover the pan. When the bubbles begin to rise on the surface the crêpe should be

golden underneath, so turn it over, cooking until golden on that side. Remove and store in a warm place.
TOTAL CALORIES: 600
CALORIES PER CREPE: 75
SERVES 4

Crêpe Fillings
Make the fillings, as below, and divide into eight. Spread a spoonful of filling on each pancake, and roll up. Arrange in an ovenproof dish, cover with foil and bake in a preheated moderately hot oven, 200°C (400°F) or Gas Mark 6, for 20 minutes.
SERVES 4

Mixed vegetables: mix together 175 g/6 oz low fat cheese with herbs and garlic, a dash of Tabasco (hot pepper sauce) and 1 tbsp plain yogurt. Stir in 1 × 250 g/8 oz packet mixed vegetables, cooked and cooled, 1 tbsp freshly chopped parsley, seasoning and mix well.
TOTAL CALORIES FOR FILLING: 395

Prawn and chive: mix together 250 g/8 oz peeled prawns (shrimp), 2 tbsp freshly chopped chives, 150 ml/¼ pint (⅔ cup) plain yogurt, grated rind and juice of 1 lemon, and a dash of Tabasco (hot pepper sauce).
TOTAL CALORIES FOR FILLING: 330

Smoked haddock: mix together 250 g/8 oz poached, cooled and flaked smoked haddock, 15 g/½ oz (1 tbsp) butter, grated rind and juice of 1 lemon, 2 tbsp plain yogurt, 2 tbsp parsley, pepper.
TOTAL CALORIES FOR FILLING: 415

Crunchy Salad

Metric/Imperial
2 crisp apples, cored and diced
juice of 1 lemon
2 sticks celery, chopped
25 g/1 oz walnuts
75 g/3 oz white cabbage, finely sliced
50 g/2 oz Gouda cheese, diced
75 g/3 oz green pepper, seeded and diced
25 g/1 oz cucumber, diced
half quantity Blue Cheese Dressing (page 115)
1 tbsp sunflower seeds, toasted

American
2 crisp apples, cored and diced
juice of 1 lemon
2 celery stalks, chopped
¼ cup walnuts
1¼ cups finely sliced white cabbage
⅓ cup diced Gouda cheese
3 oz green pepper, seeded and diced
¼ cup diced cucumber
half quantity Blue Cheese Dressing (page 115)
1 tbsp sunflower seeds, toasted

Toss the apples in the lemon juice. Add the celery, walnuts and cabbage and mix well. Stir in the cheese, green pepper and cucumber and spoon over the dressing.

TOTAL CALORIES: 610
CALORIES PER SERVING: 305
SERVES 2

Cucumber Appetizer

Metric/Imperial
6 cm/2½ in length of cucumber
25 g/1 oz cottage cheese
25 g/1 oz peeled prawns, chopped
freshly chopped parsley

American
2½ in length of cucumber
1 tbsp cottage cheese
1 tbsp shelled shrimp, chopped
freshly chopped parsley

Halve the cucumber lengthwise and scoop out the seeds. Mix together the cottage cheese and prawns (shrimp) and season. Fill the cucumber slices and sprinkle with parsley.

TOTAL CALORIES: 55
SERVES 1

Cucumber and Mint Soup

Metric/Imperial
175 g/6 oz cucumber, peeled and diced
300 ml/½ pint consommé
150 ml/¼ pint tomato juice
150 ml/¼ pint cold water
150 ml/¼ pint plain yogurt
125 g/4 oz peeled prawns
few drops of Tabasco
1–2 tbsp roughly chopped mint
1–2 cloves garlic, roughly chopped
salt and freshly ground black pepper
juice and grated rind of 1 lemon
few cucumber slices

American
1½ cups peeled and diced cucumber
1¼ cups consommé
⅔ cup tomato juice
⅔ cup cold water
⅔ cup plain yogurt
⅔ cup shelled shrimp
few drops of hot pepper sauce
1–2 tbsp roughly chopped mint
1–2 cloves garlic, roughly chopped
salt and freshly ground black pepper
juice and grated rind of 1 lemon
few cucumber slices

Place all the ingredients, except the cucumber slices, in a blender. Blend until smooth. Chill for 2–3 hours in the refrigerator. Adjust the seasoning and serve garnished with the cucumber slices.

TOTAL CALORIES: 250
CALORIES PER SERVING: 65
SERVES 4

Curried Mushroom Salad

Metric/Imperial
2 tsp curry powder
1 clove garlic, crushed
2 tbsp plain yogurt
1 tbsp low calorie mayonnaise
1 tbsp freshly chopped parsley
1 tbsp chopped chives
300 g/10 oz button mushrooms
175 g/6 oz endive
25 g/1 oz lean back bacon, grilled until crisp
1 tbsp sunflower seeds, toasted

American
2 tsp curry powder
1 clove garlic, crushed
2 tbsp plain yogurt

Crêpes with Prawn Filling, Mixed Vegetable Filling and Smoked Haddock Filling. Right: Curried Mushroom Salad

1 tbsp low calorie mayonnaise
1 tbsp freshly chopped parsley
1 tbsp chopped chives
2½ cups button mushrooms
6 oz chicory
1 slice lean bacon, broiled until crisp
1 tbsp sunflower seeds, toasted

Place the curry powder and garlic in a bowl. Stir in the yogurt and mayonnaise and mix well. Cover and leave in the refrigerator for 4-6 hours.

Add the parsley and chives to the dressing, then stir in the mushrooms and leave to chill for a further 1 hour.

Arrange the endive (chicory) on a serving dish and spoon the mushroom mixture into the centre. Crumble the bacon over the top and sprinkle with sunflower seeds.

TOTAL CALORIES: 400
CALORIES PER SERVING: 200
SERVES 2

Fennel and Orange Salad

Metric/Imperial

175 g/6 oz plaice or sole fillets,
    skinned
3 tbsp dry white wine
1 bouquet garni
salt and freshly ground black pepper
2 heads fennel, thinly sliced
2 medium oranges, peeled and cut
    into segments
half quantity Avocado Salad Cream
    (page 115)
1 head endive

American

6 oz flounder or sole fillets, skinned
3 tbsp dry white wine
1 bouquet garni
salt and freshly ground black pepper
2 heads fennel, thinly sliced
2 medium oranges, peeled and cut
    into segments
half quantity Avocado Salad Cream
    (page 115)
1 head chicory

Place the fish in a non-stick frying pan. Pour over the wine, add the bouquet garni and season well. Slowly bring to the boil and simmer for 2–3 minutes until the fish is just tender. Turn off the heat and leave the fish to cool in the liquor. When cool, drain and flake the flesh.

Place the fennel, orange segments and fish in a bowl. Spoon over the salad cream and toss lightly.

Arrange the endive (chicory) on a serving plate and spoon the salad into the centre. Serve at once.
TOTAL CALORIES: 420
CALORIES PER SERVING: 210
SERVES 2

Fillet Steak with Green Peppercorns and Herbs

Metric/Imperial

1 × 150 g/5 oz fillet steak, trimmed of
    all fat
2 tsp green peppercorns, drained if
    necessary
1 tsp freshly chopped thyme
25 g/1 oz button mushrooms, sliced
2 tbsp dry red wine
dash of Worcestershire sauce
½ tsp French mustard
1 spring onion, chopped
extra chopped thyme, to serve

American

1 × 5 oz fillet steak, trimmed of all fat
2 tsp green peppercorns, drained if
    necessary
1 tsp freshly chopped thyme
¼ cup sliced button mushrooms
2 tbsp dry red wine
dash of Worcestershire sauce
½ tsp Dijon-style mustard

1 scallion, chopped
extra chopped thyme, to serve

Season the steak with salt and press the peppercorns into both sides. Heat a non-stick or dry frying pan (skillet) and add the steak. Cook for 2–3 minutes on each side until browned, then add the remaining ingredients. Bring to the boil and cook for a further 1 minute. Remove the steak from the pan (skillet), place on a hot serving plate and keep it warm.

Increase the heat and boil the pan mixture rapidly for 1–2 minutes, until it has reduced slightly. Spoon over the steak and serve at once, sprinkled with thyme.
TOTAL CALORIES: 290
SERVES 1

Fish Pie

Metric/Imperial

175 g/6 oz cod or other white fish
    fillet, skinned
150 ml/¼ pint dry white wine
1 tsp mixed dried herbs
small strip of lemon rind
125 g/4 oz peeled prawns
300 ml/½ pint white sauce (page
    123), using fish liquor and milk
    (see below)
175 g/6 oz mashed potato
1 tbsp freshly chopped parsley
2 tsp freshly chopped chives
1 tomato, sliced

American

6 oz cod or other white fish fillet,
    skinned
⅔ cup dry white wine
1 tsp mixed dried herbs
small strip of lemon rind
¼ lb peeled shrimp
1¼ cups white sauce (page 123),
    using fish liquor and milk (see
    below)
¾ cup mashed potato
1 tbsp freshly chopped parsley
2 tsp freshly chopped chives
1 tomato, sliced

Put the fish in a frying pan (skillet) and add the wine, dried herbs and lemon rind. Gradually bring to the boil, then simmer for 5–7 minutes until the fish is tender. Remove the fish from the pan and flake the flesh. Strain the cooking liquid and reserve for the white sauce.

Put the fish and prawns (shrimp) into a shallow ovenproof dish and spoon over the sauce. Mix the mashed potato and fresh herbs together and spoon or pipe the mixture over the fish. Arrange tomato slices on top and bake in a preheated moderate oven, 200°C (400°F) or Gas

Mark 6, for 20-25 minutes or until the potato is golden brown.
TOTAL CALORIES: 900
CALORIES PER SERVING: 450
SERVES 2

Fish Stuffed with Prawns and Lemon

Metric/Imperial

175 g/6 oz plaice fillets or haddock
    fillet, skinned
100 g/3½ oz peeled prawns
grated rind of ½ lemon
2 tsp fresh dill
salt and freshly ground black pepper
6 tbsp dry white wine
1 bouquet garni
1 tbsp toasted sesame seeds

American

6 oz flounder fillet or haddock fillet,
    skinned
½ cup shelled shrimp
grated rind of ½ lemon
2 tsp fresh dill
salt and freshly ground black pepper
6 tbsp dry white wine
1 bouquet garni
1 tbsp toasted sesame seeds

Clockwise from the front: Fennel and Orange Salad, French Vegetable Quiche, Fillet Steak with Green Peppercorns and Herbs

Lay the fish fillets on a board. Mix the prawns (shrimp), lemon rind and dill together and season well. Arrange the prawns (shrimp) in the centre of the fish and roll them up. Place in an ovenproof dish and pour over the wine. Add the bouquet garni, cover and cook in a preheated moderate oven, 180°C (350°F) or Gas Mark 4, for 12–15 minutes until the fish is cooked and tender. Drain the fish and arrange on a hot serving dish. Remove the bouquet garni and boil the liquor for 5–10 minutes until reduced and thickened. Spoon over the fish, sprinkled with the sesame seeds and serve at once.
TOTAL CALORIES: 480
SERVES 1

French Onion Soup

Metric/Imperial
1 tsp butter
110 g/4 oz onion, chopped
150 ml/¼ pint beef stock
salt and freshly ground black pepper
50 g/2 oz French bread slices
25 g/1 oz hard cheese, grated

American
1 tsp butter
¼ lb onion, chopped
⅔ cup beef stock
salt and freshly ground black pepper
2 oz French bread slices
¼ cup grated hard cheese

Melt the butter in a saucepan and cook the onion gently for 5 minutes until soft. Add the stock, simmer for 20 minutes and adjust the seasoning. Pour into a flameproof soup bowl, place the bread slices on top and sprinkle with cheese. Place under a preheated grill (broiler) until the cheese is bubbling and lightly browned on top. Serve at once.

TOTAL CALORIES: 280
SERVES 1

French Vegetable Quiche

Metric/Imperial
50 g/2 oz plain flour
50 g/2 oz wholemeal flour
pinch of salt
pinch of cayenne pepper
50 g/2 oz margarine
ice-cold water
Filling:
2 eggs
150 ml/¼ pint skimmed milk
100 g/3½ oz low fat cream cheese
   with garlic and herbs
2 tomatoes, skinned, seeded and
   chopped
1 onion, finely chopped
1 clove garlic, crushed
1 courgette, diced
½ green or red pepper, diced
½ tsp mixed dried herbs
salt and freshly ground black pepper
25 g/1 oz Edam cheese, thinly sliced

American
½ cup all-purpose flour
½ cup wholewheat flour
pinch of salt
pinch of cayenne

¼ cup margarine
ice-cold water
Filling:
2 eggs
⅔ cup skimmed milk
½ cup low fat cream cheese with
   garlic and herbs
2 tomatoes, skinned, seeded and
   chopped
1 onion, minced
1 clove garlic, crushed
1 zucchini, sliced
½ green or red pepper, diced
½ tsp mixed dried herbs
salt and freshly ground black pepper
¼ cup thinly sliced Edam cheese

Place the flours in a bowl with the salt and cayenne. Rub (cut) the margarine into the flour until the mixture resembles fine breadcrumbs. Stir in 2 teaspoons of cold water at a time, until the dough is firm. Lightly knead the dough on a floured board, roll out and use to line 4 7.5 cm (3 in) tins.

Beat the eggs, milk and cream cheese together. Place the prepared vegetables in a saucepan with the herbs and season well. Bring to the boil and simmer, uncovered, for 10 minutes or until the vegetables are softened and the mixture is reduced. Cool, then spoon into the pastry cases (pie shells). Spoon over the egg mixture and arrange the sliced cheese on top. Bake in a preheated oven, 190°C (375°F) or Gas Mark 5, for 20-25 minutes until set and golden brown. Serve hot or cold.

TOTAL CALORIES: 1040
CALORIES PER SERVING: 260
SERVES 4

Gazpacho

Metric/Imperial
350 g/12 oz fresh tomatoes, skinned
   and roughly chopped
2 cloves garlic, crushed
2 spring onions, chopped
¼ cucumber, chopped
1 red pepper, seeded and chopped
1 green pepper, seeded and chopped
1 sprig of thyme
1 sprig of parsley
1 sprig of basil
2 tbsp lemon juice
300 ml/½ pint tomato juice
few drops of Tabasco
salt and freshly ground black pepper
freshly chopped parsley

American
1½ cups skinned and roughly
   chopped tomatoes
2 cloves garlic, crushed
2 scallions, chopped
¼ cucumber, chopped
1 red pepper, seeded and chopped
1 green pepper, seeded and chopped
1 sprig of thyme
1 sprig of parsley
1 sprig of basil
2 tbsp lemon juice
1¼ cups tomato juice
few drops of hot pepper sauce
salt and freshly ground black pepper
freshly chopped parsley

Place all the ingredients, except the chopped parsley, in a blender and blend until very smooth. Chill in the refrigerator. Adjust the seasoning and serve sprinkled with parsley.

TOTAL CALORIES: 140
CALORIES PER SERVING: 70
SERVES 2

Gazpacho Garnishes
Arrange the following in small dishes to accompany the soup: 1 tomato, diced; 1 green pepper, seeded and finely diced; 1 small courgette (zucchini), finely diced; 1 slice bread, toasted and cut into small pieces.

Gnocchi with Tomato Sauce

Metric/Imperial
250 g/8 oz potato, boiled and mashed
1 egg
15 g/½ oz flour
salt and freshly ground black pepper
20 g/¾ oz Edam cheese. grated, to
   serve
Tomato Sauce:
1 tbsp oil
50 g/2 oz onion, chopped
250 g/8 oz canned tomatoes
freshly chopped basil or parsley

American
½ lb potato, boiled and mashed
1 egg
½ oz flour
salt and freshly ground black pepper
¾ oz Edam cheese. grated, to serve
Tomato Sauce:
1 tbsp oil
2 oz onion, chopped
½ lb canned tomatoes
freshly chopped basil or parsley

Place the mashed potato in a bowl, add the egg, flour and seasoning and mix well. Mould into small walnut-sized balls and place in a sieve (strainer). Lower into a saucepan of boiling water and cook until gnocchi rise to surface. Drain and keep warm.

Heat the oil in a saucepan and fry (sauté) the onion gently until soft. Add the tomatoes and seasoning. Simmer until the liquid has reduced, then stir in the herbs. Pour the sauce over and sprinkle with cheese.

TOTAL CALORIES: 550
SERVES 1

Green Fruit Salad

Metric/Imperial
125 g/4 oz ogen melon
125 g/4 oz honeydew melon
2 kiwi fruit, peeled and sliced
50 g/2 oz green grapes, pipped
175 g/6 oz pear, peeled, cored and
    chopped
juice and grated rind of 1 orange
125 g/4 oz banana

American
¼ lb cantaloupe melon
¼ lb honeydew melon
2 kiwi fruit, peeled and sliced
½ cup pitted green grapes
6 oz pear, peeled, cored and chopped
juice and grated rind of 1 orange
4 oz banana

Cube the melon or shape into balls, using a melon baller. Place in a bowl with the kiwi fruit and grapes. Add the pear to the other fruit with the orange rind and juice. Lastly, slice and add the banana just before serving.

TOTAL CALORIES: 340
CALORIES PER SERVING: 85
SERVES 4

Ham and Cider Sauce

Metric/Imperial
250 g/8 oz gammon joint
1 bay leaf
few peppercorns
few whole cloves
120 ml/4 fl oz cider
Cider Sauce:
2 tsp brown sugar
1 tbsp raisins
4 tbsp cider
salt and freshly ground black pepper
1 tsp cornflour

American
½ lb fresh ham (rump portion)
1 bay leaf
few peppercorns
few whole cloves
½ cup cider
Cider Sauce:
2 tsp brown sugar
1 tbsp raisins
4 tbsp cider
salt and freshly ground black pepper
1 tsp cornstarch

Place the gammon (ham) in a large saucepan with the bay leaves and peppercorns, with enough water to cover. Bring to the boil and simmer for 1–1½ hours until tender. Drain the gammon (ham) and remove the skin and most of the fat. Stud with cloves and place in a roasting pan with 120 ml/4 fl oz (½ cup) cider. Bake in a preheated moderate oven, 180°C (350°F) or Gas Mark 4, for 15 minutes, basting occasionally with the cider. Remove the meat and keep warm while making the sauce.

Place the brown sugar, raisins, cider and seasoning in a saucepan. Add the cider and meat juices from the roasting pan. Mix the cornflour (cornstarch) with a little water and stir into the sauce. Bring to the boil, then simmer, stirring. Serve the sauce with the sliced gammon (ham).

TOTAL CALORIES: 680
CALORIES PER SERVING: 340
SERVES 2

Herb Chicken

Metric/Imperial
4 × 100 g/3½ oz chicken breasts
50 g/2 oz low fat cream cheese with
    garlic and herbs
1–2 cloves garlic, crushed
25 g/1 oz button mushrooms, very
    finely chopped
2 tsp freshly chopped thyme
salt and freshly ground black pepper
grated rind of ½ lemon
150 ml/¼ pint dry white wine
1 fresh bouquet garni (parsley,
    rosemary, thyme and sage)

American
4 × 3½ oz chicken breasts
¼ cup low fat cream cheese with
    garlic and herbs
1–2 cloves garlic, crushed
¼ cup very finely chopped button
    mushrooms
2 tsp freshly chopped thyme
salt and freshly ground black pepper
grated rind of ½ lemon
⅔ cup dry white wine
1 fresh bouquet garni (parsley,
    rosemary, thyme and sage)

Make a horizontal cut into each chicken breast to make a pocket (make sure not to cut right through). Mix together the cream cheese, garlic, mushrooms and thyme. Season well and stir in the grated lemon rind. Divide the mixture into 4 and spoon into the chicken breast pockets. Sew up the chicken neatly using string and a trussing needle.

Place the chicken breasts in a non-stick frying pan and pour over the wine. Add the bouquet garni and season well. Bring to the boil, then cover the pan and simmer for 20–25 minutes or until tender. Arrange the chicken on a hot serving dish and keep warm. Discard the bouquet garni and boil the juices for 5–10 minutes or until reduced by about half. Spoon the juices over the chicken and serve at once.

TOTAL CALORIES: 720
CALORIES PER SERVING: 180
SERVES 4

Herring with Mustard Sauce

Metric/Imperial
1 × 150 g/5 oz herring
150 ml/¼ pint White Sauce (page
    123)
1 tsp dry mustard
1 tsp wine vinegar

American
1 × 5 oz herring
⅔ cup white sauce (page 123)
1 tsp dry mustard
1 tsp wine vinegar

Place the herring under a preheated grill (broiler) and cook for 5–7 minutes on each side until the flesh is tender. Meanwhile, prepare the white sauce and stir in the mustard and vinegar. Serve the fish at once with the sauce.

TOTAL CALORIES: 365
SERVES 1

Hot Crab

Metric/Imperial
1 × 500 g/1 lb cooked crab, cleaned
2 spring onions, finely chopped
grated rind and juice of ½ lemon
pinch of cayenne pepper
salt
½ tbsp fresh brown breadcrumbs
½ tbsp freshly grated Parmesan
    cheese
fresh thyme and lemon wedges

American
1 × 1 lb cooked crab, cleaned
2 scallions, finely chopped
grated rind and juice of ½ lemon
pinch of cayenne
salt
½ tbsp soft fresh brown bread
    crumbs
½ tbsp freshly grated Parmesan
    cheese
fresh thyme and lemon wedges

Remove the crabmeat from the shell and reserve the shell. Flake the crabmeat in a bowl and add the spring onion (scallion), lemon rind and juice, cayenne and salt. Pile this mixture into the crab shell and sprinkle over the breadcrumbs and Parmesan cheese.

Place on a baking sheet and cook in a preheated moderate oven, 180°C (350°F) or Gas Mark 4, for 20 minutes until heated through and golden brown. Serve at once with fresh thyme and lemon wedges.

TOTAL CALORIES: 250
SERVES 1

Indian Chicken

This recipe needs to be prepared the day before.

Metric/Imperial
175 g/6 oz boneless chicken breast
lemon wedges and shredded lettuce
Marinade:
¼ tsp chilli powder
small piece root ginger, finely
    chopped
1 clove garlic, crushed
¼ tsp ground coriander
¼ tsp ground cumin
½ tsp paprika
4 tbsp plain yogurt
squeeze of lemon juice
½ tsp grated lemon rind

American

6 oz boneless chicken breast
lemon wedges and shredded lettuce

Marinade:

¼ tsp chili powder
small piece ginger root, minced
1 clove garlic, crushed
¼ tsp ground coriander
¼ tsp ground cumin
½ tsp paprika
4 tbsp plain yogurt
squeeze of lemon juice
½ tsp grated lemon rind

To make the marinade, mix the chilli powder, ginger, garlic, coriander, cumin, paprika, yogurt, lemon juice and rind in a bowl. Score the chicken on both sides and place in the marinade. Chill overnight.

Remove the chicken from the marinade and place on a piece of foil large enough to completely cover it. Place in a roasting tin (pan), spoon over the marinade and seal the foil. Bake in a preheated moderate oven, 180°C (350°F) or Gas Mark 4, for 30 minutes, basting occasionally. Open the foil and return the chicken to the oven for a further 5–7 minutes.

Remove the chicken, drain off the marinade and place on a serving plate. Serve at once with lemon wedges and shredded lettuce.

TOTAL CALORIES: 270
SERVES 1

Irish Stew

Metric/Imperial

250 g/8 oz lean lamb, diced
2 medium onions, sliced
250 g/8 oz potato, sliced
salt and freshly ground black pepper
300 ml/½ pint beef stock
4 tsp tomato purée
freshly chopped parsley

American

1 cup diced lean lamb
2 medium onions, sliced
1⅓ cups sliced potato
salt and freshly ground black pepper
1¼ cups beef stock
4 tsp tomato paste
freshly chopped parsley

Place the lamb, onion and potato in layers in a casserole dish with plenty of seasoning. Finish with a layer of potatoes. Mix the stock and tomato purée (paste) together and pour over the ingredients. Cover and cook in a preheated moderate oven, 180°C (350°F) or Gas Mark 4, for 1–1½ hours. Reduce the oven temperature to 150°C (300°F) or Gas Mark 2 and take the top off the casserole for the last 30 minutes to brown the potatoes. Serve sprinkled with chopped parsley.

TOTAL CALORIES: 770
CALORIES PER SERVING: 385
SERVES 2

Jacket Potatoes

1 × 175 g/6 oz potato, scrubbed

Fillings

1 Boursin cheese and chives: mix together 25 g/1 oz (2 tbsp) soft low fat cheese with herbs and garlic, 1 tbsp freshly chopped chives and a dash of Tabasco.

TOTAL CALORIES: 110

2 Cottage cheese, spring onion (scallion) and curry powder: mix together 50 g/2 oz (¼ cup) sieved cottage cheese, 2 finely chopped spring onions (scallions) and ¼ tsp curry powder.

TOTAL CALORIES: 80

3 Ham and sweetcorn (kernel corn): mix together 25 g/1 oz (2 tbsp) diced, cooked ham, 25 g/1 oz drained sweetcorn (kernel corn), 1 tsp grated onion and 1 tsp chopped parsley.

TOTAL CALORIES: 100

4 Prawn (shrimp) and tuna: mix together 25 g/1 oz drained and flaked tuna, 25 g/1 oz peeled prawns (shelled shrimp), 1 chopped spring onion (scallion) and 2 tsp finely chopped parsley.

TOTAL CALORIES: 115

Prick the potato and bake in a preheated moderately hot oven, 200°C (400°F) or Gas Mark 6, for about 1 hour, until soft.

Cut the potato in half lengthwise. Scoop out the flesh and mash until smooth. Add any of the above fillings to the potato and mix well. Spoon the mixture back into the potato shells. Place on a baking sheet and return to the oven for 12–15 minutes until hot. Serve at once.

TOTAL CALORIES PER 1 × 175 g/6 oz POTATO: 180 (plus filling)

From the front: Hot Crab, Green Fruit Salad, Jacket Potatoes

Kidneys in Red Wine

Metric/Imperial

1 tsp oil
1 small onion, chopped
1 small carrot, sliced
1 stick celery, sliced
6 lambs' kidneys, halved, skinned and cored
2 tsp tomato purée
300 ml/½ pint stock
4 tbsp red wine
salt and freshly ground black pepper
freshly chopped parsley

American

1 tsp oil
1 small onion, chopped
1 small carrot, sliced
1 celery stalk, sliced
6 lambs' kidneys, halved, skinned and cored
2 tsp tomato paste
1¼ cups stock
4 tbsp red wine
salt and freshly ground black pepper
freshly chopped parsley

Heat the oil in a heavy saucepan and gently cook the onion, carrot and celery for 10 minutes. Add the kidneys and cook until browned. Mix together the tomato purée (paste), stock and wine, pour over the kidneys and season well. Cover and simmer gently for 12–15 minutes. Remove the kidneys and keep warm. Boil the sauce rapidly until reduced and thickened. Add the kidneys and heat through. Adjust the seasoning and serve sprinkled with parsley.
TOTAL CALORIES: 340
CALORIES PER SERVING: 170
SERVES 2

Lamb Kebab

Metric/Imperial

2 small tomatoes
3 squares red or green pepper, blanched
75 g/3 oz marinated lamb, sliced
4 button onions or quarters of a large onion

American

2 small tomatoes
3 squares red or green pepper, blanched
3 oz marinated lamb, sliced
4 pearl onions or quarters of a large onion

Thread the tomatoes, pepper, lamb and onions alternately onto a skewer. Grill (broil) for 7–8 minutes each side, turning once, until all the ingredients are cooked and tender.
TOTAL CALORIES: 160
SERVES 1

Lamb Noisette with Garlic and Rosemary

Metric/Imperial

1 × 100 g/3½ oz lamb noisette, trimmed of all fat
1 clove garlic, thinly sliced
few sprigs fresh rosemary
½ tsp French mustard with herbs or coarse grain mustard
salt and freshly ground black pepper
juice of ½ lemon

American

1 × 3½ oz lamb noisette, trimmed of all fat
1 clove garlic, thinly sliced
few sprigs fresh rosemary
½ tsp Dijon-style mustard with herbs, or coarse grain mustard
salt and freshly ground black pepper
juice of ½ lemon

Make small incisions all over the lamb and insert the slices of garlic and a few sprigs of rosemary. Spread the mustard on both sides of the meat, season with a little salt and pepper, and sprinkle over the lemon juice.

Leave to marinate for about 30 minutes. Preheat the grill (broiler) and cook the lamb for 4–6 minutes each side or until cooked as preferred.
TOTAL CALORIES: 220
SERVES 1

Lamb with Apricot Stuffing

Metric/Imperial

1 × 1.5 kg/3½ lb leg of lamb, boned
thyme sprigs
parsley sprigs
Stuffing:
6 dried apricots, chopped
½ tsp thyme
2 tbsp freshly chopped parsley
50 g/2 oz walnuts, chopped
1 small onion, chopped
75 g/3 oz wholewheat breadcrumbs
salt and freshly ground black pepper
2 sticks celery, chopped
beaten egg, to bind

American

1 × 3½ lb leg of lamb, boned
thyme sprigs
parsley sprigs
Stuffing:
6 dried apricots, chopped
½ tsp thyme
2 tbsp freshly chopped parsley
½ cup chopped walnuts
1 small onion, chopped
1½ cups soft fresh wholewheat bread crumbs
salt and freshly ground black pepper
2 celery stalks, chopped
beaten egg, to bind

Clockwise: Lamb Kebab, Lentil Soup, Liver Provençal

Mix all the stuffing ingredients together using only just enough egg to bind. Fill the leg of lamb with the mixture and sew or tie firmly using a trussing needle and string. Place in a roasting pan and sprinkle with some thyme sprigs. Place in a preheated moderately hot oven, 200°C (400°F) or Gas Mark 6, for 1½–1¾ hours. Serve sliced, with parsley sprigs.
TOTAL CALORIES: 2350
CALORIES PER SERVING: 590
SERVES 4

Lasagne

Metric/Imperial

25 g/1 oz lasagne (about 2 sheets)
150 ml/¼ pint white sauce (page 123)
15 g/½ oz grated Parmesan cheese
Meat sauce:
200 g/7 oz lean minced beef
2 tomatoes, skinned and chopped
1 onion, chopped
2 tsp tomato purée
1 tsp mixed dried herbs
salt and freshly ground black pepper
150 ml/¼ pint beef stock

American

1 oz lasagne (about 2 sheets)
⅔ cup white sauce (page 123)
2 tbsp grated Parmesan cheese
Meat sauce:
1 cup lean ground beef
2 tomatoes, skinned and chopped
1 onion, chopped
2 tsp tomato paste
1 tsp mixed dried herbs
salt and freshly ground black pepper
⅔ cup beef stock

Put the beef, tomatoes and onion in a saucepan and cook gently for 5 minutes, stirring. Stir in the tomato purée (paste) to the beef mixture, then add the herbs, seasoning and stock. Simmer for 20 minutes. Meanwhile, cook the lasagne in boiling salted water, then drain well. Put a layer of lasagne in an ovenproof dish, cover with half the meat sauce and white sauce, then repeat the layers, finishing with the white sauce. Sprinkle over the Parmesan and place in a preheated moderate oven, 180°C (350°F) or Gas Mark 4, for 25–30 minutes, until browned and heated through.
TOTAL CALORIES: 700
CALORIES PER SERVING: 350
SERVES 2

Note: For a quicker recipe, buy lasagne that does not need pre-cooking and layer it as directed.

Leek and Potato Ramekins

Metric/Imperial

175 g/6 oz potato, roughly chopped
125 g/4 oz potato, diced
2 eggs
8 tbsp single cream
2 tbsp skimmed milk
125 g/4 oz leeks, thinly sliced, blanched and drained
freshly grated nutmeg

American

6 oz potato, roughly chopped
¼ lb potato, diced
2 eggs
8 tbsp light cream
2 tbsp skimmed milk
¼ lb leeks, thinly sliced, blanched and drained
freshly grated nutmeg

Boil the chopped potatoes, then drain and mash. Mix with the diced potato, eggs, cream and skimmed milk. Stir in the leeks, nutmeg and seasoning. Grease 4 ramekin dishes and spoon in the mixture. Bake in a preheated moderate oven, 180°F (350°F) Gas Mark 5, for 20–25 minutes until golden brown.

TOTAL CALORIES: 950
CALORIES PER SERVING: 240
SERVES 4

Leek and Thyme Quiche

Metric/Imperial
50 g/2 oz plain flour
50 g/2 oz wholemeal flour
pinch of salt
pinch of cayenne pepper
50 g/2 oz margarine
ice-cold water
Filling:
200 g/7 oz leeks, trimmed and thinly
    sliced
3 eggs
150 ml/¼ pint skimmed milk
50 g/2 oz Cheddar cheese, finely
    grated
salt and cayenne pepper
2 tsp freshly chopped thyme

American
½ cup all-purpose flour
½ cup wholewheat flour
pinch of salt
pinch of cayenne
¼ cup margarine
ice-cold water
Filling:
1½ cups thinly sliced leeks
3 eggs
⅔ cup skimmed milk
⅔ cup freshly grated Cheddar
    cheese
salt and cayenne
2 tsp freshly chopped thyme

Place the flours in a bowl with the salt and cayenne. Rub (cut) the margarine into the flour until the mixture resembles fine breadcrumbs. Stir in 2 teaspoons of cold water at a time until the dough is firm.

Lightly knead the pastry on a floured board. Roll out and use to line 4 individual tins (pans), 7.5 cm (3 in) in diameter. Chill for 20 minutes while making the filling.

Blanch the leeks in boiling salted water for 2 minutes, then drain and dry on kitchen paper towels. Mix the eggs, milk, cheese, salt, cayenne and thyme together. Divide the leeks into 4 portions and arrange in the bottom of the pastry cases (pie shells). Spoon over the egg mixture.

Bake in a preheated moderately hot oven, 200°C (400°F) or Gas Mark 6, for 20-25 minutes or until set and golden brown. Serve hot or cold.
TOTAL CALORIES: **1230**
CALORIES PER SERVING: **310**
SERVES **4**
✳*Note: If frozen, allow to thaw, then place in a moderate oven, 180°C (350°F) or Gas Mark 4, for 10–12 minutes until heated through. Do not re-freeze.*

Lentil Soup

Metric/Imperial
25 g/1 oz lentils, soaked overnight
1 onion, chopped
2 sticks celery, chopped
1 carrot, sliced
300 ml/½ pint stock
salt
grated nutmeg
freshly chopped parsley and mint

American
2 tbsp lentils, soaked overnight
1 onion, chopped
2 celery stalks, chopped
1 carrot, sliced
1¼ cups stock
salt
grated nutmeg
freshly chopped parsley and mint

Place the lentils, onion, celery, carrot and stock in a saucepan. Bring to the boil and simmer for 20–30 minutes or until the lentils are quite soft. Cool slightly, then purée in a blender. Season with salt and nutmeg, and adjust the consistency with a little more stock, if necessary. Serve sprinkled with parsley and mint.
TOTAL CALORIES: **130**
SERVES **1**

Liver Provençal

Metric/Imperial
200 g/7 oz calves' or lambs' liver
seasoned wholemeal flour
2 tsp oil
150 g/5 oz onion, chopped
200 g/7 oz tomatoes, skinned and
    chopped
½ tsp mixed dried herbs
salt and freshly ground black pepper

American
7 oz calf or lamb liver
seasoned wholewheat flour
2 tsp oil
1¼ cups chopped onion
¾ cup skinned and chopped
    tomatoes
½ tsp mixed dried herbs
salt and freshly ground black pepper

Cut the liver into thin strips and coat lightly in the seasoned flour. Heat the oil in a frying pan (skillet) and cook the onion gently for about 5 minutes until soft. Add the liver, tomatoes and herbs and season well. Simmer very gently for 5 minutes, taking care not to overcook the liver. Serve at once.
TOTAL CALORIES: **460**
CALORIES PER SERVING: **230**
SERVES **2**

Low Fat Dressing

Metric/Imperial
4 tbsp plain yogurt
2 tbsp sunflower seed oil
1 tbsp lemon juice
2 tbsp freshly chopped herbs
   (chervil, dill, chives, etc)
dash of Tabasco

American
4 tbsp plain yogurt
2 tbsp sunflower seed oil
1 tbsp lemon juice
2 tbsp freshly chopped herbs
   (chervil, dill, chives, etc)
dash of hot pepper sauce

Using a small whisk, beat the yogurt until smooth, then add the other ingredients and beat until well mixed. This can be served over any salad, either mixed green or *salades composés*.

TOTAL CALORIES: 50 per tbsp

Low Fat Gravy

This recipe may be used to serve with roasted meat, or when a dry frying pan is used to cook steaks and chops.

Metric/Imperial
sediment from the pan
150 ml/¼ pint dry white or red wine
pinch of mixed dried herbs
dash of Worcestershire sauce or
   Tabasco
salt and freshly ground black pepper

American
sediment from the pan
⅔ cup dry white or red wine
pinch of mixed dried herbs
dash of Worcestershire sauce or hot
   pepper sauce
salt and freshly ground black pepper

Drain any fat from the pan, or use a special fat-removing brush to do this. Place the pan over a low heat and cook until it becomes 'sticky'. Add the wine (use red wine for red meat and white wine for pork, veal and poultry), stirring constantly. Add a little Worcestershire sauce or Tabasco (hot pepper sauce) and seasoning. Serve at once.

TOTAL CALORIES: 100
CALORIES PER SERVING: 50
SERVES 2

Liver Stroganoff

Metric/Imperial
250 g/8 oz calves' liver
salt and freshly ground black pepper
2 tsp oil
50 g/2 oz onions, sliced
125 g/4 oz button mushrooms, sliced
3 tbsp sherry or dry white wine
5 tbsp soured cream
freshly chopped parsley

American
½ lb calf liver
salt and freshly ground black pepper
2 tsp oil
½ cup sliced onions
1 cup chopped button mushrooms
3 tbsp sherry or dry white wine
5 tbsp sour cream
freshly chopped parsley

Cut the liver into thin strips and season with salt and pepper. Heat the oil in a non-stick frying pan (skillet), add the onions and fry (sauté) until lightly browned. Add the liver, mushrooms and sherry or wine and simmer for 5 minutes. Season and stir in the soured cream and sprinkle with parsley just before serving.

TOTAL CALORIES: 630
CALORIES PER SERVING: 315
SERVES 2

Note: If freezing, omit the soured cream and parsley and add when reheated, just before serving.

Liver with Orange

Metric/Imperial
1 small onion, sliced
2 tsp butter
125 g/4 oz calves' or lambs' liver,
   thinly sliced
2 tsp flour
150 ml/¼ pint stock
salt and freshly ground black pepper
¼ tsp French mustard
1 tbsp red wine
2 slices of orange
25 g/1 oz brown rice, boiled in stock,
   to serve

American
1 small onion, sliced
2 tsp butter
¼ lb calf or lamb liver, thinly sliced
2 tsp flour
⅔ cup stock
salt and freshly ground black pepper
¼ tsp Dijon-style mustard
1 tbsp red wine
2 slices of orange
2 tbsp brown rice, boiled in stock, to
   serve

Place the onion and butter in a frying pan (skillet) and cook gently for 5 minutes until the onion is soft. Add the liver and cook for a further 7 minutes, turning once. Remove the liver and keep warm. Add the flour to the pan and cook for 1 minute, stirring. Stir in the stock and bring to the boil. Add seasoning with the mustard, red wine and orange slices. Simmer for 1 minute, then pour over the liver and serve with rice.

TOTAL CALORIES: 430
SERVES 1

Mediterranean Seafood Sauce

Metric/Imperial
100g/3½oz onion, finely chopped
150ml/¼ pint dry white wine
100g/3½oz tomatoes, skinned, seeded and chopped
1 or 2 cloves garlic, crushed
1 fresh bouquet garni (thyme, rosemary and parsley)
1 tsp French mustard
dash of Worcestershire sauce
pinch of cayenne pepper
100g/3½oz crabmeat
200g/7oz peeled prawns
100g/3½oz scallops, cleaned and quartered
salt and freshly ground black pepper
freshly chopped parsley

American
¾ cup minced onion
⅔ cup dry white wine
½ cup skinned, seeded and chopped tomatoes
1 or 2 cloves garlic, crushed
1 bouquet garni (thyme, rosemary and parsley)
1 tsp Dijon-style mustard
dash of Worcestershire sauce
pinch of cayenne
½ cup crab meat
1 generous cup shelled shrimp
3½oz scallops, cleaned and quartered
salt and freshly ground black pepper
freshly chopped parsley

Place the onion, wine, tomatoes, garlic, bouquet garni, mustard, Worcestershire sauce and cayenne into a saucepan. Bring to the boil and cook rapidly for 15-20 minutes, stirring occasionally, until thickened and reduced. Add the shellfish and seasoning, then simmer for 5 minutes. Serve sprinkled with parsley.

TOTAL CALORIES: 580
CALORIES PER SERVING: 145
SERVES 4

Melon, Pear and Cucumber Salad

Metric/Imperial
1 ripe ogen melon
1 ripe comice pear
¼ cucumber, diced
125g/4oz peeled prawns
Lemon Dressing (page 115)
salt and freshly ground black pepper
15g/½oz pinenuts, toasted
1 tbsp sesame seeds, toasted
2 whole prawns and lemon twists

American
1 small ripe honeyball melon
1 ripe comice pear
¼ cucumber, diced
½ cup shelled shrimp
Lemon Dressing (page 115)
salt and freshly ground black pepper
2 tbsp pine nuts, toasted
1 tbsp sesame seeds, toasted
2 whole shrimp and lemon twists

Halve the melon, remove seeds and scoop out the flesh. Peel, core and dice the pear and add to the melon flesh with the cucumber and prawns (shrimp). Add the dressing, seasoning and pinenuts and spoon into the shells. Garnish with sesame seeds, whole prawns (shrimp) and lemon.

TOTAL CALORIES: 390
CALORIES PER SERVING: 200
SERVES 2

Middle Eastern Rice

Metric/Imperial
25g/1oz butter
25g/1oz flaked almonds
25g/1oz cashew nuts
1 medium onion, thinly sliced
2 carrots, coarsely grated
175g/6oz brown rice
2 cloves garlic, thinly sliced
1 tsp ground cumin
1 tsp ground coriander
1 tsp turmeric
½ tsp ground cinnamon
¼ tsp ground cloves
salt and freshly ground black pepper
3 tbsp raisins
1 medium eating apple, peeled, cored and chopped
300ml/½ pint consommé, diluted to make 600ml/1 pint
150ml/¼ pint dry white wine
100g/3½oz frozen peas

American
2 tbsp butter
¼ cup flaked almonds
¼ cup cashew nuts
1 medium onion, thinly sliced
2 carrots, coarsely grated
¾ cup brown rice
2 cloves garlic, thinly sliced
1 tsp ground cumin
1 tsp ground coriander
1 tsp turmeric
½ tsp ground cinnamon
¼ tsp ground cloves
salt and freshly ground black pepper
3 tbsp raisins
1 medium eating apple, peeled, cored and chopped
1¼ cups consommé, diluted to make 2½ cups
⅔ cup dry white wine
½ cup frozen peas

Melt the butter in a large saucepan and fry (sauté) the nuts for 1-2 minutes until brown. Add the carrots, rice, garlic, spices and seasoning and fry for 2 minutes. Stir in the raisins, apple, consommé and wine, and simmer for 30–35 minutes. Add the peas and cook for 1 minute, then sprinkle with the nuts.

TOTAL CALORIES: 1380
CALORIES PER SERVING: 345
SERVES 4

Minestrone

Metric/Imperial
1 rasher streaky bacon, chopped
1 medium onion, chopped
75g/3oz green cabbage, chopped
2 tomatoes, skinned and chopped
2 tsp tomato purée
1 carrot, diced
150ml/¼ pint stock
salt and freshly ground black pepper
75g/3oz canned haricot beans, drained

American
1 slice bacon, chopped
1 medium onion, chopped
1 cup chopped green cabbage
2 tomatoes, skinned and chopped
2 tsp tomato paste
1 carrot, diced
⅔ cup stock
salt and freshly ground black pepper
3oz canned haricot beans, drained

Cook the bacon and onion in a heavy saucepan until the onion is soft. Add the cabbage, tomatoes, tomato purée (paste), carrot, stock and seasoning. Simmer for 20 minutes, then stir in the haricot beans. Adjust the seasoning before serving. Serve with 40g/1½oz (1 slice) wholewheat bread and 25g/1oz grated Edam cheese.

TOTAL CALORIES: 240
SERVES 1

Mixed Seafood Salad

Metric/Imperial
100g/3½oz scallops, cleaned
100g/3½oz peeled prawns
100g/3½oz crabmeat
25g/1oz button mushrooms, sliced
2 spring onions, chopped
grated rind and juice of 1 lime
2 tsp freshly chopped parsley
2 tsp freshly chopped thyme
1 clove garlic, crushed (optional)
salt and freshly ground black pepper
2 large Spanish tomatoes, each weighing 200g/7oz
few crisp lettuce leaves
2 whole prawns and lime slices

American
3½oz scallops, cleaned
½ cup shelled shrimp
½ cup crab meat
¼ cup sliced button mushrooms
2 scallions, chopped
grated rind and juice of 1 lime
2 tsp freshly chopped parsley
2 tsp freshly chopped thyme
1 clove garlic, crushed (optional)
salt and freshly ground black pepper
2 large tomatoes, each weighing 7oz
few crisp lettuce leaves
2 whole shrimp and lime slices

Wash the scallops and pat dry. Poach them in simmering water for 1–2 minutes until cooked and tender. Drain and cool.

Mix the scallops, prawns (shrimp) and crabmeat together; add the mushrooms, spring onions (scallions), lime juice and rind and mix well. Stir in the herbs, garlic (if using) and seasoning.

Cut the tomatoes in half, scoop out the seeds and carefully remove the flesh, leaving a little around the skin so that the tomato does not collapse. Chop up the tomato flesh and fold into the fish mixture. Pile the mixture into the four tomato shells.

Arrange the lettuce leaves on a serving dish and put the tomato shells on top. Spoon any remaining mixture around the tomatoes and serve with the whole prawns (shrimp) and slices of lime.

TOTAL CALORIES: 400
CALORIES PER SERVING: 200
SERVES 2

Orange and Pear Fruit Salad

Metric/Imperial
175g/6oz dried pears
150ml/¼ pint natural unsweetened orange juice
1 tbsp brandy
15g/½oz raisins
3 oranges, cut into segments
1 tbsp pistachio nuts

American
6oz dried pears
⅔ cup natural unsweetened orange juice
1 tbsp brandy
1½ tbsp raisins
3 oranges, cut into segments
1 tbsp pistachio nuts

Soak the pears in the orange juice and brandy for 2 hours. Transfer to a saucepan, bring to the boil, add the raisins and simmer, covered, for 20–25 minutes until the pears are tender. Leave to cool in a serving dish. Mix the orange segments and pistachios together, and spoon over the pears. Chill before serving.

TOTAL CALORIES: 500
CALORIES PER SERVING: 125
SERVES 4

Orange and Tomato Soup

Metric/Imperial
4 tomatoes, skinned and chopped
1 carrot, sliced
3 peppercorns
300 ml/½ pint stock
1 small onion, chopped
pinch of salt
1 rounded tsp arrowroot
juice of ½ orange
shredded orange rind

American
4 tomatoes, skinned and chopped
1 carrot, sliced
3 peppercorns
1¼ cups stock
1 small onion, chopped
pinch of salt
1 rounded tsp arrowroot
juice of ½ orange
shredded orange rind

Place the tomatoes, carrots, peppercorns, stock and seasoning in a saucepan and simmer for 30 minutes. Cool slightly, remove the peppercorns, then purée in a blender or rub through a sieve (strainer). Mix the arrowroot with 1 tablespoon of cold water and stir into the soup. Return to the clean saucepan and bring to the boil, stirring constantly. Add the orange juice and reheat. Garnish with shredded orange rind and serve with 40g/1½oz (1 slice) wholewheat bread.
TOTAL CALORIES: 100
SERVES 1

Oriental Red Mullet

Metric/Imperial
1 × 175g/6oz red mullet, gutted
2 spring onions, chopped
50g/2oz button mushrooms, thinly
  sliced
small piece root ginger, cut into
  julienne strips
1 tbsp soy sauce
lemon slices or wedges and fresh
  coriander leaves

American
1 × 6oz red mullet, cleaned
2 scallions, chopped
½ cup thinly sliced button
  mushrooms
small piece ginger root, cut into
  matchstick strips
1 tbsp soy sauce
lemon slices or wedges and fresh
  coriander leaves

Wash the fish and dry well. Mix the spring onions (scallions), mushrooms, ginger and soy sauce together. Place the fish in an ovenproof dish, spoon the mushroom mixture into the cavity of the fish and the remaining mixture around it. Cook in a preheated moderate oven, 180°C (350°F) or Gas Mark 4, for 12–15 minutes until tender. Serve, covered, with lemon and coriander.

TOTAL CALORIES: 220
SERVES 1
Note: If mullet is unavailable, use trout of the same weight. Total calories will then be 150.

Clockwise from the front: Oriental Red Mullet, Poached Salmon Steak, Peach and Orange Sorbet

Peach and Orange Sorbet

Metric/Imperial
75 g/3 oz sugar
250 ml/8 fl oz water
350 g/12 oz peaches, skinned and
  stones removed
3 tbsp unsweetened orange
1 egg white
1½ tbsp icing sugar

American
⅓ cup sugar
1 cup water
¾ lb peaches, skinned and pits
  removed
3 tbsp unsweetened orange juice
1 egg white
1½ tbsp confectioners' sugar

Dissolve the sugar in the water in a heavy-based saucepan over a low heat. Gradually bring to the boil and boil rapidly for 3 minutes, then allow to cool. Place the peaches in a blender with the sugar syrup and purée. Add to the orange juice and mix well. Pour the mixture into a plastic freezer container with lid. Freeze until the mixture is half frozen.

Whisk the egg white until stiff, then gradually whisk in the icing (confectioners') sugar. Then whisk in the semi-frozen peach and orange purée until smooth and combined. Pour the mixture back into the freezer container and freeze until set. When serving, spoon or scoop into bowls and serve at once.
TOTAL CALORIES: 670
CALORIES PER SERVING: 170
SERVES 4

Pepperoni

Metric/Imperial
2 tsp butter
½ small green pepper, cored, seeded
  and sliced
½ small red pepper, cored, seeded
  and sliced
1 small onion, sliced
½ clove garlic, crushed (optional)
salt and freshly ground black pepper

American
2 tsp butter
½ small green pepper, cored, seeded
  and sliced
½ small red pepper, cored, seeded
  and sliced
1 small onion, sliced
½ clove garlic, crushed (optional)
salt and freshly ground black pepper

Melt the butter in a small saucepan and add the peppers, onion and garlic (if using). Cook gently for about 15 minutes until soft. Season lightly.
TOTAL CALORIES: 120
SERVES 1

Piperade

Metric/Imperial
25 g/1 oz butter
4 spring onions, chopped
1 green pepper, seeded and sliced
1 red pepper, seeded and sliced
2 courgettes, sliced
1 clove garlic, crushed
100 g/3½ oz very lean rashers bacon,
  chopped
2 tomatoes, skinned, seeded and
  chopped
½ tsp mixed dried herbs
4 eggs, beaten
chopped parsley and chives

American
2 tbsp butter
4 scallions, chopped
1 green pepper, seeded and sliced
1 red pepper, seeded and sliced
2 zucchini, sliced
1 clove garlic, crushed
4 very lean bacon slices, chopped
2 tomatoes, skinned, seeded and
  chopped
½ tsp mixed dried herbs
4 eggs, beaten
chopped parsley and chives

Heat the butter in a non-stick frying pan and gently fry (sauté) the spring onions (scallions), green and red pepper for 2 minutes, stirring occasionally. Add the courgettes (zucchini) and garlic, then increase the heat, add the bacon, and cook for 2 minutes. Stir in the tomatoes and herbs and cook, uncovered, for 5 minutes. Stir in the eggs and cook until just scrambled. Pile onto a warmed serving dish. Sprinkle with the parsley and chives and serve at once.
TOTAL CALORIES: 750
CALORIES PER SERVING: 190
SERVES 4

Poached Salmon Steak

Metric/Imperial
few peppercorns
1 bay leaf
juice of ½ lemon
½ medium onion, sliced
½ carrot, sliced
1 × 150 g/5 oz salmon steak

American
few peppercorns
1 bay leaf
juice of ½ lemon
½ medium onion, sliced
½ carrot, sliced
1 × 5 oz salmon steak

Place the peppercorns, bay leaf, lemon juice, onion and carrot in a saucepan and add sufficient water to just cover the vegetables. Place the salmon on top, cover the pan and poach gently for 10–12 minutes until the flesh is cooked and tender. Drain the salmon, discarding the vegetables, and serve at once.
TOTAL CALORIES: 200
SERVES 1

Pork Casserole

Metric/Imperial
175 g/6 oz pork fillet, cubed
1 small onion, chopped
3 tsp tomato purée
2 tsp soy sauce
1 tsp sugar
200 ml/⅓ pint stock
salt and freshly ground black pepper
1 tsp cornflour

American
6 oz pork tenderloin, cubed
1 small onion, chopped
3 tsp tomato paste
2 tsp soy sauce
1 tsp sugar
⅞ cup stock
salt and freshly ground black pepper
1 tsp cornstarch

Place the pork, onion, tomato purée (paste), soy sauce, sugar, stock and seasoning in a saucepan. Stir well, bring to the boil and simmer for about 45 minutes or until the meat is tender. Mix the cornflour (cornstarch) with a little water and stir into the casserole. Bring to the boil, stirring, and adjust the seasoning.
TOTAL CALORIES: 460
CALORIES PER SERVING: 230
SERVES 2

Pork Chop with Cider

Metric/Imperial
1 small onion, sliced
1 × 175 g/6 oz pork chop, trimmed of
  all fat
150 ml/¼ pint stock
150 ml/¼ pint dry cider
salt and freshly ground black pepper
50 g/2 oz cooking apple, sliced
freshly chopped parsley

American
1 small onion, sliced
1 × 6 oz centre cut pork chop,
  trimmed of all fat
⅔ cup stock
⅔ cup hard cider
salt and freshly ground black pepper
½ cup sliced apple
freshly chopped parsley

Put the onion in a small flameproof casserole and place the chop on top. Add the stock, cider and seasoning. Cover and place in a preheated moderately hot oven, 190°C (375°F) or Gas Mark 5, for about 1 hour.

Remove the chop to a serving dish and keep warm. Place the casserole on top of the stove, add the apple and bring to the boil, stirring. Adjust the seasoning and simmer for 15 minutes until the sauce is thickened and reduced. Spoon the sauce over the chop and serve sprinkled with parsley.
TOTAL CALORIES: 500
SERVES 1

Pork Curry

Metric/Imperial
1 tbsp oil
100 g/3½ oz onions, sliced
1½ tsp ground coriander
½ tsp ground turmeric
1 tsp ground cumin
¼ tsp ground ginger
½–1 tsp chilli powder
500 g/1 lb very lean pork fillet, diced
small piece root ginger, finely
  chopped
2–3 cloves garlic, crushed
1 × 397 g/14 oz can tomatoes
salt and freshly ground black pepper
1 tbsp freshly grated coconut

American
1 tbsp oil
¾ cup sliced onions
1½ tsp ground coriander
½ tsp ground turmeric
1 tsp ground cumin
¼ tsp ground ginger
½–1 tsp chili powder
1 lb very lean pork tenderloin, diced
small piece ginger root, minced
2–3 cloves garlic, crushed
1 can (16 oz) tomatoes
salt and freshly ground black pepper
1 tbsp freshly grated coconut

Heat the oil in a pan, add the onions and fry (sauté) until lightly browned. Add the spices and cook for a further 2 minutes. Add the pork and brown on all sides (do not allow the onion and spices to burn). Pour off any excess fat, then add the ginger, garlic, tomatoes with their juice and season well. Bring to the boil, cover and simmer for 30 minutes. Sprinkle over the coconut and simmer, uncovered, for a further 30 minutes, stirring occasionally, until the meat is tender and the sauce thickened. Serve immediately.
TOTAL CALORIES: 1280
CALORIES PER SERVING: 320
SERVES 4

resembles fine breadcrumbs. Then add just enough milk to mix into a soft dough. Knead well until thoroughly mixed. Flatten into 2 rounds about 13 cm (5 in) in diameter and place on a greased baking sheet. Season.

Top with remaining ingredients finishing with cheese. Bake in a preheated hot oven, 220°C (425°F) or Gas Mark 7, for 15–20 minutes.

TOTAL CALORIES: 900

CALORIES PER SERVING: 450

SERVES 2

Ratatouille

Metric/Imperial
1 courgette, sliced
2 tomatoes, skinned, seeded and chopped
½ small onion, sliced
¼ small aubergine, sliced
150 ml/¼ pint stock or tomato juice
½ clove garlic, crushed
salt and freshly ground black pepper

American
1 zucchini, sliced
2 tomatoes, skinned, seeded and chopped
½ small onion, sliced
¼ small egg plant, sliced
⅔ cup stock or tomato juice
½ clove garlic, crushed
salt and freshly ground black pepper

Put all the ingredients in a saucepan and season well. Bring to the boil, stirring occasionally, for 15–20 minutes until the vegetables are soft and the liquid reduced.

TOTAL CALORIES: 35

SERVES 1

Ratatouille Pies

Metric/Imperial
50 g/2 oz wholemeal flour
50 g/2 oz plain flour
pinch of salt
ice-cold water
Filling:
15 g/½ oz butter
1 medium onion, thinly sliced
1 small aubergine, diced
1 courgette, thinly sliced
2 tomatoes, skinned, seeded and chopped
1 tbsp tomato purée
salt and freshly ground black pepper
2 tsp coriander seeds

American
½ cup wholewheat flour
½ cup all-purpose flour
pinch of salt
ice-cold water

Pork Fillet with Prunes

Metric/Imperial
150 g/5 oz pork fillet
salt and freshly ground black pepper
5 prunes, soaked and stoned
150 ml/¼ pint dry white wine

American
5 oz pork tenderloin
salt and freshly ground black pepper
5 prunes, soaked and pitted
⅔ cup dry white wine

Cut a pocket in the pork, sprinkle with salt and pepper and fill with the prunes. Tie up securely with string and place on a rack in a roasting pan with the wine. Roast in a preheated moderately hot oven, 190°C (375°F) or Gas Mark 5, for about 35 minutes, basting occasionally with the wine. When cooked, remove the meat from the pan, remove string, and keep warm. Strain the juices into a saucepan and bring to the boil, stirring. Continue boiling until reduced by half. Pour the juices over the meat and serve immediately.

TOTAL CALORIES: 305

SERVES 1

Front: Ratatouille
Back: Quick Pizza

Potato, Carrot and Onion Soup

Metric/Imperial
110 g/4 oz potato, sliced
½ onion, chopped
1 carrot, diced
1 leek, sliced
150 ml/¼ pint skimmed milk
salt and freshly ground black pepper

American
¼ lb potato, sliced
½ onion, chopped
1 carrot, diced
1 leek, sliced
⅔ cup skimmed milk
salt and freshly ground black pepper

Place all the ingredients in a saucepan, bring to the boil and simmer for 30 minutes. Cool slightly, then purée the soup in a blender or press through a sieve (strainer). Reheat in the clean saucepan and serve with 75 g/3 oz French bread.

TOTAL CALORIES: 175

SERVES 1

Quick Pizza

Metric/Imperial
Pizza Base:
125 g/4 oz self-raising flour
pinch bicarbonate of soda
25 g/1 oz butter
4–5 tbsp skimmed milk
Topping:
salt and freshly ground black pepper
50 g/2 oz cooked peas
4 tomatoes, sliced
75 g/3 oz mushrooms, sliced
50 g/2 oz feta cheese, crumbled

American
Pizza Base:
1 cup self-rising flour
pinch of baking soda
2 tbsp butter
4–5 tbsp skimmed milk
Topping:
salt and freshly ground black pepper
½ cup cooked peas
4 sliced tomatoes
1 cup sliced mushrooms
¼ cup feta cheese, crumbled

First make the base: sift the flour and soda into a large mixing bowl. Rub (cut) in the butter until the mixture

Filling:
1 tbsp butter
1 medium onion, thinly sliced
1 small eggplant, diced
1 zucchini, thinly sliced
2 tomatoes, skinned, seeded and
*   chopped*
½ green pepper, seeded and
*   chopped*
1 tbsp tomato paste
salt and freshly ground black pepper
2 tsp coriander seeds

Place the flours in a bowl and mix together with the salt. Add 2 tsp cold water at a time to give a firm dough. Knead lightly. Roll out and use to line 4 × 7.5 cm (3 in) individual flan tins (pie pans). Prick the bottoms and chill for 30 minutes.

Melt the butter in a saucepan, add the onion and aubergine (eggplant) and cook gently for 10 minutes. Stir in the courgette (zucchini), tomatoes, pepper and tomato purée (paste). Add seasoning and the coriander seeds. Bring to the boil, cover and simmer for 2 minutes.

Line the pastry cases (pie shells) with foil or greaseproof (waxed) paper and beans and bake in a preheated moderately hot oven, 200°C (400°F) or Gas Mark 6, for 12–15 minutes until golden brown. Remove the foil or paper and cook for a further 2–3 minutes. Spoon in the filling and serve hot or cold.
TOTAL CALORIES: 580
CALORIES PER SERVING: 145
SERVES 4

Red Cabbage with Apple

Metric/Imperial
75 g/3 oz apple, sliced
75 g/3 oz red cabbage, sliced
50 g/2 oz onion, chopped
15 g/½ oz raisins
¼ tsp freshly grated nutmeg
2 tsp cider or wine vinegar
salt and freshly ground black pepper

American
3 oz apple, sliced
3 oz red cabbage, sliced
2 oz onion, chopped
½ oz raisins
¼ tsp freshly grated nutmeg
2 tsp cider or wine vinegar
salt and freshly ground black pepper

Arrange the apple slices, cabbage, onion and raisins in layers in a small ovenproof dish, sprinkling with nutmeg and vinegar, and seasoning to taste. Place in a moderate oven, 180°C (350°F) or Gas Mark 4, and bake for 1 hour. Adjust the seasoning before serving.
TOTAL CALORIES: 90
SERVES 1

Red Fruit Salad

Metric/Imperial
125 g/4 oz redcurrants
25 g/1 oz thin honey
grated rind of 1 lemon
250 g/8 oz strawberries
250 g/8 oz raspberries
50 g/2 oz cherries, stoned and halved

American
1 cup redcurrants
1½ tbsp thin honey
grated rind of 1 lemon
1½ cups strawberries
1½ cups raspberries
½ cup cherries, pitted and halved

Place the redcurrants in a saucepan with the honey and lemon rind. Stew for 3–4 minutes until tender. Cool, then rub through a strainer.

Halve the strawberries, if large, and put into a bowl with the raspberries and cherries. Pour over the redcurrant sauce, mix and chill.
TOTAL CALORIES: 240
CALORIES PER SERVING: 60
SERVES 4

Salad Dressings

Avocado Salad Cream
Place ½ avocado in a blender with 2 roughly chopped spring onions (scallions), juice of ½ lemon, a pinch of ground ginger, 15 g/½ oz (¼ cup) skimmed milk powder, 5 tbsp (⅓ cup) warm water, a dash of Tabasco (hot pepper sauce) and salt and freshly ground black pepper. Blend until smooth. Add a little cold water if the dressing is too thick. Use at once, as avocado discolours.
TOTAL CALORIES: 250

Blue Cheese Dressing
Chop 100 g/3½ oz (about ½ cup) blue brie cheese and place in a blender with 2 tbsp plain yogurt. Add freshly ground black pepper, a dash of Tabasco (hot pepper sauce) and 1 tbsp chives and blend until smooth. Store in the refrigerator for up to 1 week.
TOTAL CALORIES: 325

Cottage Cheese and Chive Dressing
Sieve (strain) 50 g/2 oz (¼ cup) cottage cheese. Stir in the juice of 1 lemon, 1 crushed clove garlic, a pinch of cayenne pepper, salt and 2–3 tbsp warm water. Mix until smooth. Store in the refrigerator for up to 1 week.
TOTAL CALORIES: 65

Cucumber and Yogurt Dressing
Put 175 g/6 oz (1½ cups) roughly chopped cucumber into a blender with 150 ml/¼ pint (⅔ cup) plain yogurt. Add 5 tbsp (⅓ cup) warm water, the juice and grated rind of 1 lemon, 1 crushed clove garlic, a bunch of mint leaves and salt and freshly ground black pepper. Blend until smooth. Store in the refrigerator for a few days.
TOTAL CALORIES: 100

Egg and Caper Dressing
Place a roughly chopped hard-boiled egg in a blender with ¼ tsp French (Dijon-style) mustard, 1 clove garlic, 2 tsp lemon juice and 1 tbsp capers. Gradually add 2 tbsp olive oil, drop by drop, and blend until smooth. Store in the refrigerator for up to about 1 week.
TOTAL CALORIES: 325

Egg Dressing
Remove the shell from 1 hard-boiled egg while it is still warm. Put the egg into a blender with 3 tbsp plain yogurt, ½ tsp French (Dijon-style) mustard, 1 crushed clove garlic, dash of Worcestershire sauce, a small bunch of parsley and salt and freshly ground black pepper. Blend until smooth and use at once as this dressing will not keep.
TOTAL CALORIES: 125

French Dressing
Mix together 2 tbsp lemon juice and 4 tbsp olive oil (preferably green) or walnut oil in a bowl. Add ½–1 tsp thin honey, ¼ tsp mixed dried herbs, ¼ tsp French (Dijon-style) mustard and salt and freshly ground black pepper. Mix well and store in the refrigerator.
TOTAL CALORIES: 600

Herb Dressing
Place 200 ml/½ pint (⅞ cup) plain yogurt in a bowl and add 1 crushed clove garlic, a dash of Worcestershire sauce, salt and freshly ground black pepper and 1 tbsp each of freshly chopped parsley, mint, chives and thyme. Stir in 2 tsp grated lemon rind and 1 tsp lemon juice. Store tightly covered in the refrigerator.
TOTAL CALORIES: 105

Lemon and Mustard Dressing
Grate the rind from a medium-sized lemon and squeeze the juice. Mix the juice and rind with 1 tsp French (Dijon-style) mustard and stir in 1 tsp each of freshly chopped parsley, chives and thyme. Mix thoroughly. Store in the refrigerator for up to 2 weeks.
TOTAL CALORIES: 20

Lemon and Tarragon Dressing
Place 2 tbsp lemon juice in a bowl, stir in ½ tsp thin honey, 1 tbsp finely chopped tarragon and ½ tsp grated lemon rind. Season with salt and freshly ground black pepper. Use at once.
TOTAL CALORIES: 30

Thousand Island Dressing
Place a roughly chopped hard-boiled egg in a blender with ½ canned pimento, 4 stuffed olives, 1 roughly chopped shallot, a squeeze of lemon juice and 7 tbsp plain yogurt. Season with salt and freshly ground black pepper and blend until smooth. Store in the refrigerator for 1 week.
TOTAL CALORIES: 155

Tomato Dressing
Place 150 ml/¼ pint (⅔ cup) tomato juice into a screw-topped jar with 1 crushed clove garlic (or 1 tbsp minced onion), a dash of Worcestershire sauce and ½ tsp grain mustard. Add salt and freshly ground black pepper and shake well. Store in the refrigerator and use within 3–4 days.
TOTAL CALORIES: 30

Scampi Provençal

Metric/Imperial
150 ml/¼ pint water
1 slice of onion
few peppercorns
2 tbsp dry white wine
250 g/8 oz fresh scampi
1 onion, chopped
1 clove garlic, crushed
2 tsp tomato purée
2 tomatoes, chopped
75 g/3 oz mushrooms, sliced

American
⅔ cup water
1 slice of onion
few peppercorns
2 tbsp dry white wine
½ lb jumbo shrimp
1 onion, chopped
1 clove garlic, crushed
2 tsp tomato paste
2 tomatoes, chopped
¾ cup sliced mushrooms

Put the water, onion slice, peppercorns and white wine in a saucepan, add the scampi (shrimp) and poach for 5–10 minutes. Drain, reserving the stock, and keep the scampi (shrimp) warm.

Place the chopped onion, garlic, tomato purée (paste), tomatoes and 150 ml/¼ pint (⅔ cup) of the reserved stock in a saucepan. Bring to the boil, then simmer for a few minutes until slightly thickened. Stir the scampi (shrimp) into the sauce with the mushrooms and cook for a further 1 minute. Adjust the seasoning and serve.
TOTAL CALORIES: 350
CALORIES PER SERVING: 175
SERVES 2

Skewered Chicken

This recipe needs to be made the day before.

Metric/Imperial
175 g/6 oz boneless chicken breast
1 tsp French mustard with herbs
1 tsp freshly chopped thyme
grated rind and juice of 2 limes or
    1 lemon
6 sage leaves
lime wedges

American
6 oz boneless chicken breast
1 tsp Dijon-style mustard with herbs
1 tsp freshly chopped thyme
grated rind and juice of 2 limes or
    1 lemon
6 sage leaves
lime wedges

Cut the chicken into cubes. Place the mustard, thyme, lime or lemon juice and rind in a bowl. Add the chicken and toss well until it is coated with the marinade. Chill overnight.

Thread the chicken and sage leaves alternately onto a skewer. Place under a preheated grill (broiler) for 10-12 minutes, turning occasionally and basting. Serve at once with lime wedges.

TOTAL CALORIES: 230
SERVES 1

Smoked Haddock Roulade

Metric/Imperial
4 eggs, separated
salt
pinch of cayenne pepper
pinch of grated nutmeg
Filling:
175 g/6 oz fresh smoked haddock
175 g/6 oz cottage cheese, sieved
2 tbsp freshly chopped chives
grated rind of ½ lemon
1 tbsp freshly grated Parmesan
    cheese

American
4 eggs, separated
salt
pinch of cayenne
pinch of grated nutmeg
Filling:
6 oz fresh smoked haddock
¾ cup strained cottage cheese
2 tbsp freshly chopped chives
grated rind of ½ lemon
1 tbsp freshly grated Parmesan
    cheese

Place the egg yolks, salt, cayenne and nutmeg in a bowl and mix well. Whisk the egg whites until stiff, then carefully fold them into the yolk mixture. Spread evenly in a lined and greased 30 × 20 cm (12 × 8 in) Swiss roll tin (jelly roll pan). Bake in a preheated moderately hot oven, 200°C (400°F) or Gas Mark 6, for 10-15 minutes until well risen and brown.

Meanwhile, make the filling. Poach the haddock in water for 8–10 minutes, drain well and remove the skin and bones. Flake the fish and add the cottage cheese, chives and lemon rind. Heat together in a saucepan, stirring for 2–3 minutes.

Turn the roulade onto a piece of waxed paper sprinkled with the Parmesan cheese. Carefully peel off the lining paper, spread with the filling and roll up like a Swiss (jelly) roll. Serve immediately.

TOTAL CALORIES: 740
CALORIES PER SERVING: 185
SERVES 4

Smoked Salmon Quiche

Metric/Imperial
50 g/2 oz plain flour
50 g/2 oz wholemeal flour
pinch of salt
pinch of cayenne pepper
50 g/2 oz margarine
ice-cold water
Filling:
3 eggs
150 ml/¼ pint skimmed milk
100 g/3½ oz cottage cheese, sieved
2 tbsp freshly chopped chives
salt and freshly ground black pepper
½ tsp grated lemon rind
150 g/5 oz smoked salmon

American
½ cup all-purpose flour
½ cup wholewheat flour
pinch of salt
pinch of cayenne
¼ cup margarine
ice-cold water
Filling:
3 eggs
⅔ cup skimmed milk
½ cup strained cottage cheese
2 tbsp freshly chopped chives
salt and freshly ground black pepper
½ tsp grated lemon rind
5 oz smoked salmon

Place the flours in a bowl and add the salt and cayenne. Rub (cut) the margarine into the flour until the mixture resembles fine breadcrumbs. Stir in 2 teaspoons of water at a time, until the dough is firm. Lightly knead the dough on a floured board, roll out and use to line 4 individual tins (pans), 7.5 cm (3 in) in diameter. Chill for 20 minutes.

Beat the eggs, milk and cottage cheese together. Add the chives, seasoning and lemon rind. Roughly chop the smoked salmon and arrange in the bottom of the pastry cases (pie shells). Spoon over the egg and cheese mixture.

Bake in a preheated moderately hot oven, 200°C (400°F) or Gas Mark 6, for 20–25 minutes until set and golden brown. Serve hot or cold.

TOTAL CALORIES: 920
CALORIES PER SERVING: 230
SERVES 4

Note: If frozen, allow to thaw, then place in a moderate oven, 180°C (350°F) or Gas Mark 4, for 10–12 minutes until heated through. Do not re-freeze.

Smoked Trout and Bean Salad

Metric/Imperial
200 g/7 oz canned red kidney beans,
    drained
250 g/8 oz smoked trout fillets
50 g/2 oz leek, thinly sliced
50 g/2 oz cauliflower florets
15 g/½ oz shelled pistachio nuts
25 g/1 oz cucumber, diced
half quantity Cottage Cheese and
    Chive Dressing (page 115)
crisp lettuce leaves
small bunch watercress

American
7 oz canned red kidney beans,
    drained
½ lb smoked trout fillet
½ cup thinly sliced leek
½ cup cauliflower florets
1 tbsp shelled pistachio nuts
¼ cup diced cucumber
half quantity Cottage Cheese and
    Chive Dressing (page 115)
crisp lettuce leaves
small bunch watercress

Wash the kidney beans in a colander and drain well. Flake the smoked trout and put into a bowl with the beans, leek, cauliflower, pistachios and cucumber. Spoon over the dressing and mix well. Arrange the lettuce and watercress in a bowl and spoon the salad into the centre.

TOTAL CALORIES: 680
CALORIES PER SERVING: 340
SERVES 2

Sole Florentine

Metric/Imperial
175 g/6 oz lemon sole fillets, rolled up
120 ml/4 fl oz dry white wine
1 bouquet garni
175 g/6 oz fresh spinach
salt and freshly ground black pepper
freshly grated nutmeg
2 tbsp plain yogurt

American
6 oz sole fillets, rolled up
½ cup dry white wine
1 bouquet garni
6 oz fresh spinach
salt and freshly ground black pepper
freshly grated nutmet
2 tbsp plain yogurt

Place the sole in a non-stick saucepan with the wine and bouquet garni and poach for 2–3 minutes until tender. Drain and keep hot. Cook the spinach in the water left on the leaves after washing. Drain well and season with salt, pepper and a little nutmeg. Return to the clean pan and heat through, then remove from the heat and stir in the yogurt. Serve the sole on a bed of sauce.

TOTAL CALORIES: 320
SERVES 1

Sole with Herbs and Wine

Metric/Imperial
2 × 150 g/5 oz lemon or Dover sole
  fillets
1 tbsp freshly chopped dill
1 tbsp freshly chopped parsley
1 tsp freshly chopped lemon thyme
grated rind of ½ lemon
5 tbsp dry white wine
salt and freshly ground black pepper
750 g/1½ lb chopped cooked
  spinach

American
2 × 5 oz sole fillets
1 tbsp freshly chopped dill
1 tbsp freshly chopped parsley
1 tsp freshly chopped lemon thyme

grated rind of ½ lemon
5 tbsp dry white wine
salt and freshly ground black pepper
3 cups chopped cooked spinach

Put the fish into a large ovenproof dish. Sprinkle with the herbs and lemon rind and spoon over the wine. Season well and leave to marinate for 1 hour.

Cook in a preheated moderate oven, 180°C (350°F) or Gas Mark 4, for 12–15 minutes or until the fish is tender. Serve at once on a bed or chopped cooked spinach.
TOTAL CALORIES: 540
CALORIES PER SERVING: 270
SERVES 2

Sole with Lemon and Prawns

Metric/Imperial
150 g/5 oz lemon or Dover sole fillets
25 g/1 oz peeled prawns
grated rind and juice of ½ lemon
2 tsp freshly chopped parsley
1 tsp freshly chopped chives
salt and freshly ground black pepper

American
5 oz sole fillets
2 tbsp shelled shrimp
grated rind and juice of ½ lemon
2 tsp freshly chopped parsley
1 tsp freshly chopped chives
salt and freshly ground black pepper

Place the sole fillets on a board. Divide the prawns (shrimp) into 2 portions and arrange down the centre of each fillet. Sprinkle over the lemon rind and herbs, and season well. Roll up the fish and place in an ovenproof dish. Pour over the lemon juice and cover with foil. Place in a preheated moderately hot oven, 190°C (375°F) or Gas Mark 5, for 10–15 minutes until the fish is tender and flakes easily. Serve at once.
TOTAL CALORIES: 160
SERVES 1

Soufflé Cheese Omelette

Metric/Imperial
2 eggs, separated
1 tbsp cold water
25 g/1 oz hard cheese, grated
pinch of mixed dried herbs
salt and freshly ground black pepper

American
2 eggs, separated
1 tbsp cold water
¼ cup grated hard cheese
pinch of mixed dried herbs
salt and freshly ground black pepper

Place the egg yolks and water in a bowl and mix well. Stir in the cheese, herbs and seasoning. Whisk the egg whites until stiff and fold into the yolk mixture. Heat an 18–20 cm (7–8 in) non-stick omelette pan, pour in the egg mixture and cook over a low heat until the mixture is almost set and the underneath is light golden brown. Place the pan under a preheated hot grill (broiler) for about a minute to cook the top. Fold the omelette in half, slide onto a warmed plate and serve immediately.
TOTAL CALORIES: 250
SERVES 1

Clockwise from the front: Smoked Salmon Quiche, Smoked Trout and Bean Salad, Skewered Chicken

Spinach and Cottage Cheese Quiche

Metric/Imperial
50 g/2 oz plain flour
50 g/2 oz wholemeal flour
pinch of salt
pinch of cayenne pepper
50 g/2 oz margarine
ice-cold water
Filling:
2 eggs
150 ml/¼ pint skimmed milk
2 spring onions, chopped
100 g/3½ oz cottage cheese, sieved
50 g/2 oz Camembert cheese, finely
  chopped
pinch of cayenne pepper
1 tsp freshly chopped parsley
100 g/3½ oz cooked spinach,
  drained and finely chopped

American
½ cup all-purpose flour
½ cup wholewheat flour
pinch of salt
pinch of cayenne
¼ cup margarine
ice-cold water
Filling:
2 eggs
⅔ cup skimmed milk
2 scallions, chopped
½ cup strained cottage cheese
½ cup finely chopped Camembert
  cheese
pinch of cayenne
1 tsp freshly chopped parsley
½ cup cooked and finely chopped
  spinach

Place the flours in a bowl and add the salt and cayenne. Rub (cut) the margarine into the flour until the mixture resembles fine breadcrumbs. Stir in 2 teaspoons of water at a time until the dough is firm.

Lightly knead the dough on a floured board. Roll it out and use to line 4 individual tins (pans), 7.5 cm (3 in) in diameter. Chill for 20 minutes while making the filling.

Mix together the eggs, milk, spring onion (scallion), cheeses, cayenne, parsley and spinach. Spoon the mixture into the pastry cases (pie shells). Bake in a preheated moderately hot oven, 190°C (375°F) or Gas Mark 5, for 20–25 minutes until set and golden brown. Serve hot or cold.
TOTAL CALORIES: 800
CALORIES PER SERVING: 200
SERVES 4

Note: If frozen, allow to thaw, then place in a moderate oven, 180°C (350°F) or Gas Mark 4, for 10–12 minutes until heated through. Do not re-freeze.

Spinach Roulade

Metric/Imperial
300 g/10 oz fresh spinach
4 eggs, separated
salt
pinch of cayenne pepper
pinch of grated nutmeg
Filling:
100 g/3½ oz low fat cream cheese
   with herbs and garlic
25 g/1 oz mature Cheddar cheese,
   grated

American
10 oz fresh spinach
4 eggs, separated
salt
pinch of cayenne
pinch of grated nutmeg
Filling:
½ cup low fat cream cheese with
   herbs and garlic
¼ cup grated sharp Cheddar cheese

Steam the spinach for 3 minutes, drain well and chop finely.

Place half the spinach in a bowl and mix with the egg yolks, salt, cayenne and nutmeg. Whisk the egg whites until very stiff and fold into the spinach mixture. Spread the mixture evenly in a lined and greased 30 × 20 cm (12 × 8 in) Swiss roll tin (jelly roll pan). Bake in a preheated moderately hot oven, 200°C (400°F) or Gas Mark 6, for 10–15 minutes.

Meanwhile put the remaining spinach, cream cheese and grated cheese into a small pan. Heat through until the cheese has melted and the mixture is hot. Season with salt and cayenne.

Turn the roulade onto a piece of waxed paper and carefully peel off the paper. Spread with the filling and roll up like a Swiss (jelly) roll. Serve immediately.
TOTAL CALORIES: 680 (980)
CALORIES PER SERVING: 170(245)
SERVES 4

Spinach Soufflé

Metric/Imperial
25 g/1 oz butter
50 g/2 oz wholemeal flour
300 ml/½ pint skimmed milk
pinch of mixed dried herbs
salt and cayenne pepper
¼ tsp dry mustard
3 eggs, separated
100 g/3½ oz fresh spinach,
   blanched, drained and finely
   chopped
100 g/3½ oz mature Cheddar
   cheese, grated

American
2 tbsp butter
½ cup wholewheat flour
1¼ cups skimmed milk
pinch of mixed dried herbs
salt and cayenne
¼ tsp dry mustard
3 eggs, separated
½ cup blanched, drained and
   chopped fresh spinach
¾ cup grated sharp Cheddar cheese

Melt the butter in a saucepan, stir in the flour and cook for 1 minute. Gradually stir in the milk; bring to the boil, stirring constantly, and cook for 2 minutes. Add the herbs, salt, cayenne and mustard. Stir until mixed together, then remove from the heat and quickly mix in the egg yolks, spinach and cheese.

Whisk the egg whites until very stiff. Fold into the spinach mixture and divide between 4 individual, greased, soufflé dishes. Bake in a preheated moderately hot oven, 190°C (375°F) or Gas Mark 5, for 20–25 minutes. Serve immediately.
TOTAL CALORIES: 1100
CALORIES PER SERVING: 275
SERVES 4

Steak and Kidney Casserole

Metric/Imperial
250 g/8 oz lean stewing steak, cubed
2 lamb's kidneys, halved, cored and
   diced
1 medium onion, chopped
200 g/7 oz tomatoes, chopped
150 ml/¼ pint beef stock
salt and freshly ground black pepper
2 tsp cornflour
1 tbsp water

American
½ lb lean stewing steak, cubed
2 lamb kidneys, halved, cored and
   diced
1 medium onion, chopped
¾ cup chopped tomatoes
⅔ cup beef stock
salt and freshly ground black pepper
2 tsp cornstarch
1 tbsp water

Put the steak, kidneys, onion, tomatoes and stock into a small flameproof casserole dish. Season and cook in a preheated moderate oven, 180°C (350°F) or Gas Mark 4, for about 1½ hours or until meat is tender. Mix the cornflour (cornstarch) with the water, add a little hot stock and stir into the casserole. Place the casserole on top of the stove, bring to the boil, stirring, and cook for a further 2 minutes. Adjust the seasoning and serve.
TOTAL CALORIES: 610
CALORIES PER SERVING: 305
SERVES 2

Strawberry Sorbet

Metric/Imperial
75 g/3 oz sugar
250 ml/8 fl oz water
grated rind of 1 lemon
2 tsp lemon juice
300 g/10 oz strawberries, puréed
1 egg white
1½ tbsp icing sugar

American
⅓ cup sugar
1 cup water
grated rind of 1 lemon
2 tsp lemon juice
2 cups strawberries, puréed
1 egg white
1½ tbsp confectioners' sugar

Dissolve the sugar in the water in a heavy-based saucepan over a low heat. Gradually bring to the boil and boil rapidly for 3 minutes, then allow to cool. Add the lemon rind and juice and strawberries. Mix well and pour into a plastic freezer container with a lid. Freeze until half frozen.

Whisk the egg white until stiff, then gradually whisk in the icing (confectioners') sugar. Then whisk in the semi-frozen strawberry purée until smooth and combined. Pour the mixture into a freezer container and freeze until set. When serving, scoop into bowls and serve at once.
Note: It is best to remove the sorbet from the freezer 30 minutes before required so that it is not too hard.
TOTAL CALORIES: 480
CALORIES PER SERVING: 120
SERVES 4

Stuffed Aubergine

Metric/Imperial
1 × 200 g/7 oz aubergine
2 tomatoes, chopped
50 g/2 oz mushrooms, chopped
1 small onion, chopped
75 g/3 oz cooked chicken, diced
salt and freshly ground black pepper
300 ml/½ pint stock

American
1 × 7 oz (medium) eggplant
2 tomatoes, chopped
½ cup chopped mushrooms
1 small onion, chopped
⅓ cup diced cooked chicken
salt and freshly ground black pepper
1¼ cups stock

Halve the aubergine (eggplant) and scoop out most of the flesh. Chop the flesh and mix about half with the tomatoes, mushrooms, onion, chicken and seasoning. Pile the mixture back into the aubergine (eggplant) shells and place them in an ovenproof dish. Pour the stock around the aubergine (eggplant), cover and cook in a preheated moderate oven, 180°C (350°F) or Gas Mark 4, for about 1 hour or until tender.
TOTAL CALORIES: 180
SERVES 1

Stuffed Pepper with Tomato Sauce

Metric/Imperial
1 large green pepper
75 g/3 oz lean minced beef
1 tsp flour
1 tomato, skinned and chopped
1 small onion, chopped
1 tsp tomato purée
pinch of mixed dried herbs
salt and freshly ground black pepper
little stock
Tomato Sauce:
2 tomatoes, chopped
1 small onion, chopped
1 tsp wine vinegar
1 tsp sugar
150 ml/¼ pint stock
1 bay leaf
salt and freshly ground black pepper

American
1 large green pepper
½ cup loosely packed, lean ground
   beef
1 tsp flour
1 tomato, skinned and chopped
1 small onion, chopped
1 tsp tomato paste
pinch of mixed dried herbs
salt and freshly ground black pepper
little stock
Tomato Sauce:
2 tomatoes, chopped
1 small onion, chopped
1 tsp wine vinegar
1 tsp sugar
⅔ cup stock
1 bay leaf
salt and freshly ground black pepper

Cut a slice from the stalk end of the pepper and discard the seeds and white pith. Place the beef in a bowl and sprinkle with the flour, then mix in the tomato, onion, tomato purée (paste), herbs and seasoning. Place the meat mixture in a non-stick frying pan and cook gently until the meat is browned, stirring constantly. Add a little stock, if necessary.

Fill the pepper, replace the top slice and place in a small ovenproof dish. Bake in a preheated moderately hot oven, 190°C (375°F) or Gas Mark 5, for 25 minutes.

Meanwhile prepare the tomato sauce by placing the tomatoes, onion, vinegar, sugar, stock, bay leaf and seasoning in a saucepan. Bring to the boil and simmer, uncovered, for about 15 minutes. Remove the bay leaf, adjust the seasoning and pour the sauce over the pepper. Serve at once.

TOTAL CALORIES: 280
SERVES 1

Stuffed Roast Shoulder of Lamb

Metric/Imperial
1 × 1 kg/2 lb boned shoulder of lamb
Stuffing:
150 g/5 oz sausagemeat
250 g/8 oz chestnut purée
1 tbsp freshly chopped parsley
1 tsp freshly chopped rosemary
1 small onion, finely chopped
salt and freshly ground black pepper
rosemary sprigs
parsley sprigs

American
1 × 2 lb boneless lamb shoulder
Stuffing:
⅔ cup sausage meat
1 cup chestnut purée
1 tbsp freshly chopped parsley
1 tsp freshly chopped rosemary
1 small onion, minced
salt and freshly ground black pepper
rosemary sprigs
parsley sprigs

First, make the stuffing. Mix together the sausagemeat, chestnut purée, parsley, rosemary, onion and seasoning. Stuff the lamb, roll up and tie securely with string. Place in a roasting pan and strew with rosemary sprigs. Roast in a preheated moderate oven, 180°C (350°F) or Gas Mark 4, for 1½–2 hours, basting occasionally. Turn oven up to 200°C (400°F) or Gas Mark 6 for about 15 minutes to crisp the outside. Serve sliced with parsley sprigs and gravy (see page 110).

TOTAL CALORIES: 2380
CALORIES PER SERVING: 400–595
SERVES 4–6

Stuffed Veal (Veal Olives)

Metric/Imperial
2 × 125 g/4 oz veal escalopes, beaten flat
1 tsp oil
1 stick celery, sliced
1 carrot, sliced
2 tsp tomato purée
150 ml/¼ pint light stock
Marinade:
2 tsp lemon juice
grated rind of ½ lemon
freshly ground black pepper
pinch of mace
2 tbsp dry white wine
Stuffing:
1 small onion, chopped
2 bacon rashers, grilled and chopped
25 g/1 oz wholewheat breadcrumbs
2 tsp mixed dried herbs
beaten egg

American
2 × ¼ lb veal scaloppini, beaten flat
1 tsp oil
1 celery stalk, sliced
1 carrot, sliced
2 tsp tomato paste
⅔ cup light stock
Marinade:
2 tsp lemon juice
grated rind of ½ lemon
freshly ground black pepper
pinch of mace
2 tbsp dry white wine
Stuffing:
1 small onion, chopped
2 bacon slices, broiled and chopped
½ cup soft fresh wholewheat bread crumbs
2 tsp mixed dried herbs
beaten egg

Place the escalopes (scaloppini) in a flat dish, mix the marinade ingredients, pour over the veal and leave to marinate for several hours.

To make the stuffing, place all the dry ingredients in a bowl, season well and mix with just enough egg to bind. Divide between the escalopes (scaloppini) and roll them into olive shapes. Tie securely with string.

Heat the oil in a heavy-based saucepan and brown the olives on all sides. Add the marinade and remaining ingredients. Bring to the boil, cover and simmer gently for about 30–35 minutes or until tender. Remove the veal olives, cut off the string, and keep warm. Boil the sauce until reduced by half. Strain and pour over the veal.

TOTAL CALORIES: 580
CALORIES PER SERVING: 290
SERVES 2

Front: Stuffed Roast Shoulder of Lamb   Back: Spinach Roulade

Sweet and Sour Chicken

Metric/Imperial
1 tsp oil
50 g/2 oz onion, chopped
2 tsp flour
200 ml/⅓ pint stock
2 tsp dark brown sugar
2 tsp soy sauce
2 tsp vinegar
salt and freshly ground black pepper
175 g/6 oz cooked, diced chicken
1 carrot, cut into fine strips
3 water chestnuts, sliced
6 spring onions, sliced

American
1 tsp oil
½ cup chopped onion
2 tsp flour
⅞ cup stock
2 tsp dark brown sugar
2 tsp soy sauce
2 tsp vinegar
salt and freshly ground black pepper
⅔ cup cooked diced chicken
1 carrot, cut into fine strips
1 celery stalk, cut into fine strips
3 water chestnuts, sliced
6 scallions, sliced

Heat the oil in a saucepan, add the onions and fry (sauté) lightly until browned. Add the flour, cook for 1 minute and gradually stir in the stock. Bring to the boil and then add the sugar, soy sauce, vinegar and seasoning. Simmer for about 5 minutes, then add the chicken. Continue simmering for 10 minutes before adding the carrot, celery and water chestnuts. Keep over the heat for 1 minute longer, then sprinkle with the spring onions (scallions).
TOTAL CALORIES: **440**
CALORIES PER SERVING: **220**
SERVES **2**

Swiss Steak

Metric/Imperial
250 g/8 oz lean stewing steak
1 medium onion, sliced
200 g/7 oz tomatoes, skinned and chopped
freshly chopped herbs
salt and freshly ground black pepper
200 ml/⅓ pint beef stock
1 tsp cornflour
75 g/3 oz button mushrooms, sliced
freshly chopped basil or parsley

American
½ lb lean stewing steak
1 medium onion, sliced
⅞ cup skinned and chopped tomatoes
freshly chopped herbs
salt and freshly ground black pepper
⅞ cup beef stock
1 tsp cornstarch

Clockwise from the front: Three Bean Salad, Vegetable Curry, Swiss Steak

¾ cup sliced button mushrooms
freshly chopped basil or parsley

Cut the steak into 4 pieces. Place in a small saucepan with the onion, tomatoes, herbs and seasoning. Cover with the stock and simmer for 1–1½ hours until the meat is tender. Mix the cornflour (cornstarch) with a little water and use to thicken the sauce, stirring constantly. Add the mushrooms, adjust the seasoning, and simmer for a further 5 minutes. Serve at once, sprinkled with herbs.
TOTAL CALORIES: **510**
CALORIES PER SERVING: **255**
SERVES **2**

Three Bean Salad

Metric/Imperial
125 g/4 oz canned red kidney beans, drained
125 g/4 oz canned cannellini beans, drained
125 g/4 oz canned flageolet beans, drained
2 spring onions, finely chopped
125 g/4 oz tuna, drained of all oil
100 g/3½ oz cauliflower florets
100 g/3½ oz peeled prawns
few stoned black olives
dressing of your choice (page 115)
2 radicchio or chicory heads

American
¼ lb canned red kidney beans, drained
¼ lb canned cannellini beans, drained
¼ lb canned flageolet beans, drained
2 scallions, finely chopped
¼ lb tuna, drained of all oil
¾ cup cauliflower florets
½ cup shelled shrimp
few pitted black olives
dressing of your choice (page 115)
2 radicchio or endive

Wash the kidney beans in a colander and drain well. Mix the beans together in a bowl. Stir in the spring onions (scallions), tuna, cauliflower, prawns (shrimp) and olives. Spoon over the chosen dressing and mix well. Arrange the radicchio or chicory (endive) on a serving dish and pile the salad in the centre.
TOTAL CALORIES: **840** (without dressing)
CALORIES PER SERVING: **420** (without dressing)
SERVES **2**
Note: Egg Dressing (page 115) is very good with this salad.

Thyme and Parsley Stuffing
This is sufficient for about 4 portions and will be enough for a small chicken.

Metric/Imperial
125 g/4 oz fresh wholewheat breadcrumbs
2 tbsp freshly chopped parsley
good pinch dried thyme
salt and freshly ground black pepper
grated rind of ½ lemon
2 tsp lemon juice
skimmed milk, to bind

American
2 cups soft fresh wholewheat bread crumbs
2 tbsp freshly chopped parsley
good pinch dried thyme
salt and freshly ground black pepper
grated rind of ½ lemon
2 tsp lemon juice
skimmed milk, to bind

Mix all the ingredients together well.
TOTAL CALORIES: **290**
CALORIES PER SERVING: **75**

Clockwise from the front: Three Bean Salad, Vegetable Curry, Swiss Steak

Trout with Almonds

Metric/Imperial
1 × 200 g/7 oz trout, cleaned
juice of ¼ lemon
15 g/½ oz flaked almonds
watercress and lemon wedges

American
1 × 7 oz trout, cleaned
juice of ¼ lemon
2 tbsp flaked almonds
watercress and lemon wedges

Sprinkle the trout with lemon juice and place under a preheated moderate grill (broiler) and cook gently for about 5–7 minutes each side or until tender. Meanwhile, place the almonds in a small frying pan (skillet) and heat gently until golden brown. Sprinkle over the trout and serve with sprigs of watercress and lemon wedges.
TOTAL CALORIES: **350**
SERVES **1**

Veal Escalope with Ham

Metric/Imperial
150 g/5 oz veal escalope
1 slice lean ham
salt and freshly ground black pepper
1 tsp oil
1 tomato, sliced

American
5 oz veal scaloppini
1 slice lean ham
salt and freshly ground black pepper
1 tsp oil
1 tomato, sliced

Beat the veal between 2 sheets of greaseproof (waxed) paper until thin and flat. Place the ham on half the veal, season well and fold over, securing with string. Heat the oil in a frying pan (skillet) and cook the veal for 8–10 minutes on each side until tender. Drain well on kitchen paper towels, remove the string, and serve at once garnished with fresh tomato slices.

TOTAL CALORIES: 245
SERVES 1

Veal Florentine

Metric/Imperial
150 g/5 oz veal escalope
150 g/5 oz spinach
salt and freshly ground black pepper
2 tbsp marsala
25 g/1 oz mozarella cheese, sliced

American
5 oz veal scaloppini
5 oz spinach
salt and freshly ground black pepper
2 tbsp marsala
1 oz mozarella cheese, sliced

Place the veal under a preheated hot grill (broiler) and cook for 5–6 minutes each side. Meanwhile, cook the spinach in the water still clinging to the leaves after washing. When cooked, drain the spinach well and place in an ovenproof dish. Place the veal on top, season and pour over the marsala. Arrange the cheese over the veal and return to the grill (broiler) until the cheese has melted.

TOTAL CALORIES: 340
SERVES 1

Vegetable Curry

Metric/Imperial
1 tbsp corn oil
2 tsp ground coriander
1½ tsp ground cumin
½ tsp turmeric
½ tsp ground ginger
2 large cloves garlic, thinly sliced
100 g/3½ oz carrots, sliced diagonally
4 spring onions, chopped
2 sticks celery, sliced diagonally
2 leeks, sliced
3 courgettes, sliced
1 small cauliflower, broken into florets
300 ml/½ pint stock, (homemade if possible)
150 ml/¼ pint plain yogurt
25 g/1 oz cashew nuts

American
1 tbsp corn oil
2 tsp ground coriander
1½ tsp ground cumin
½ tsp tumeric
½ tsp ground ginger
2 large cloves garlic, thinly sliced
⅔ cup sliced carrots
4 scallions, chopped
2 celery stalks, sliced diagonally
2 leeks, sliced
3 zucchini, sliced
1 small cauliflower, broken into florets
¼ cup stock (homemade if possible)
⅔ cup plain yogurt
¼ cup cashew nuts

Heat the oil in a saucepan, add the spices and cook for 5 minutes without browning. Add the garlic, carrots, spring onions (scallions) and celery. Cook for 2 minutes, then add the leeks, courgettes (zucchini) and cauliflower. Pour over the stock, bring to the boil, and simmer gently for 8–10 minutes. Stir in the yogurt and heat gently, without boiling. Sprinkle with cashew nuts and serve at once.

TOTAL CALORIES: 500
CALORIES PER SERVING: 125
SERVES 4

Vegetable Lasagne

Metric/Imperial
250 g/8 oz courgettes, sliced lengthwise
125 g/4 oz flat mushrooms, sliced
4 tomatoes, skinned and sliced
2 medium onions, sliced
1 tsp mixed dried herbs
600 ml/1 pint skimmed milk
3 eggs, beaten
125 g/4 oz mature Cheddar cheese, grated

American
½ lb zucchini, sliced lengthwise
1 cup sliced flat mushrooms
4 tomatoes, skinned and sliced
2 medium onions, sliced
1 tsp mixed dried herbs
2½ cups skimmed milk
3 eggs, beaten
1 cup grated sharp Cheddar cheese

Layer the courgettes (zucchini), mushrooms, tomatoes and onions, alternately in a dish, seasoning well and sprinkling with herbs. Mix the milk, eggs and cheese together and spoon over the vegetables. Cook in a preheated moderately hot oven, 190°C (375°F) or Gas Mark 5, for 25 minutes.

TOTAL CALORIES: 1040
CALORIES PER SERVING: 260
SERVES 4

Vegetable Terrine

Metric/Imperial
600 ml/1 pint aspic
2 tbsp dry sherry
1 tbsp freshly chopped parsley
1 tbsp freshly chopped basil
250 g/8 oz fresh asparagus, trimmed
175 g/6 oz carrots, thinly sliced
175 g/6 oz small turnips, thinly sliced
4–6 canned artichoke hearts, sliced
175 g/6 oz courgettes, thinly sliced
125 g/4 oz French beans, halved

American
2½ cups aspic
2 tbsp dry sherry
1 tbsp freshly chopped parsley
1 tbsp freshly chopped basil
½ lb fresh asparagus, trimmed
6 oz carrots, thinly sliced
6 oz small turnips, thinly sliced
4–6 canned artichoke hearts, sliced
6 oz zucchini, thinly sliced
¼ lb green beans, halved

Blanch and drain all the fresh vegetables. Mix the liquid aspic with the sherry and fresh herbs. Spoon a thin layer over the base of a 1 kg/2 lb loaf tin or terrine and chill until set. Dip each of the selection of vegetables in the aspic, then arrange in layers in the terrine, pouring a thin layer of aspic over each time. Set each layer in the refrigerator. Continue layering until all the vegetables and aspic are used, finishing with the aspic. Chill for 2 hours. To turn out quickly, dip the terrine in a bowl of boiling water, then invert onto a serving dish. Garnish with parsley and basil if desired.

TOTAL CALORIES: 280
CALORIES PER SERVING: 70
SERVES 4 as a starter or light meal

Vegetable Salad

Metric/Imperial
3 tbsp tomato juice
1 shallot, finely chopped
1 tbsp dry white wine
dash of Tabasco
6 coriander seeds
1 bouquet garni
1 clove garlic, crushed (optional)
2 courgettes, sliced diagonally
2 sticks celery, chopped
few cauliflower florets
50 g/2 oz button mushrooms, sliced
1 carrot, grated coarsely
1 tbsp green peppercorns, drained

American
3 tbsp tomato juice
1 shallot, finely chopped
1 tbsp dry white wine
dash of hot pepper sauce
6 coriander seeds
1 bouquet garni
1 clove garlic, crushed (optional)
2 zucchini, sliced diagonally
2 celery stalks, chopped
few cauliflower florets
¼ cup sliced button mushrooms
1 carrot, grated coarsely
1 tbsp green peppercorns, drained

Place the tomato juice, shallot, wine, Tabasco (hot pepper sauce), coriander seeds, bouquet garni and garlic in a saucepan, bring to the boil and simmer for 5 minutes. Turn off the heat and leave until completely cold, then strain into a jug.

Place the vegetables and peppercorns in a bowl and pour over the dressing. Toss well to mix, then spoon into a serving dish.

TOTAL CALORIES: 90
CALORIES PER SERVING: 45
SERVES 2

Watercress Soup

Metric/Imperial
½ oz butter
1 bunch watercress, chopped
1 small onion, chopped
2 tsp flour
salt and freshly ground black pepper
450 ml/¾ pint skimmed milk

American
1 tbsp butter
1 bunch watercress, chopped
1 small onion, chopped
2 tsp flour
salt and freshly ground black pepper
2 cups skimmed milk

Melt the butter in a saucepan and add the watercress and onion. Cook gently for 5–7 minutes and then sprinkle over the flour and seasoning. Stir well and continue to cook for 1 minute. Gradually pour in the milk and bring to the boil. Simmer for about 10 minutes, then cool slightly and purée in a blender. Return to the clean pan and adjust the seasoning. Serve either hot or cold.

TOTAL CALORIES: 390
CALORIES PER SERVING: 195
SERVES 2

Whipped Cream Topping

Metric/Imperial
5 tbsp whipping cream
5 tbsp plain yogurt
1 egg white

American
1⅓ cups whipping cream
⅓ cup plain yogurt
1 egg white

Whip the cream until thick, then gradually beat in the yogurt. Beat the egg white until stiff, then fold into the cream and yogurt mixture.

TOTAL CALORIES: 340

White Sauce

Metric/Imperial
1½ tsp butter
25 g/1 oz flour
300 ml/½ pint skimmed milk
salt and freshly ground black pepper

American
1½ tsp butter
¼ cup flour
1¼ cups skimmed milk
salt and freshly ground black pepper

Melt the butter in a saucepan and stir in the flour. Cook, stirring, for 1 minute and then gradually add the milk. Keep on stirring all the time to prevent lumps. Bring to the boil and simmer for 2 minutes, stirring until smooth, and season well.

Makes 300 ml/½ pint (1¼ cups).
TOTAL CALORIES: 260

Wholewheat Macaroni with Cheese and Ham

Metric/Imperial
50 g/2 oz Bel Paese cheese, diced
50 g/2 oz low fat soft cheese with herbs and garlic
50 g/2 oz Gruyère cheese, grated

Clockwise from the front:
Wholewheat Spaghetti with Tomato and Basil Sauce, Vegetable Salad, Winter Fruit Compote

1–2 cloves garlic, crushed
2 tsp freshly chopped thyme
2 tsp freshly chopped parsley
2 tsp freshly chopped chives
125 g/4 oz very lean ham, diced
salt and freshly ground black pepper
175 g/6 oz wholewheat macaroni

American
⅓ cup diced Bel Paese cheese
¼ cup low fat soft cheese with herbs and garlic
½ cup grated Gruyère cheese
1–2 cloves garlic, crushed
2 tsp freshly chopped thyme
2 tsp freshly chopped parsley
2 tsp freshly chopped chives
½ cup diced lean ham
salt and freshly ground black pepper
6 oz wholewheat macaroni

Put the cheeeses and garlic into a saucepan, add the herbs and heat through very slowly. Stir in the diced ham and season well with salt and pepper.

Cook the macaroni in boiling salted water for 7–9 minutes or until 'al dente'.

Drain the macaroni and add to the sauce. Mix well, turn onto a heated serving dish and serve at once.

TOTAL CALORIES: 1500
CALORIES PER SERVING: 375
SERVES 4

Wholewheat Pan Pizza

Metric/Imperial
125 g/4 oz wholemeal bread mix
lukewarm water
Topping:
50 g/2 oz tomato purée
100 g/3½ oz tomatoes, skinned and sliced
1 clove garlic, sliced
¼ tsp dried basil
¼ tsp dried marjoram
1 × 350 g/12 oz can asparagus, drained
100 g/32 oz tiny button mushrooms
few stuffed olives
75 g/3 oz Bel Paese cheese, thinly sliced
salt and freshly ground black pepper

American
¼ lb wholewheat bread mix
lukewarm water
Topping:
2 tbsp tomato paste
½ cup skinned and sliced tomatoes
1 clove garlic, sliced
¼ tsp dried basil
¼ tsp dried marjoram
1 can (12 oz) asparagus, drained
1 cup tiny button mushrooms
few stuffed olives
⅓ cup thinly sliced Bel Paese cheese
salt and freshly ground black pepper

Mix together the contents of the bread mix and measure the required amount. Place in a bowl and stir in sufficient lukewarm water to form a firm but elastic dough. Knead for 5 minutes, then cover and leave in a warm place for 50 minutes or until the dough has doubled in size. Lightly grease a non-stick heavy-based 18–20 cm (7–8 in) frying pan (skillet). Knead the dough again and roll out to the size of the pan. Place in the pan (skillet) and work a little dough up the sides.

Spread the tomato purée (paste) over the bottom, then cover with the sliced tomatoes. Sprinkle with the garlic and herbs, and arrange the asparagus and mushrooms on top with the olives and cheese. Season well.

Cook over a medium heat for 15–20 minutes, then place under a pre-heated grill (broiler) until the cheese is golden. Transfer to a heated serving dish and serve hot.

TOTAL CALORIES: 740
CALORIES PER SERVING: 185
SERVES 4

Wholewheat Spaghetti with Chicken Livers

Metric/Imperial
100 g/3½ oz chicken livers
1 small onion, finely chopped
25 g/1 oz button mushrooms, sliced
1 clove garlic, crushed
pinch of chilli powder
¼ tsp mixed dried herbs
1 tbsp dry sherry
salt and freshly ground black pepper
25 g/1 oz wholewheat spaghetti
2 tbsp plain yogurt
freshly chopped thyme

American
½ cup chicken liver
1 small onion, minced
¼ cup sliced button mushrooms
1 clove garlic, crushed
pinch of chili powder
¼ tsp mixed dried herbs
1 tbsp dry sherry
salt and freshly ground black pepper
1 oz wholewheat spaghetti
2 tbsp plain yogurt
freshly chopped thyme

Place the chicken livers, onion and mushrooms in a non-stick frying pan (skillet). Cook for 5 minutes, stirring occasionally, until the chicken livers are browned. Add the garlic, chilli powder, herbs, sherry and seasoning. Cover and simmer, stirring occasionally, for 5 minutes.

Cook the spaghetti in boiling salted water for 9 minutes or until 'al dente'. Drain well.

Pour the yogurt onto the chicken liver mixture; heat gently but do not boil. Add the spaghetti and mix well. Serve at once, sprinkled with thyme.

TOTAL CALORIES: 300
SERVES 1

Wholewheat Spaghetti with Tomato and Basil

Metric/Imperial
500 g/1 lb tomatoes, skinned, seeded and chopped
100 g/3½ oz onion, very finely chopped
2 tbsp freshly chopped basil
salt and freshly ground black pepper
dash of Worcestershire sauce
150 g/5 oz wholewheat spaghetti
25 g/1 oz freshly grated Parmesan cheese

American
2 cups skinned, seeded and chopped tomatoes
⅞ cup minced onion
2 tbsp freshly chopped basil
salt and freshly ground black pepper
dash of Worcestershire sauce
5 oz wholewheat spaghetti
¼ cup grated Parmesan cheese

Put the tomatoes, onion, basil and seasoning into a saucepan. Boil rapidly for 15–20 minutes, stirring, until the sauce has thickened. Add the Worcestershire sauce; season.

Meanwhile, cook the spaghetti in boiling salted water for 6–8 minutes until it is 'al dente'. Drain, spoon over the sauce and sprinkle with cheese.

TOTAL CALORIES: 750
CALORIES PER SERVING: 375
SERVES 2

Winter Fruit Compote

Metric/Imperial
175 g/6 oz dried apricots
125 g/1 oz dried figs
50 g/2 oz dried apples
300 ml/½ pint apple juice
grated rind and juice of 2 lemons

American
1 cup dried apricots
⅔ cup prunes
1 tbsp dried figs
½ cup dried apples
1¼ cups apple juice
grated rind and juice of 2 lemons

Place the dried fruit, apple juice, lemon rind and juice in a bowl and soak for 4 hours. Transfer to a saucepan, cover and slowly bring to the boil, then simmer for 20–30 minutes until tender. Chill before serving.

TOTAL CALORIES: 880
CALORIES PER SERVING: 220
SERVES 4

Index

ACKNOWLEDGEMENTS

The following pictures were taken specially for Octopus Books:
Christian von Alvensleben 69; Sandra Lousada 4-5. All other
photographs by Charlie Stebbings.